I thought finally that of all the nostalgias that haunt the human heart the greatest of them all, for me, is an everlasting longing to bring what is youngest home to what is oldest, in us all.

LAURENS VAN DER POST

Contents

≈

Jeremiah Abrams
Introduction: The Inner Child   1

Part 1 The Promise of the Inner Child

Introduction   19

1. Edith Sullwold
   A Fresh Experiment: The Archetype of the Inner Child   21
2. C. G. Jung
   The Psychology of the Child Archetype √   30
3. June Singer
   The Motif of the Divine Child   39
4. Ralph Metzner
   Rebirth and the Eternal Child   45

Part 2 The Abandoned Child

Introduction   53

5. James Hillman
   Abandoning the Child   56
6. Marion Woodman
   The Soul Child   69
7. M. Scott Peck
   Love and the Fear of Abandonment √   75

8. Ursula K. LeGuin
    The Ones Who Walk Away from Omelas   81

Part 3 Eternal Youth and Narcissism: The Child's Dilemma

Introduction   93
9. Joel Covitz
    Narcissism: The Disturbance of Our Time   97
10. Alice Miller
    The Search for the True Self ✓   105
11. Marie-Louise von Franz
    Puer Aeternus   121
12. Jeffrey Satinover
    The Childhood Self and the Origins of Puer Psychology 129

Part 4 The Wounded Child Within

Introduction   149
13. Hal Stone and Sidra Winkelman
    The Vulnerable Inner Child   152
14. Alexander Lowen
    Why Are You So Angry with Me?   165
15. Alice Miller
    Advocating for the Child   171
16. Robert M. Stein
    On Incest and Child Abuse   177

Part 5 Recovering the Child

Introduction   185
17. Lucia Capacchione
    The Power of Your Other Hand   187
18. John Bradshaw
    Liberating Your Lost Inner Child   197

19. Jean Houston
    Recalling the Child   210
20. Joseph Campbell
    Killing the Dragon   216

Part 6 Inner Child/Outer Child: The Future of Parenting

Introduction   221
21. James Hillman
    A Note on Story   224
22. Bruno Bettelheim
    Exploring Childhood as an Adult   228
23. Erik H. Erikson
    The Historical Relevance of Human Childhood   237
24. Theodore Reik
    Out of the Mouths of Babes   240
25. Samuel Osherson
    The Wounded Father Within   248

Epilogue
'*May You Stay Forever Young*'   256

Notes   258
Notes on Contributors   264
Bibliography   268
Permissions and Copyrights   273

ACKNOWLEDGMENTS

≈

A project such as this is the work of many hands. Without the generous, creative, and cooperative energies of the many, the one work would not exist.

I am especially indebted to my loving wife, Barbara Shindell, who has sacrificed to keep things going during my distraction, and who has been my mainstay, chief reader, and enthusiastic supporter.

I am most grateful to my editor, Connie Zweig, that rare and gifted kind of person who has been able to be a dear friend as well as book-mother and book-midwife to this endeavour.

Many other individuals also deserve special thanks for their specific aid to this book: Bob Stein and Joel Covitz gave unflinching intellectual and emotional support to this endeavour throughout, as readers, believers, critics, and contributors. Mark Dowie and Mark Libarle helped me to get the book off to a great start. Bill and Vivienne Howe generously allowed me to turn their library into a research facility. Sharon Heath gave infusions of support from her parallel project. Lotte Stein, Joanna Karp, Bruce and Carla Burman, and Alys Graveson provided invaluable critical support as readers. Kathleen Dickey rescued and commandeered the manuscript preparation with grace. The support from Jeremy Tarcher and his staff has been attentive and professional throughout. And, obviously, I am indebted to the individual authors and publishers who have generously allowed their written work to be woven into this tapestry.

I especially want to acknowledge those clients and personal friends who have shared their innermost beings with me over the years, who have given reality to my own experience of the inner child and to the healing possibilities within us all.

Introduction:

THE INNER CHILD
Jeremiah Abrams

> *It is the Child that sees the primordial secret in Nature and it is*
> *the child of ourselves we return to. The child within us is simple*
> *and daring enough to live the Secret.*
>
> CHUANG TSU

Most of us feel a strong resonance with the inner child. We know
intuitively what it is, what its meaning is for us. We sense, perhaps
secretly, that a part of us remains whole, untouched by life's
sorrows, capable of great joy and wonder at small things.

This child image is one of subtle complexity and truth. Its message
is that *we all carry within us an eternal child*, a young being of innocence and wonder. *And that symbolic child also carries us*, who we
have been, the record of our formative experiences, our pleasures
and pains.

As a symbolic and poetic reality, the inner child appears in our
imaginations, our dreams, our art, and in mythologies throughout
the world representing renewal, divinity, a zest for life, a sense of
wonder, hope, the future, discovery, courage, spontaneity and
immortality. As such, the inner child is a uniting symbol and brings
together the separated or dissociated parts of the individual personality. Marie-Louise von Franz, eminent Jungian analyst and scholar,
says: 'If I trust my naive reaction, then I am whole; I am wholly in
the situation and wholly in life . . . That is why child therapists let
children play, and in two minutes they reveal their whole problem,
for in that way they are themselves.'

The inner child is both a developmental actuality and a symbolic possibility. It is the soul of the person, created inside of us through the experiment of life, and it is the primordial image of the Self, the very centre of our individual being. As Carl Gustav Jung suggested, the child represents a 'wholeness which embraces the very depths of Nature'.

'The Child is the father of the Man,' said Wordsworth. The child is father to the whole person.

Most of us continue to have contact with the child in adulthood through childish habits and desires and childlike behaviour, and through contact with real children. Jung said that the tendency to engage in regressive activity has the positive function of keeping us connected to the child, of activating the inner child. He said regression is a 'genuine attempt to get at something necessary: the universal feeling of childhood innocence, the sense of security, of protection, of reciprocal love, of trust, of faith – a thing that has many names.'[1]

WE HAVE ALL BEEN CHILDREN

Our inner child possesses the spirit of truthfulness, absolute spontaneity, and genuineness. Its actions bespeak a naturalness in us, the ability to do the right thing, the capacity to save a situation. Culver Barker, a British psychologist, observed how important it is to become aware of the child within, to relate to it consciously and be reinforced by it. He wrote:

> When I talk about the child within, I mean that aspect within us adults which still reflects some of the qualities of the divine child . . . When we are too unconscious of it, for whatever reason, and so do not mediate it, this force contains all the potentialities for constructive and destructive activities. So it can hold the creative dynamics of the human personality, its motive power.[2]

'Only when I make room for the voice of the child within me,' says renowned Swiss psychoanalyst Alice Miller, 'do I feel myself to be genuine and creative.'

The child's voice is essential to the process of becoming oneself. Individuation, the lifelong process of personality development, is tied to and circles around the unique identity of the childhood self. Von Franz concurs with Miller on this point when she says, 'The child within is the genuine part, and the genuine part within one is that which suffers ... Many grown-ups split off this part and thereby miss individuation, for only if one accepts it and the suffering it imposes on one, can the process of individuation go on.'

The inner child's voice is one that each and every one of us will recognize, for we know it well. We have all been children. And the child we have been remains within us – for better or worse – a container of our personal history and an ever-present symbol of our hopes and creative possibilities.

The child, by whatever means we achieve contact with it, is the key to our achieving fullest expression as individuals. This child entity, the self we truly are and have always been, lives within us in the here and now. If, for instance, we observe the self-image of exceptionally gifted individuals – people who have fully realized their talents in life – it is striking how much their self-concept is tied to the unique and personal experience of the childhood self.

Albert Einstein is a well-known example of the genius forever wedded to the inner child's naturalness. It is said that Einstein didn't even speak until he was nearly five years old! 'Even at the age of nine he was not fluent,' says biographer Ronald W. Clark.[3] The authenticity of his child self was not contaminated by words, but rather contained in a nonverbal sense of wonder. Einstein recognized this quality of the child in himself. He honoured it faithfully in the face of adversity. In his autobiographical notes, written at the age of sixty-seven, he mused:

It is, in fact, nothing short of a miracle that the modern methods of instruction have not yet entirely strangled the holy curiosity of inquiry; for this delicate little plant, aside from stimulation, stands mostly in need of freedom; without this it goes to wreck and ruin without fail. It is a very grave mistake to think that the enjoyment of seeing and searching can be promoted by means of coercion and a sense of duty.[4]

This naturalness, freedom, and perpetual sense of wonder, assiduously preserved into adult life, remained the mark of Einstein's character even in old age.

In contrast, the life of Wolfgang Amadeus Mozart provides an example of a one-sided inversion of the positive tendencies in the inner child. Here we have a childhood genius who, according to his biographers, was unable to achieve balance by developing the socialized adult self in his personality. His child self was a prisoner of conditional love, inflated with grandiosity and compelled to seek the approval of his father, his monarch and his world. His musical gift burned pure, but his puerile behaviour led to a premature demise.

For other gifted individuals, maturity and adulthood result in a diminution of the vibrant power of the child. Consider, for example, the flattening effects of maturation on the gifts of many child prodigies. The process of socialization somehow has a stifling effect on the natural gifts of most children. This is the narcissistic dilemma.

Perhaps the scenario goes like this: The real child, being forced to adapt, becomes a little adult and identifies with a false self. The treasures of the true child self are then hidden protectively in such a well-concealed sanctum that when the adult self matures, it fails to recall and to reclaim the inner child. The child within is abandoned, lost. Eventually, rationalization or bitterness replaces the natural spontaneity and clarity of that radiant self. As J. Robert Oppenheimer, the dark genius who fathered the atomic age, lamented, 'There are children playing in the street who could solve some of my top problems in physics, because they have modes of sensory perception that I lost long ago.'[5]

'WHERE IS THE LIFE WE HAVE LOST IN LIVING?'

For others, the child within has been far from inspiring, for it is hardly a reality. The experience of their childhood stories has been obliterated by pain and time, obscured by rationality, driven out by ambition, or distorted by the pressure to grow up and conform.

Few of us had a childhood free of anxiety, filled with contact and understanding involvement with adults, a childhood of freedom to engage in imaginative play and to follow distraction to delight, an emotional environment where it was safe to feel vulnerable. For many, the inner child is a traumatized and wounded being, a sufferer we would rather not acknowledge, stunted by experiences we would rather not remember as adults.

The child of our experience, says child therapist Edith Sullwold, 'is the child which we all desire to heal, so that we can reclaim the energy for adult action that still resides in the reactive patterns of defence and protection, which developed in response to early painful experiences.'

We have played and suffered, grown and learned. The youthful, soulful part persists, though for some only as an occasional twinkle in the eyes or an intonation of voice. Many people experience the inner child unconsciously as one who has not had its needs recognized or met. This experience and the longing that accompanies it are a great source of humiliation and shame, very difficult to identify or share with others. Thus the child can be a tremendous inhibition in adult human relatedness.

We always encounter the inner child in marriage and other close associations with others, where the wounding love relationships of our past are most deeply felt. 'Those childhood wounds to the soul,' says author and Jungian analyst Robert M. Stein, 'make it extremely difficult, if not impossible, for one to experience an intimate and creatively evolving human connection. In this sense the wounded child also represents that aspect of the soul which needs and demands union with another.'

Healing this wounded problem child is possible, and necessary if we are to achieve inner wholeness. Healing requires an internal transformation, the creation of a positive inner attitude that supports and nourishes the child within compassionately. In her book *The Drama of the Gifted Child*, Alice Miller describes the shift that takes place during the healing process:

> *If a person is able . . . to experience that he was never 'loved' as a child for what he was, but for his achievements, success, and good qualities, and that he sacrificed his childhood for this 'love', this will shake him very deeply but one day he will feel the desire to end this courtship. He will discover in himself a need to live according to his 'true self' and no longer be forced to earn love, a love that at root, still leaves him empty-handed since it is given to the 'false self', which he has begun to relinquish.*

THE LIGHT OF THE WORLD CAN SHINE THROUGH

The inner child is the carrier or our personal stories, the vehicle for our memories of both the actual child and an idealized child from the past. It is the *truly alive* quality of being within us. It is the soul, our experiencer throughout the cycles of life. It is the sufferer. And it is the bearer of renewal through rebirth, appearing in our lives whenever we detach and open to change.

In the poem 'The Holy Longing', Goethe, the great European renaissance man of the eighteenth and nineteenth centuries, sang his praise to this remarkable quality in the human being:

> *Tell a wise person, or else keep silent,*
> *because the massman will mock it right away.*
> *I praise what is truly alive,*
> *what longs to be burned to death . . .*

And so long as you haven't experienced
this: to die and so to grow,
you are only a troubled guest
on the dark earth.[6]

To experience this process of renewal is to experience the creative possibilities of the symbolic inner child. To 'die' – that is, to let go at a time of transition – allows some new possibility to be born. 'Give up what thou hast and thou shalt receive', goes the Latin proverb. When something passes out of being, the child is constellated as an inner possibility. It enters our sphere filled with a naive vitality.

'The process of psychologically dying while one is still alive is followed by a psychological rebirth, or renewal,' says Ralph Metzner in his book *Opening to the Light*. A new being is born – a new way of being – imagined as the symbolic radiant child. 'The newborn child is still connected to the Tao, to the source of its life and its arising, and this is why we should emulate it,' adds Metzner. 'As Chuang Tsu says, "Can you be like a newborn child? The baby cries all day and yet his voice never becomes hoarse. That is because he has not lost nature's harmony."'

At the core of our being this eternal child exists, truly alive, awaiting embodiment in our actions and our attitudes. And the light of the world can shine through it.

'It Takes a Long Time to Become Young'

The inner child motif, though it has emerged as a concept in the popular culture only in the past thirty years, is both timeless and contemporary. It is as ancient as religion, and as current as a Hollywood comedy. In the film *Big*, for instance, a boy gets his wish to be grown-up instantaneously, and we see him succeed in the adult world in his new adult's body by simply remaining his natural child self, innocent and ebullient. This is not substantially different from the child-god Hermes we meet in the Homeric Hymns, who, through his cleverness (and all on the very day he is born!) invents music and song by creating a lyre as a toy from a tortoise's shell, steals from and appeases his older brother, the archer Apollo, and wins the approval of his most famous father, Zeus.

The child within is an evolving concept, originating in primordial times with the very earliest forms of nature worship and solar religions. Those child-gods gave way before the beginning of our eon to the emergence of divine mythological children throughout the world. The Romulus and Remus fable gave us the glory that was Roman civilization. The messiah concept of the Hebrews eventually produced what has become the primary inner symbol of the self in our times, the Christ child. During the Middle Ages, when unsanctioned religious practices were forced underground, the alchemists imagined their great work accomplished in a synthesis of the opposites, the creation of an inner soul child, the Philosopher's Child. In the East, to this day, devotion to the child Krishna suffuses family life with an awareness of divine presence in everyday living.

In the West, religious thought has given rise to secular thought on the subject of the child. Tremendous growth has taken place in the social sciences in our era – a period of time once imagined by Victorian scientistic sensibilities to be the coming 'century of the Child'. Most especially expanded in our immediate times is the realm of psychological ideas. By the 1960s, revisionist work in educational theory and practice had fully taken hold of modern ideas of child psychology and developmental theory. The analytic insights of the depth psychologies of Freud, Adler, Jung, Reich, Reik, and others had grown in influence and were making perfectly clear what the more mystical traditions had valued through the ages – namely, that we are not all of a piece, that each of us contains a multitude of internal influences, the child and childhood being the most immediate and important.

This ripe intellectual context gave ferment to the rising ideas of the inner child. The concept emerges in the serious and the popular psychological literature of the 1960s, most notably in the works of the preeminent Swiss psychologist C. G. Jung ('The Psychology of the Child Archetype', 1959 American edition), who wrote about the inner child as a symbol of wholeness in the psyche, as a bridge between the personal and collective realms. American psychiatrist W. Hugh Missildine (*Your Inner Child of the Past*, 1963) wrote one of the original books in the self-help genre, giving encouraging advice on how to bring the inner child of experience into harmony with the outer adult's personality. The extremely popular work of California psychiatrist Eric Berne (*Transactional Analysis*, 1961) placed the inner child in an interactive role with an inner parent and inner adult, a versatile model that worked well in psychotherapeutic settings, enabling the inner child to take a constructive role in healing the whole person.

There are important reasons why the image of the inner child has such a compelling message for us today. The following six catalysing factors, though not a complete explanation in themselves, are what make the inner child a theme of pressing interest.

The Expansion of Interest in Psychology

Psychology – itself a child of this century – has brought us to an appreciation of the relevance of human childhood, stressing its developmental importance and emphasizing the reality of childhood experience. Sigmund Freud, whose brilliance was midwife to modern psychological inquiry, is reported to have said at the end of his pioneering career that 'the real value of psychoanalysis is to improve parenting.' Almost all subsequent thought in the field of psychology has given a prominent place to the child and child studies.

Jung, whose discoveries have advanced psychological thinking well into the next century, did not underestimate the promise of psychology for the modern temperament when he asked waggishly:

Why is it that just now especially we interest ourselves in psychology? The answer is, everyone is in dire need of it. Humanity seems to have reached today a point where previous concepts are no longer adequate and where we begin to realize that we are confronted with something strange, the language of which we no longer understand. We live in a time when there dawns upon us a realization that the people living on the other side of the mountain are not made up exclusively of red-headed devils responsible for all the evil on this side of the mountain.[7]

A Parallel Growth in Psychotherapy

The 'talking cure', which originated with Freud and his followers, has evolved and become differentiated in its focus, but nevertheless continues to honour the soul, to validate the inner life of the adult, and to acknowledge the existence of the inner child in need of healing.

In the past three decades the phenomenon of the inner child has risen in prominence largely because of a growing interest in Jungian depth psychology in general and in the treatment of narcissistic personality disorders in particular. Both of these disciplines identify the image of the inner child as the vulnerable soul, the wounded child in need of integration, and the injured Self. Archetypal psychologist James Hillman echoes Jung when he says, 'What depth psychology has come to call regression is nothing other than a return to the child.'

With the rise and popularization of psychotherapy, therapists have come into contact with the neglected child within themselves and have found it necessary to heal their own inner children in order to effectively help others. According to author Charles L. Whitfield, many therapists have in turn extended this work to their clientele and have made recovery of the inner child a key feature of the therapeutic relationship, expanding the currency of the inner child in many circles.

The Adult Children of Alcoholics (ACA) Program

This rapidly growing phenomenon, a spin-off of the enormously popular twelve-step self-help recovery movement of the Alcoholics

Anonymous fellowship, makes broad use of the child-within concept. It has been estimated that the *ACA* program is growing at a rate of one new group nationwide every day. The success of the concept seems to lie in the identification of the previously unacknowledged suffering of those who were raised in alcoholic households; specifically, the recognition of the disastrously damaging effects on the child self of such persons. Utilizing a family and systems approach to alcoholism recovery, the *ACA* model makes it plain that families that are dysfunctional for any reason, not just alcoholic or chemically dependent ones, do incalculable damage to the children and to the inner childhood of their members. This is a very influential phenomenon, with a burgeoning membership and literature, helping to break the denial of the genuine, suffering part of us that is the inner child.

The Ever-Widening Acknowledgment of Child Abuse

The rise in incidence, reporting, prosecution, and publicity of child abuse forces us to consider the perpetuation of such behaviour by the abused inner children of adult offenders. Jungian analyst and author Joel Covitz, in his book *Emotional Child Abuse*, calls this cross-generational phenomenon 'the family curse'. He says that when we look at the adult perpetrator of abuse,

> *we almost always find this root: as a child, this person's healthy narcissistic needs were not met . . . and when the child grows up, the devastating effects of these disturbances are passed on to his own children. Patterns of abuse will not be altered until parents realize more fully the effect their actions have on their children.*

What is it in our culture that is manifesting in this epidemic of child abuse? This is a complicated problem, requiring a deeper consideration of collective attitudes toward the inner child. 'Actual child abuse always reflects a lack of connection to and respect for the internal or psychic child,' according to Robert M. Stein, a leading thinker in the field, whose writing challenges us to look at this problem with greater sensitivity and awareness. The growing attention and awareness of child abuse in our culture, and the insight that most perpetrators have been abused themselves, give work on the inner child an important mandate.

Today's Increased Parental Burden

The child-rearing task, under siege now as never before, cries out for support and attention. Attitudes toward children and their development are changing rapidly. What would have been thought of as inappropriate thirty years ago, such as widespread child care outside the home for six-month-old babies, is now widely accepted practice. Rapidly changing values in postindustrial culture have irrevocably altered the family structure and are radically affecting child-rearing practices. Women have entered the workforce in large numbers in response to economic pressures and in an effort to expand their sense of identity and purpose. This trend, along with the increased incidence of single-parent households, has necessitated wholesale rethinking of the parental task as we approach the end of the century. The cohort, tidal-wave generation of new parents, the postwar baby boom, is now proliferating in considerable numbers. These people need and want to expand the collective awareness of good parenting. Parents more than ever *want* all the help they can get. Yet parenting and the art of child-rearing seem to be subject to greater isolation and social abandonment, as are our children.

These circumstances bring special attention to the child within the parent, as well as to the inner life of the child: The quality and success of parenting is deeply enhanced when parents can realize their own neglected child selves and transform them into compassionate resources for the care of their own children. The way one treats the inner child strongly determines the way one treats the outer child.

Hunger for Spirituality and Meaning

The spiritual uncertainty of the times calls for a birth of new meaning and hope in each of us.

Things fall apart; the centre cannot hold;
Mere anarchy is loosed upon the world,
The blood-dimmed tide is loosed, and everywhere
The ceremony of innocence is drowned . . .[8]

W. B. YEATS, 'THE SECOND COMING'

We suffer from what Jung has called 'an unprecedented impoverishment of symbols'. There is a great hunger for spirituality and meaning in our era, a longing for a second coming of a divine inner child whose appearance would announce the beginning of a new millennium of hope.

On the personal level, we feel a compelling necessity to contact and to live the inner child's destiny in order to find spiritual salvation. 'Our childhood bears witness to the childhood of man, of the being touched by the glory of living', says Gaston Bachelard.

Or as Jungian psychologist June Singer puts it, 'The divine child within us gives meaning to our immature strivings; he shows us the unconscious side of the limitations which we experience, and that is a vision of potentiality coming into flower.'

In psychological terms, we might say the appearance of the divine child is a manifestation of the Self, causing a restructuring of the personality to accommodate an expanded comprehension of meaning and a fuller expression of vitality.

'As one searches the literature of mysticism and spiritual guidance and the life stories of those who seem to have become mature selves,' writes John Loudon in his essay 'Becoming a Child', 'the goal seems common: an integration that embraces the fullness of human potentiality that is at the same time uncomplicated, wise, joyful, and even playful'. In short, a return to the child. This motif is reflected in the great mythologies of the world's religions, where the birth of a special child means that the old gods have to go, and a new beginning emerges.

The appearance of the archetype of the divine child – the collective inner child – presages a transformation in the individual or the collective psyche, the possibility of renewal and expansion. 'There is within us', writes Edith Sullwold in the opening essay of this book, 'a creative force which is beckoning, forcing us out of its own essential nature, to leave the old and familiar world view and step forward into the new'.

'SING, MUSE, THE CHILD!'

This child awareness in our midst is a healthy sign for our culture, portending good things for our children. As Homer made his ancient invocation, 'Sing, Muse, the Child!', so we might now look to the child within for inspiration.

This book has come into being to satisfy that objective. It brings together, for the first time, major writings on the subject of the inner child. The intentions of the book are simple and direct: to give structure to a field of inquiry that is both compelling and timely; and to supply the reader with the best, most readable, inspiring material available. The project has been guided by synchronicity, persistence, and the good faith of many people. Chance encounters and suggestions from many unnamed helpmeets have played no small part. Such an endeavour becomes itself a practice in discovery, in developing that sense of choosing the right thing to do, and in trusting one's naive reaction as it occurs. This has been an unexpected blessing, a beneficial gift which the child has brought along.

The selection of material for this collection has been made after an extensive literature search, each contribution chosen for its particular quality of thought, point of view, and passion for the subject. The selections are clustered around six major themes, focused topics that emerged once the breadth of the subject was fully surveyed. The section introductions provide a skeletal structure for the book, describing each main theme and giving a general context for the essays in each section. Shorter, lead-in descriptions preceding each essay provide more specific contextual information.

Part 1 examines the mythic dimensions of the inner child theme, the innate images of childhood and childlikeness that we all carry. Here we meet the archetype of the child and the divine child, the poetic and mysterious child-god filled with promise and possibility, reverie and wonder, rebirth and renewal, the very highest and best in all of us.

Part 2 carries the theme of abandonment – figurative, literal, intentional, unintentional; the abandoned, repressed, unloved, or lost child, the victim of fate, circumstance, and neglect.

Part 3 focuses on the paradigmatic problem of narcissistic disturbances, the minefield most children have to cross, the inner dilemma of our time. Here we learn about the effects of inner conflicts on the formation of self, self-concept, and character. We meet the *puer aeternus*, the eternal youth who, in order to avoid further loss, hovers above life, living only provisionally. Though exuberant and charming, this disturbed inner child is not yet willing to take life for real.

Part 4 is about the wounded child, the child as victim, abused, abandoned, neglected, a product of dysfunctional family life or societal indifference. Where there is wounding there is also healing, and all the pieces in this section also address the healing of that wounded inner child.

Part 5 moves up and out, beyond the vale of tears and injury, to the practical tasks of recovering the younger self, of realizing the child's gifts and embracing its vitality.

Finally, part 6 examines the revitalization of child-rearing practices through knowledge and awareness of the child within.

* * * * *

We came on this trek
To find our life.
For we are all,
We are all,
We are all the children of . . .
A brilliantly coloured flower,
A flaming flower.
And there is no one,
There is no one,
Who regrets what we are.

HUICHOL INDIAN CHANT[9]

Part One

THE PROMISE OF THE INNER CHILD

≈

INTRODUCTION

≈

In every adult there lurks a child – an eternal child, something that is always becoming, is never completed, and calls for unceasing care, attention, and education. That is the part of the human personality which wants to develop and become whole.

C. G. JUNG

We begin, first of all, with the archetype of the child, what we might call the 'big' image of the child within, since it is the child each of us carries, both as a part of ourselves and as an encoded form of the collective human experience of the child. In the beginning was the newly created being, the child, as in the garden of Eden, filled with innocence, wonder, happiness, all the possibilities of human life and the future. The promise that child holds is within us. It is in our origins and in our hopes.

This promise begins with a birth. When a child is born a star lights up, a world of possibilities opens. Each writer in this section discusses the inner possibilities that the child carries for both the individual life and for the collective life of man.

Edith Sullwold introduces us to the archetypal world of the child, suggesting that each birth, each child's life, is a fresh experiment in humankind's spiritual evolution. She differentiates for us the personal world of the inner child from the larger realm of the mythic child.

Carl Jung's essay, laden with the freight of complex ideas, is the definitive work on the mythic dimensions of the inner child. The child is a symbol, says Jung, that expresses 'the all-embracing nature of psychic wholeness'. In describing the child archetype, he says that 'it is a well-nigh hopeless undertaking to tear a single archetype out of the living tissue of the psyche; but despite their interwovenness they do form units of meaning that can be apprehended intuitively'. (Therefore, we recommend using your intuitive faculties, rather than your analytic ones, in tackling Jung's article.)

June K. Singer, whose essay forms Chapter 3, treats the divine child as an extension of our collective awareness, saying it symbolically represents 'the ideals of a culture which it is not able, in reality, to fulfil'. Her provocative ideas on the child motif expand on the Jungian archetypal perspective. She also introduces us to the *puer aeternus* archetype, the eternal child who is the subject of Part 3 of this book.

This section ends with the great mystery of rebirth and the idea of becoming a child again through a metaphoric process of death-rebirth. Ralph Metzner's succinct essay makes it clear that renewal is the birth of a spiritual attitude, often taking the form of a realization of the inner child. 'Out of the turmoil and darkness of dying', he says, 'comes the sparkling vitality of the newborn self. This new self is connected to the eternal source of all life, that source from which we all derive, the divine essence within. It is therefore aptly named "the eternal child." '

A FRESH EXPERIMENT: THE ARCHETYPE OF THE INNER CHILD

Edith Sullwold

Edith Sullwold brings considerable energy, understanding, and sensitivity to the difficult task of distinguishing the personal from the archetypal qualities of the inner child. Her warm and particular feelings for the child's inner life are blended here with scholarship, interpretive skill, and a storyteller's knowledge of her material. This essay was originally delivered by the author on November 20, 1987, as the keynote address at the conference Reawakening the Inner Child, in Washington, D.C. Dr Sullwold, who is a child therapist and therapist supervisor, generously agreed to expand and adapt her talk expressly for this collection, to once again sound the keynote on the inner child.

One of my favourite quotations regarding the child comes from a rather unlikely source, the pen of George Bernard Shaw. In an essay that asks, what is a child?, he answers:

> *An experiment. A fresh attempt to produce the just man made perfect, that is, to make humanity divine. And you will vitiate the experiment if you make the slightest attempt to abort it into some fancy figure of your own, for example, your notion of a good man or a womanly woman . . . If you begin with its holiest aspirations, and suborn them for your own purposes, there is hardly any limit to the mischief you may do.*[1]

This statement seems to speak with a profound understanding of the nature of both the outer and inner child. The idea that a child is a 'fresh experiment' implies that the child is viewed as an individual with gifts and limitations particular to his or her own unique nature – a being who can contribute to the exploration of life's meaning, who can contribute to the richness of life's possibilities.

This new being, out of necessity for nurturance and guidance, finds himself in a particular family, a particular culture, a particular education. Within these particulars are rules, values, and systems to which the child beings to adapt, becoming shaped by them. This shaping often happens to such an extent that the child is no longer connected to those aspects of his being which do not fit within the structure of these outer forms and expectations. For some, adaptation means that those gifts which do not fit within the structure or are not valued are submerged and consequently lost, not only to the individual but to the culture as well.

In others, the vitality of these gifts cannot be so easily submerged. Lacking appropriate channels for expression, the energy behind these gifts will cause pain, as can any energy when it is blocked and pushes for a chance to live.

This experience can be like that which Wordsworth so well describes, 'Shades of the prison-house begin to close/Upon the growing Boy'[2] ('The Boy' refers to the Divine or Self aspect). Every time I read this line I feel within my own body the double strain of restriction from the outside and the organic pressure of growth from the inside.

While writing this, on the first glorious day of spring, I went outside to watch our tulips open in the sun. I noticed some day lilies that had struggled to come up through a few boards left over from our winter building project. The force of these fragile shoots in a vital push for growth was amazing, but because of the restriction of the boards they were bent, distorted, and somewhat yellow. Once out into the light and free of the boards, perhaps they would be able to straighten up, continue to grow, and eventually to blossom. But they might never gain the fullness of other flowers nearby that had only the open space of sun, air, and rain to meet as they emerged.

So it is often with the child. The board once used to provide structure may crush or distort the natural organic life of our children. We need to be continually vigilant in looking under those boards – examining our value systems and our assumptions about reality.

Where shall we turn for the inspiration and encouragement to lift up the debris of the old and restricting structure – our notions of the 'good man' or 'womanly woman' of which Shaw speaks? Unfortunately, these images are often formed out of an unconscious acceptance of the collective definitions of success, health and normality.

Here Shaw's last phrase is important – the idea that the child has his or her own 'holiest aspirations', own unique path. In this context, the word 'holiest' may have two meanings. The aspirations or intentions are seen to have a holy or spiritual source. And we know the word 'holy' is related to 'whole'. To take this gift of life we are given and carefully, respectfully help it to grow to its fullest can be the 'holiest' task. This growth must include all aspects of our being as individuals, not only those that are sanctioned by collective values. This urge to grow is as natural in each of us as the urge to push up past the boards was in the day lily. C. G. Jung says in his essay on 'The Psychology of the Child Archetype' that the image of the child 'represents the strongest, the most ineluctable urge in every being, namely the urge to realize itself'.[3]

The divine aspect of the inner child that resides in us all is a source that when consciously realized can give us the courage and enthusiasm of exploration to break out of our 'prison doors'. I use the word 'divine' to distinguish this aspect from the inner child which has been formed by memory of personal experience – that is, the neglected, abused, unfed, unloved, overdisciplined, overjudged child, as well as the vulnerable and needful aspects of the child we once were. This is the child – our child of experience – which we all desire to heal, so that we can reclaim the energy for adult action that still resides in the reactive patterns of defence and protection that we developed in response to early painful experiences. To heal this child also means that we will not unconsciously continue these patterns with the 'fresh experiments' that are our own children.

The actual child of our memory is no longer who we are. Though we have survived beyond it, we frequently continue to live our lives unaware of patterns we adopted when we were young, and thus we limit the scope of our living in the present. The consequences of the hurt, fear, anger, and loneliness of early years have been given much recognition in recent years in psychological theory and therapeutic practice. However, when the spotlight is thrown on early experiences, other memories also can return – positive images of events that supported the child's natural exuberance, curiosity and adventurous exploration, the deliciousness of the senses and the richness of the imagination. These memories, allowed to emerge, give us a sense of the history of our pleasure and pains, reconnecting us to the being we are now as adults. How we live in the present is a consequence of all the events which have come to us in our experiment with living.

In addition to memories of actual events, we often carry within us an image of the ideal childhood, one with perfect nurturance and guidance. It is the childhood we would have liked, constructed out of the limitations of our own experience. By comparison, we find our own childhood wanting. This image is sometimes projected on others whom we perceive as having had a perfect childhood, and we increase our loneliness and pain as we mourn for the ideal. Frequently this image is also projected on our children as we try to provide a perfect childhood for them, at the same time creating an image of ourselves as the perfect parents.

One antidote for this paradisical idealization of childhood is to share our stories and history with others, discovering thereby that the common human condition of children and parents is a complex blend of successes and failures, gifts and limitations.

Behind these images of the actual and the ideal childhood is the image of the divine inner child mentioned earlier, which comes from the deepest archetypal level of our being. This archetypal image has as its universal function the task of seeing that our experiment with living remains fresh. The divine inner child has innocence, which the Zen master Suzuki Roshi called 'beginner's mind'. It represents spontaneity and the deep urge of the human soul to expand, to grow, and to explore vast and unlimited territories.

Sometimes this inner child makes very strong demands, presenting itself in emotions of anxiety, depression, anger, hopelessness, or in physical symptoms. Sometimes it brings us subtle and fragile new shoots of inspiration – a sudden idea, a dream, a fantasy, or a feeling of longing for something renewing. The natural, vital force of this archetype wants recognition by us and cannot be ignored without consequences. If we do not claim its enlivening energy for ourselves, we often project it outwardly. If we place the archetypal child onto our outer, physical children, then they will carry the burden of our own creative development.

This inspiring image of the inner child represents the creative aspects of life, both within the individual human being and in the collective. It is expressed in myth, the metaphorical realm of history. In every culture there are stories of the birth of the special child – child of the gods, goddesses, and heroes – timeless stories that belong to the species. As we hear these ancient stories we can perhaps resonate with them as songs of our primal origins. Here we can rediscover and remember the roots of our own nature, our instincts, and creativity, and recognize elements of our being we once knew instinctively. They can remind us of our incipient wholeness, which was in our origins.

Perhaps it is best to give an example of such a story. My favourite one among the Greek epiphanies is the story of Hermes as a child. Hermes is born of a union of Zeus and the wood nymph Maia. Maia's name reminds us of the month of May; of Mary the mother of another Divine Child, Jesus; and of Maya, the mother of Buddha. To protect Hermes from Zeus's jealous wife Hera, Maia keeps the infant in a cave, as if in a second womb. Zeus has abandoned his new son and has returned to Olympus and his old family.

Maia, a spirit of nature, cares for Hermes. A trickster in character, the child escapes the cave in the early morning of the first day of his life, creates a lyre from a tortoise shell, and steals his brother Apollo's cattle. Apollo apprehends his younger brother and takes him to trial at the court of Zeus. Hermes, according to Homer, replies to all-knowing Zeus's accusations, 'How could I have done such a thing? I was only born yesterday', and winks at Zeus. At that, Zeus laughs, and all those on Olympus laugh with him. Zeus's only dictum is that harmony be established between the two brothers, a feat that is ultimately achieved when Hermes plays the new instrument of harmony he has created, the lyre.

In this story we find the universally common elements of mythic tales recounting the birth of the divine child. Although there are variations of plot, circumstance, and costume, these mythic dramas seem to share a skeletal structure that defines the general qualities and characteristics of the inner child, attributes that have much meaning to us psychologically.

In the first place, these children are born under circumstances of unusual conception and delivery – unusual from the point of view of ordinary human birth. These conceptions are sometimes the result of the union of spirit and human, as in the immaculate conception of Mary or in the case of Buddha's mother, who is impregnated by an elephant. Sometimes the union is that of a god with some aspect of nature, as Hermes born from Zeus and the wood nymph. The birth itself can be unusual, directly out of primal elements of water or fire (Venus), or out of the head of Zeus (Athena), or from his thigh (Dionysus).

These unusual births speak metaphorically of the emergence in us of a new beginning that comes from unknowable, unexpected, out-of-the-ordinary sources and creates spontaneous birthings within our own psyches. These may come as hunches, dreams, visions, or emotions. If the outer personality or the culture has developed in a one-sided, restricted manner, the appearance of the divine inner child will presage the possibility of renewal and expansion. The inner birth may be conceived through an outer event that startles or surprises us. Perhaps seen as an accident of fate, it awakens us to a new insight of life possibility.

The child, so unusually conceived and delivered, comes into a particular situation, culture, or order that is already formed, whether in the realm of the gods, the underworld, or the human sphere. This world has its own established patterns and principles represented by those in power, and this unusually created and creative child is in most cases in great danger from the old order. Even Apollo attempts to destroy his precocious baby brother, Hermes. Herod kills the young in order to be sure of destroying the Christ child. Hera, always jealous of Zeus's mating with the new and virginal elements, seeks to destroy the progeny of such unions. These rulers represent in us the old structure that does not want to lose its power to the new and divinely conceived being. To incorporate the new, the old must give way to change.

To be sensitive and responsive to the promptings and demands of this inner child, who is constantly urging us to be more, opens us for change. On the other hand, the discomfort of this experience will often result in attempts to placate, distract, or tranquillize this inner child, or to ignore it and deny it time and attention. Thus we jeopardize our own 'holiest aspirations'.

In addition to danger from the existing order that wants to maintain its established power, these divine children of myth and psyche are exposed and vulnerable because they are often abandoned by one or both parents, as Zeus abandons Hermes. Within our own psyches this may indicate that the ordinary familiar parents, patterns of what we already know, abandon this child to his own devices to find his own singular, nonconventional place in the order of things.

Although abandoned by his divine parents, the child is often protected by guardians from the earth realm, representations of the natural forces in our own simple, primitive nature that can nurture this special child quietly, with a kind of earth-peasant knowledge. This natural force can allow the child to become earthed, to become incarnated in us in its own natural organic timing.

The child's place of birth often offers some protection. Hermes is born in a cave, a kind of second womb. So was his father, Zeus, protecting him from being devoured by *his* father, Chronos. Christ is born in a stable, since there is no room at the collective inn. And here again it is the animals and shepherds who first surround him. In this protected place, the child can gain strength until ready to enter the threatening world. Psychologically, this protection may represent some development in us – a creative idea, a dream, or a new attitude or relation to life – that should not be manifested or brought out into the light before it has a certain maturity and can survive on its own and, consequently, can bring effective and integrated change to the old order. Christ is twelve when he returns and speaks to the elders in the temple.

Paradoxically, this abandoned and threatened child that needs protection is already full of creative individuality and indestructible power. It is the extraordinary gift of Hermes that creates the lyre and threatens Apollo with the magical power of trickery. Buddha, just born, walks seven steps from his mother and, pointing both upward and downward, declares himself Prince of all that is above and below. It is this power that draws the three Kings of the Orient to come and worship the Christ child.

In fact, it is precisely this recognized, prophesized, intuited power that is such a threat to the old order. It is not just an ordinary event, this birth. In psychological terms it can be seen as a manifestation of the Self, which demands a restructuring of the personality. This can lead to a painful disintegration of the old form and often a time of confusion, loneliness, and disorientation before the new order is established.

These potentially painful trials are sensed by the currently ruling principle in the personality, the ego. The ego may set up resistances in an attempt to silence the new voice. But being divine, it will not be silenced. We always have before us the choice of listening to it cry to us out of its prison, or to join its exuberant, joyful movement toward an expanded, more humane life. Then we can enter with it into the world of divine play.

Hermes brought laughter and the sound of soothing, harmonious music into the world of Olympus – a new ingredient in the kingdom to be acknowledged and appreciated, changing the quality of the realm forever.

In the modern adult, the energy of the inner child may result in dramatic changes in lifestyle and image. It may lead only to the pursuit of new interests or habits. But once born in us, this child will demand that we expand our world to include it, to suffer the abandonment of our own inner familiarities that sustained us, and to tolerate the loneliness arising from creative action conceived out of an inspired connection to the new. The prize to be won is our totality, a totality hinted at in our beginnings and to which we are inexorably drawn. It is possible that cultures can also be so renewed, old orders reexamined and reconstructed, leading toward a more harmonious world for the human race.

The archetype of the inner child, then, can bring a sense of hope to the hopelessness of our personal history and world history. It reminds us of a time as it was in the beginning, the moment of creation, the new, the unexpected, the individual difference that changes the whole. This is the promise of the 'fresh experiment', the promise of the inner child.

THE PSYCHOLOGY
OF THE CHILD ARCHETYPE
C. G. Jung

≈

*This is an excerpt from the pioneering study of the inner child. To under-
stand the child archetype requires some grounding in Jung's background
notion of the collective unconscious, which he conceived of as the reposi-
tory of humanity's psychic heritage and possibilities. It also requires some
understanding of the nature of the archetype, one of Jung's major discoveries, perhaps the fundamental concept in his work. He developed his
theory of the archetypes in stages, beginning around 1912. The realization of his own inner child came from personal encounters around the
same time (see Chapters 7 and 26 for details of these experiences). This
essay contains the quintessential musings on the inner child. It is pregnant with the very thoughts that have spawned and given reality to our
subject; it is referenced by several contributors in this volume.*

The archetype, according to Jung, 'is an irrepresentable unconscious,
pre-existent form that seems to be part of the inherited structure of the
psyche. Its form might perhaps be compared to the axial system of a
crystal, which, as it were, preforms the crystalline structure in the
mother liquid, although it has no material existence of its own . . . The
archetype in itself is empty and purely formal, nothing but a preformed
faculty, a possibility of representation which is given a priori. The representations themselves are not inherited, only the forms, and in that
respect they correspond in every way to the instincts, which are also
determined in form only. The existence of the instincts can no more be
proved than the existence of the archetypes, so long as they do not manifest themselves concretely' (CW, vol. 9, i, para. 155).

Jung also said: 'Archetypes were, and still are, living psychic forces . . .

Always they were the bringers of protection and salvation, and their viola-
tion has as its consequence the "perils of the soul" known to us from the
psychology of primitives. Moreover, they are the unfailing causes of
neurotic and even psychotic disorders, behaving exactly like neglected or
maltreated physical organs or organic functional systems' (CW, vol. 9, i,
para. 266).

The Critical Dictionary of Jungian Analysis *(Samuels, et al., 1986)*
says the following:

> *All psychic imagery partakes of the archetypal to some extent. That*
> *is why dreams and many other psychic phenomena have numi-*
> *nosity. Archetypal behaviours are most evident at times of crisis,*
> *when the ego is most vulnerable. Archetypal qualities are found in*
> *symbols and this accounts in part for their fascination, utility and*
> *recurrence. Gods are metaphors of archetypal behaviours and*
> *myths are archetypal enactments. The archetypes can neither be*
> *fully integrated nor lived out in human form. Analysis involves a*
> *growing awareness of the archetypal dimensions of a person's life*
> *... Jung's concept of the archetype is in the tradition of Platonic*
> *Ideas, which are present in the minds of the gods and serve as the*
> *models of all entities in the human realm.*

This essay in its complete form was published originally in 1940; an
English translation was made in 1949, the current translation in 1963.

THE ARCHETYPE AS A LINK WITH THE PAST

As to the *psychology* of our theme I must point out that every statement going beyond the purely phenomenal aspects of an archetype
lays itself open to criticism. Not for a moment dare we succumb to
the illusion that an archetype can be finally explained and disposed
of. Even the best attempts at explanation are only more or less
successful translations into another metaphorical language.
(Indeed, language itself is only an image.) The most we can do is to

dream the myth onwards and give it a modern dress. And whatever explanation or interpretation does to it, we do to our own souls as well, with corresponding results for our own well-being.

The archetype – let us never forget this – is a psychic organ present in all of us. A bad explanation means a correspondingly bad attitude to this organ, which may thus be injured. But the ultimate sufferer is the bad interpreter himself. Hence the 'explanation' should always be such that the functional significance of the archetype remains unimpaired, so that an adequate and meaningful connection between the conscious mind and the archetype is assured. For the archetype is an element of our psychic structure and thus a vital and necessary component in our psychic economy. It represents or personifies certain instinctive data of the dark, primitive psyche, the real but invisible roots of consciousness. Of what elementary importance the connection with these roots is, we see from the preoccupation of the primitive mentality with certain 'magic' factors, which are nothing less than what we would call archetypes. This original form of *religio* ('linking back') is the essence, the working basis of all religious life even today, and always will be, whatever future form this life may take.

There is no 'rational' substitute for the archetype any more than there is for the cerebellum or the kidneys. We can examine the physical organs anatomically, histologically, and embryologically. This would correspond to an outline of archetypal phenomenology and its presentation in terms of comparative history. But we only arrive at the *meaning* of a physical organ when we begin to ask teleological questions. Hence the query arises: What is the biological purpose of the archetype? Just as physiology answers such a question for the body, so it is the business of psychology to answer it for the archetype.

Statements like 'The child motif is a vestigial memory of one's own childhood' and similar explanations merely beg the question. But if, giving this proposition a slight twist, we were to say, 'The child motif is a picture of certain *forgotten* things in our childhood,' we are getting closer to the truth. Since, however, the archetype is always an image belonging to the whole human race and not merely to the individual, we might put it better this way: 'The child motif represents the pre-conscious childhood aspect of the collective psyche.'[1]

(It may not be superfluous to point out that lay prejudice is always inclined to identify the child motif with the concrete experience 'child', as though the real child were the cause and precondition of the existence of the child motif. In psychological reality, however, the empirical idea 'child' is only the means [and not the only one] by which to express a psychic fact that cannot be formulated more exactly. Hence by the same token the mythological idea of the child is emphatically not a copy of the empirical child but a *symbol* clearly recognizable as such: it is a wonder-child, a divine child, begotten, born, and brought up in quite extraordinary circumstances, and not – this is the point – a human child. Its deeds are as miraculous or monstrous as its nature and physical constitution. Only on account of these highly unempirical properties is it necessary to speak of a 'child motif' at all. Moreover, the mythological 'child' has various forms: now a god, giant, Tom Thumb, animal, etc., and this points to a causality that is anything but rational or concretely human. The same is true of the 'father' and 'mother' archetypes which, mythologically speaking, are equally irrational symbols.)

We shall not go wrong if we take this statement for the time being *historically*, on the analogy of certain psychological experiences which show that certain phases in an individual's life can become autonomous, can personify themselves to the extent that they result in a *vision of oneself* – for instance, one sees oneself as a child. Visionary experiences of this kind, whether they occur in dreams or in the waking state, are, as we know, conditional on a dissociation having previously taken place between past and present. Such dissociations come about because of various incompatibilities; for instance, a man's present state may have come into conflict with his childhood state, or he may have violently sundered himself from his original character in the interests of some arbitrary persona[2] more in keeping with his ambitions. He has thus become unchildlike and artificial, and has lost his roots. All this presents a favourable opportunity for an equally vehement confrontation with the primary truth.

In view of the fact that men have not yet ceased to make statements about the child god, we may perhaps extend the individual analogy to the life of mankind and say in conclusion that humanity, too, probably always comes into conflict with its childhood conditions, that is, with its original, unconscious, and instinctive state, and that the danger of the kind of conflict which induces the vision of the 'child' actually exists. Religious observances, i.e., the retelling and ritual repetition of the mythical event, consequently serve the purpose of bringing the image of childhood, and everything connected with it, again and again before the eyes of the conscious mind so that the link with the original condition may not be broken.

THE FUNCTION OF THE ARCHETYPE

The child motif represents not only something that existed in the distant past but also something that exists *now*; that is to say, it is not just a vestige but a system functioning in the present whose purpose is to compensate or correct, in a meaningful manner, the inevitable one-sidedness and extravagances of the conscious mind. It is in the nature of the conscious mind to concentrate on relatively few contents and to raise them to the highest pitch of clarity. A necessary result and precondition is the exclusion of other potential contents of consciousness. The exclusion is bound to bring about a certain one-sidedness of the conscious contents. Since the differentiated consciousness of civilized man has been granted an effective instrument for the practical realization of its contents through the dynamics of his will, there is all the more danger, the more he trains his will, of his getting lost in one-sidedness and deviating further and further from the laws and roots of his being. This means, on the one hand, the possibility of human freedom, but on the other it is a source of endless transgressions against one's instincts. Accordingly, primitive man, being closer to his instincts, like the animal, is characterized by fear of novelty and adherence to tradition. To our way of thinking he is painfully backward, whereas we exalt progress. But our progressiveness, though it may result in a great many delightful wish-fulfilments, piles up an equally gigantic Promethean debt which has to be paid off from time to time in the form of hideous catastrophes. For ages man has dreamed of flying, and all we have got for it is saturation bombing! We smile today at the Christian hope of a life beyond the grave, and yet we often fall into chiliasms a hundred times more ridiculous than the notion of a happy Hereafter. Our differentiated consciousness is in continual danger of being uprooted; hence it needs compensation through the still existing state of childhood.

The symptoms of compensation are described, from the progressive point of view, in scarcely flattering terms. Since, to the superficial eye, it looks like a retarding operation, people speak of inertia, backwardness, scepticism, fault-finding, conservatism, timidity, pettiness, and so on. But inasmuch as man has, in high degree, the capacity for cutting himself off from his own roots, he also may be swept uncritically to catastrophe by his dangerous one-sidedness. The retarding ideal is always more primitive, more natural (in the good sense as in the bad), and more 'moral' in that it keeps faith with law and tradition. The progressive ideal is always more abstract, more unnatural, and less 'moral' in that it demands disloyalty to tradition. Progress enforced by will is always *convulsive*. Backwardness may be closer to naturalness, but in its turn it is always menaced by painful awakenings. The older view of things realized that progress is only possible *Deo concedente* ('God willing'), thus proving itself conscious of the opposites and repeating the age-old *rites d'entree et de sortie* ('rites of passage') on a higher plane. The more differentiated consciousness becomes, the greater the danger of severance from the root-condition. Complete severance comes when the *Deo concedente* is forgotten. Now it is an axiom of psychology that when a part of the psyche is split off from consciousness it is only *apparently* inactivated; in actual fact it brings about a possession of the personality, with the result that the individual's aims are falsified in the interests of the split-off part. If, then, the childhood state of the collective psyche is repressed to the point of total exclusion, the unconscious content overwhelms the conscious aim and inhibits, falsifies, even destroys its realization. Viable progress only comes from the cooperation of both.

THE FUTURITY OF THE ARCHETYPE

One of the essential features of the child motif is its futurity. The child is potential future. Hence the occurrence of the child motif in the psychology of the individual signifies as a rule an anticipation of future developments, even though at first sight it may seem like a retrospective configuration. Life is a flux, a flowing into the future, and not a stoppage or a backwash. It is therefore not surprising that so many of the mythological saviours are child gods. This agrees exactly with our experience of the psychology of the individual, which shows that the 'child' paves the way for a future change of personality. In the individuation process, it anticipates the figure that comes from the synthesis of conscious and unconscious elements in the personality. It is therefore a symbol which unites the opposites;[3] a mediator, bringer of healing, that is, one who makes whole. Because it has this meaning, the child motif is capable of the numerous transformations mentioned above: it can be expressed by roundness, the circle or sphere, or else by the quaternity as another form of wholeness.[4] I have called this wholeness that transcends consciousness the 'self'[5] The goal of the individuation process is the synthesis of the self. From another point of view the term 'entelechy' might be preferable to 'synthesis' [entelechy = a vital force urging an organism toward self-fulfilment]. There is an empirical reason why 'entelechy' is, in certain conditions, more fitting: the symbols of wholeness frequently occur at the beginning of the individuation process, indeed they can often be observed in the first dreams of early infancy. This observation says much for the *a priori* existence of potential wholeness,[6] and on this account the idea of entelechy instantly recommends itself. But insofar as the individuation process occurs, empirically speaking, as a synthesis, it looks paradoxically enough, as if something already existent were being put together. From this point of view, the term 'synthesis' is also applicable.

THE CHILD AS BEGINNING AND END

Faust, after his death, is received as a boy into the 'choir of blessed youths'. I do not know whether Goethe was referring, with this peculiar idea, to the *cupids* on antique grave-stones. It is not unthinkable. The figure of the *cucullatus* points to the hooded, that is, the *invisible* one, the genius of the departed, who reappears in the childlike frolics of a new life, surrounded by the sea-forms of dolphins and tritons. The sea is the favourite symbol for the unconscious, the mother of all that lives. Just as the 'child' is, in certain circumstances (e.g., in the case of Hermes and the Dactyls), closely related to the phallus, symbol of the begetter, so it comes up again in the sepulchral phallus, symbol of a renewed begetting.

The 'child' is therefore *renatus in novam infantiam* ('reborn into a new childhood'). It is thus both beginning and end, an initial and a terminal creature. The initial creature existed before man was, and terminal creature will be when man is not. Psychologically speaking, this means that the 'child' symbolizes the pre-conscious and the post-conscious essence of man. His pre-conscious essence is the unconscious state of earliest childhood; his post-conscious essence is an anticipation by analogy of life after death. In this idea the all-embracing nature of psychic wholeness is expressed. Wholeness is never comprised within the compass of the conscious mind – it includes the indefinite and indefinable extent of the unconscious as well. Wholeness, empirically speaking, is therefore of immeasurable extent, older and younger than consciousness and enfolding it in time and space. This is no speculation, but an immediate psychic experience. Not only is the conscious process continually accompanied, it is often guided, helped, or interrupted, by unconscious happenings. The child had a psychic life before it had consciousness. Even the adult still says and does things whose significance he realizes only later, if ever. And yet he said them and did them as if he knew what they meant. Our dreams are continually saying things beyond our conscious comprehension (which is why they are so useful in the therapy of neuroses). We have intimations and intuitions from unknown sources. Fears, mood, plans, and hopes come to us with no visible causation. These concrete experiences are at the bottom of our feeling that we know ourselves very little; at the bottom, too, of the painful conjecture that we might have surprises in store for ourselves.

Primitive man is no puzzle to himself. The question 'What is man?' is the question that man has always kept until last. Primitive man has so much psyche outside his conscious mind that the experience of something psychic outside him is far more familiar to him than to us. Consciousness hedged about by psychic powers, sustained or threatened or deluded by them, is the age-old experience of mankind. This experience has projected itself into the archetype of the child, which expresses man's wholeness. The 'child' is all that is abandoned and exposed and at the same time divinely powerful; the insignificant, dubious beginning, and the triumphal end. The 'eternal child' in man is an indescribable experience, an incongruity, a handicap, and a divine prerogative; an imponderable that determines the ultimate worth or worthlessness of a personality.

THE MOTIF
OF THE DIVINE CHILD

June Singer

≈

The divine child is a universal manifestation of the child archetype. We see it in examples such as the madonna and child and the child-hero gods of myth. June Singer, practicing Jungian analyst and author, utilizes both her consulting room experience and her authoritative grasp of mythology to draw a portrait of the divine quality of the inner child. This piece is excerpted from her book Boundaries of the Soul, *a rich study of psychotherapy from a Jungian perspective.*

The archetype of the divine child tends to appear in advance of a transformation in the psyche. His appearance recalls the marking of aeons in the history of the world which were heralded by the appearance of an infant who overthrows an old order and, with passion and inspiration, begins a new one. I know of no place where the power of this archetype is better expressed than in William Blake's poem, *A Song of Liberty*, The Eternal Female, the anima, gives birth to the divine child, a sun god with flaming hair. This evokes the jealous rage of the old king, the 'starry king' of night and darkness and all the decadence that has come upon the world. Though the king flings the divine child into the western sea, the child will not be drowned. A night sea journey will take place and when it is finished the son of morning will rise in the east to bring his light to the world:

The Eternal Female groan'd! it was heard all over the Earth!
. . . In her trembling hands she took the new born terror,
  howling:
On those infinite mountains of light, now barr'd out by the
  atlantic sea, the new born fire stood before the starry
  king!
Flag's with grey brow'd snows and thunderous visages, the
  jealous wings wav'd over the deep.
The speary hand burned aloft, unbuckled was the shield;
  forth went the hand of jealousy among the flaming hair,
  and hurl'd the new born wonder thro' the starry night.
The fire, the fire is falling! . . .

The fiery limbs, the flaming hair, shot like the sinking sun
  into the western sea . . .
With thunder and fire, leading his starry hosts thro' the
  waste wilderness, [the gloomy king] promulgates his ten
  commands, glancing his beamy eyelids over the deep in dark
  dismay,
Where the son of fire in his eastern cloud, while the
  morning plumes her golden breast.
Spurning the clouds written with curses, stamps the stony
  law to dust, loosing the eternal horses from the dens of
  night, crying:
Empire is no more! And now the Lion & Wolf shall cease.[1]

In [Jungian] analysis, the motif of the child frequently appears in the course of the individuation process. At first the analysand tends to identify this with his own infantilism, and this may be appropriate to a degree. Wherever the appearance of the child in dreams or other kinds of imagery bears a resemblance to the dreamer himself, or to a form of the dreamer's behaviour, the image may be helpful in understanding the personal aspects of the material itself. It may be helpful in tracing back neurotic elements to an earlier stage of development in the individual.

However, just as fantasy material may, in part, be identifiable with the history of the one who produces it, in part, the image of the divine child may also be new, bearing no resemblance whatever to the previous experience of the individual. It is this latter element that encourages the imagination to dwell on the futurity of the archetype – that is, to ask what this image may suggest about developments which are still embryonic in the psyche but which have the potentiality for growth and change.

As our own children are, to a certain extent, extensions of our own egos, so the 'divine child' may be thought of as an extension of the collective consciousness. As we pin our hopes and dreams on our children, wishing for them the fulfilment of our unfinished tasks, the realization of what we were never able to realize, so the 'divine child' represents the ideals of a culture which it is not able, in reality, to fulfil. Often the 'saviour' becomes the scapegoat for the sins of his society, and by reason of his suffering and his sacrifice the society is enabled to continue, to have another chance.

The divine child is unusual from the very circumstances of his birth, or even of his conception. Perhaps he is taken from his mother in order to prevent some dire fate to the family or the community. Moses, Oedipus and Krishna were taken from their mothers and reared by strangers; Romulus and Remus were abandoned to the wilderness; all of these children were saved for a special mission. Some miraculous design kept them safe until the time was ripe for their task to be fulfilled. In the intervening years the child would overcome many difficulties and develop his own sense of meaning and a style of living which expresses that meaning. At the appropriate time he manifests himself and brings into reality that dynamic change for which he was appointed. Shortly thereafter he dies, having accomplished that for which he came.'

In our own dreams the appearance of the special child often carries with it a profound meaning. In my practice I have found that it is common for a child who is maimed or ill or dying to appear in a dream. This may have no correspondence to the life of the individual, and so I find myself wondering – in what way is the dreamer's innate potential being distorted or cut off? The analysis of the specific details in the unconscious material and some comparison with similar details as they appear in the archetypal situations in the literature of myth and comparative religion may enable the individual to get beyond his immediate concern and to see where he is going in terms of his life task. As Viktor Frankl pointed out in *Man's Search for Meaning*, his report on his concentration camp experiences, those who regarded their lives in the camp as 'provisional' and lived only from day to day quickly lost their strength. The few who were able to find, through their suffering in a place where their physical bodies were imprisoned, the challenge to free their spirits, these few tended to survive against nearly impossible odds. The divine child within us gives meaning to our immature strivings; he shows us the unconscious side of the limitations which we experience, and that is a vision of potentiality coming into flower.

Another archetype which we are likely to meet along the way of individuation has been called by Jung the *puer aeternus*, after the child god Iachhus in the Eleusinian mysteries.[3] He is described by Ovid in *Metamorphoses* as a divine youth, born into the mother-cult mysteries. A god of vegetation and resurrection, he has some of the qualities of the redeemer. The man who is identified with the archetype of the *puer aeternus*, with eternal youth, is one who has remained too long in adolescent psychology. In him, characteristics which are normal in a youth in his teens are continued into later life.[4] Perhaps the expression 'high living' best describes what this archetype is about: the young man indulges his high-flying fantasies, living out experiences for their sheer excitement, picking up friends when he wants amusement and dropping them when they become in any sense a responsibility. Some of the heroes of the youth culture fall into this category, and again, for some 'getting high' is the objective in and of itself. The aimless travelling, moving in and out of various groups, is characteristic of the *puer*. Homosexuality is an expression of this archetype, especially when homosexuality takes the form of casual and promiscuous relationships, compulsively arrived at. If he is heterosexually inclined, he forms one liaison after another, only to drop each one at the first suggestion that some commitment may be required of him.

Von Franz, in her study of the *puer aeternus* archetype,[5] suggests that the man who is identified with this archetype often seeks a career in flying, but that he is usually rejected on application for the reason that psychological tests show up his instability and the neurotic reasons for his interest in this profession.

The dreams of an individual who is established in his life in a secure position, who may be already middle-aged, may disclose the operation of the *puer aeternus* archetype. The motifs of flying (sometimes without any plane, just by flapping the arms), high-speed driving, deep-sea diving, climbing precarious mountain cliffs, are all typical of one whose unconscious is dominated by this archetype. They may be taken as a warning signal to be aware of the ways in which the unconscious may be preparing to intrude its autonomous will in the way of consciously determined functioning.

There is, of course, a feminine counterpart to the *puer* and that is the *puella aeterna*, the woman who is afraid to grow old, although she will never admit it. Still, the fear dominates much of her existence. She is the one who never tells her age, who falls for every diet fad and for every new make-up with the fantastic promise of rejuvenation written into the advertisements. She is a 'pal' to her children, and an everlasting coquette where men are concerned. In her dreams she is often on a pedestal, inspiring the adoration of men, or she is a siren or a whore or a nymphet. In life she generally is reckless and impulsive. When it comes to making an important decision, however, she vacillates a good deal and asks many people for advice. She then acts with surprising suddenness, and she regrets her actions almost before they are completed.

Living the archetype of 'eternal youth' is not altogether negative, as may be inferred from some of the ways we see it manifest itself. Some aspects of the *puer aeternus* or the *puella aeterna* which are most helpful are youthful enthusiasm and the boundless energy to carry it along, spontaneity of thinking, production of new ideas and new ways to solve problems, willingness to strike out in a different direction without being held in by a desire to conserve the past and its values.

The *puer* and *puella* as unconscious factors provide the needed impetus to start out on new paths. They do not necessarily offer the wisdom to discern whether the endeavour is worth the struggle, and they often do not provide the steadying and staying power to carry it through if, indeed, it is worth while. When this archetype is active great dreams and schemes will be hatched. If they are to succeed, even in the smallest part, a compensatory archetype must come into play. This is the 'senex' archetype.[6]

Senex means old or aged and, as archetype, it stands behind the forces that would preserve the traditional values, that hold out for keeping things the way they are, for applying sober judgment and consideration in the schemes of the eternal youth. At best this factor in the unconscious is expressed in mature wisdom born of experience and, at worst, it represents a hidebound orthodoxy that tolerates no interference from those who would break with established patterns.

A variant of the figure of the *puer aeternus*, sometimes even incorporating aspects of the senex, is the enchanting archetypal figure who is known as the *trickster*.

In dreams the trickster is the one who sets obstacles in our path for his own reasons; he is the one who keeps changing shape and appearing and disappearing at the oddest moments. He symbolizes that aspect of our own nature which is always nearby, ready to bring us down when we get inflated, or to humanize us when we become pompous. He is the satirist par excellence, whose trenchant wit points out the flaws in our haughty ambitions, and makes us laugh though we feel like crying. In society we find him as critic or gadfly, and he even pops up in the highest offices of our land.

REBIRTH AND THE ETERNAL CHILD

Ralph Metzner

≈

*Rebirth and renewal are often experiences of renewed hope and possi-
bilities. The child is the promise of the future, the symbol for these transformative processes. In this short excerpt from his book* Opening to
Inner Light, *Ralph Metzner describes the rebirth experience and its
path of intersection with the eternal inner child.*

The process of psychologically dying while one is still alive is
followed by a psychological rebirth, or renewal. In the words of
Ramana Maharshi, 'He who finds his way to the core of the Self,
whence arise all levels of the I, all spheres of the world, he who finds
his way home to his first source with the question "whence am I" is
born and reborn. Know that whoever is so born is the wisest of the
wise – each moment of his life he is born anew'.[1]

This rebirth phase of transformation may be experienced in
several different ways. (a) First, there is the idea of a resurrection, a
restoring to life of a personality that has died. (b) Alternatively,
rebirth is seen as the replacement of the small self by another,
greater Self or Spirit. (c) Third, it is said that one who has died,
whether actually or metaphorically, lives afterward in a different
world, a different state. (d) In the fourth variant, the new being is
actually imagined as a child: this is the archetype of the radiant,
divine, or eternal child, which, as Jung points out, symbolized 'the
potential future'[2]

(a) The idea of resurrection, the restoration to life of an adult
body that has died, is described in many mythic and shamanic tales:

≈ 45

Osiris is put together again by Isis; the twins Hunter and Jaguar of the Popul Vuh reassemble themselves after being dismembered; shamans who have 'died' may be reconstituted by their power animal or ally. Many modern practitioners of shamanic work recount how they were 'cut up', 'pulverized', 'burned', 'eviscerated', or otherwise 'killed', then reconstructed by their animal helper.[3] For example, one man reported how his animal, a 'horse', stood over his lifeless 'corpse' and passed its huge nostrils gently all over his body, 'breathing' life back into him. While, from a sceptical point of view, we could dismiss all this as the deluded fantasy of an overactive imagination, we would still have to account for the fact that this man, like others, felt better and healthier after this experience.

In the New Testament, the story of Lazarus, as well as that of Jesus himself, exemplifies this kind of physical resurrection. To a lesser degree, the modern accounts of near-death experience (NDE) coincide with this kind of pattern. In the case of Jesus, the resurrection was into a nonphysical, 'spiritual' body that yet resembled the physical in all significant respects, even to having the wounds that the physical body had suffered. The closest most of us come to this kind of experience is in suffering a near-fatal illness and then recovering – the body appears to be fully restored to health. A common feature in all these accounts, when the individual is intentionally pursuing a death-rebirth transformation, is that the new body is better than the old; it is stronger, healthier, and lighter.

(b) Another aspect of this rebirth and renewal experience is that the little self is overshadowed or replaced by the Great Self, the personal-physical ego replaced by the transpersonal Spirit, the mortal by the Immortal. Meister Eckhart says, in this experience 'the soul . . . is dead to self and alive to God'.[4] A Sufi saint wrote, 'thy being dies away, and His person covers thy person'.[5] Or, in the words of the Gospel of John. 'No one can enter the Kingdom of God without being born from water and Spirit. That which is born of the flesh is flesh, that which is born of the Spirit is spirit'.[6] People in such states feel their own ego concern and interests fade into insignificance or nothingness in the face of the awesome power and light of the Great

Self, the god within, the 'diamond essence', the *Atman*.

The encounter with the Self can be an overwhelming and annihilating self-confrontation, as was pointed out by C. G. Jung in his essay 'Concerning Rebirth', Jung wrote that

> *He who is truly and hopelessly little will always drag the revelation*
> *of the greater down to the level of his littleness, and will never*
> *understand that the day of judgment for his littleness has dawned.*
> *But the man who is inwardly great will know that the long-*
> *expected friend of his soul, the immortal one, has now really come,*
> *'to lead captivity captive'; that is, to seize hold of him by whom this*
> *immortal had always been confined and held prisoner, and to make*
> *his life flow into that greater life – a moment of deadliest peril.*[7]

As this quotation makes clear, the deadly danger exists for those identified with the small self, the personal ego. Not all encounters with Self, however, need be traumatic or even painful. There is, after all, the vast literature of mysticism that sings in rapturous tones of ecstatic union with the divine, of dyings that are peaceful and blissful, of unitive experiences that have the character of a nuptial or are likened to dissolving in an oceanic feeling of oneness.

(c) Some accounts of death-rebirth experiences emphasize the new quality of awareness and perception that comes into existence afterward. It is as if we had entered a new world in which everything looks and feels different, and a kind of pristine, shining radiance suffuses everything we perceive. Mental and emotional responses to what is perceived are also new; there is a quality of joy and spontaneity and an outpouring of affection and enthusiasm. In an anonymous medieval Hermetic treatise we read, 'The resurrection is the revelation of what is, and the transformation of things, the transition [*metabole*] into newness. For imperishability descends upon the perishable; the light flows down upon the darkness, swallowing it up.'[8] Here we find the metaphor of the newly born paralleling the metaphor of vision with the veils removed, the doors of perception having been cleansed. The mystics say that after the death-rebirth revelation, everything is seen with love and wisdom, from the perspective of the infinite and eternal (*sub specie aeternitatis*).

(d) The biblical admonition that 'except ye become as children, ye cannot enter the Kingdom of Heaven' follows naturally from the teaching that one needs to die before entering the blessed, enlightened state of this Kingdom. Here the death-rebirth metaphor leads us to the archetype of the divine child, the *puer aeternus*. While most discussions by Jungians of the *puer* or *puella* focus on the shadow side of this archetype and on its clinical manifestations in flighty, immature 'playboys' or 'babies', these represent only a limited interpretation of this powerful image. Chinese and Western alchemists spoke of the foetus of immortality, the philosophers' child that is born as a consequence of the inner conjunction of male and female. The idea of the eternal child, who comes into manifestation after a conscious 'death' experience is connected to the numerous myths, which play a central role in most religions, of the birth of a god in human form. The Indian legends of the boy Krishna and the Christian legends of the infant Jesus are only the best-known examples.

Jung, in his essay on 'The Psychology of the Child Archetype', pointed out several of the significant features or meanings of this profound symbol. He described it as an anticipation of the synthesis of conscious or unconscious, as a symbol of wholeness, or the Self. The child-god or child-hero always has an unusual, miraculous birth or a virgin conception – which corresponds to the 'psychic genesis' of the new being. The child image represents a link to the past, to our childhood, as well as a link to the future, as it anticipates a 'nascent state of consciousness'. The 'golden child' or 'eternal youth' is androgynous, because he/she represents the perfect union of opposites. Only the old self, the ordinary ego, identifies itself as male or female – and this self has now died. The 'child' is both beginning and end, 'an initial and a terminal creature', because the wholeness that it symbolizes is 'older and younger than consciousness, enfolding it in time and space'.[9]

The divine child is invincible. He/she overcomes dangerous

enemies in infancy: one of the images of the boy Krishna shows him trampling a giant serpent underfoot in a dance – a metaphor for the overcoming of reptilian instinctual aggressiveness. An example from Greek mythology is the story of the baby Herakles, who strangled a serpent that attacked him in his crib. The Child has all the power of a god, since it is a god: it is the Immortal One that replaces the mortal personality that has 'died'. Here, too, we find the notion of the divine child as representing the triumph over death. Christ demonstrated the power to resurrect – himself as well as another (Lazarus) – and many other divine heroes and yogic adepts of high degree have demonstrated similar powers, as documented particularly in Eastern mystical literature. While such powers might seem remote to the average person, the myths and images that convey them show potentials; they reveal what humans *can* attain.

In the Russian Orthodox liturgy, the triumph over death is expressed in the following words: 'Christ is risen from the dead, trampling down death by death, and upon those in the tomb bestowing life'. I suggest that this imagery refers to the change that occurs in the psyche as the healing, transformative power of the international dying is experienced. The unconscious death tendencies (*thanatos*), which function to oppose the body's life-preserving tendencies (*eros*) through disease and other destructive operations are gradually reduced; or rather, brought into balance. One of my teachers referred to 'pockets of death' within our nature that are opened up and dissolved by enlightened awareness, thus bringing about the death of death. As we consciously accept dying and 'dying', the process provides spiritual nourishment. Shakespeare expresses this idea in one of the sonnets:

> *So shalt thou feed on death,*
> *That feeds on men,*
> *And death once dead, there's*
> *No more dying then.*

In the nontheistic Chinese Taoist tradition, the archetype of the eternal child also is known and treasured. The newborn child is still connected to the Tao, to the source of its life and its arising, and this is why we should emulate it. As Chuang Tsu says: 'Can you be like a newborn child? The baby cries all day and yet his voice never becomes hoarse. That is because he has not lost nature's harmony.'[10] Characteristically, the Taoists emphasize the practical value, in terms of health and well-being, of attunement to the awareness of the infant.

For the individual in a process of transformation, the imagery and mythology of the eternal child fosters a positive and life-affirming attitude: we are encouraged to confront and transform our fear of death, to embrace the process of 'dying' as liberating and as bringing wisdom. We thus come to know that out of the turmoil and darkness of dying comes the sparkling vitality of the newborn self. This new self is connected to the eternal source of all life, that source from which we all derive, the divine essence within. It is hence aptly named 'the eternal child'.

Part Two

THE ABANDONED CHILD

≈

INTRODUCTION

≈

Mankind is an orphan were it not for God, according to St Augustine. Psychologically translated this would imply that for the abandoned child there are no 'good enough' parents ... We are indeed all, in part, orphans, and it is through the suffering of this archetypal fact of abandonment (and abandoning) that we can join together in community. This communal feeling, based on a recognition of our mutual aloneness and suffering, is a religious emotion, an existential reality, and a return to the world with a recognition that the world is all we have, and that maybe it is 'good enough'.

— PATRICIA BERRY, *CHIRON*, 1985

The child begins life in a state akin to paradise. Pure and abounding with possibilities – its needs fulfilled in a maternally enfolding, watery world that is timeless, seamless and without end – the innocent child enters, carrying the great promise of humanity.

But, alas, innocence cannot endure. What begins with infinite potential must eventually move out into the finite, unpredictable world in order to be fulfilled. Hence, an abrupt separation or abandonment is one of the early transitional experiences for each human being, a passage in which the child becomes internalized as the individual personality adapts to the demands of his or her outer circumstance. According to C. G. Jung, abandonment is, in fact, what initially defines the inner child. ' "Child," ' he said, 'means something evolving toward independence. This it cannot do without detaching itself from its origins: abandonment is therefore a necessary condition, not just a concomitant symptom.'

The experience of abandonment – actual, emotional, psychological – is therefore an initiation into life. It is a reenactment of the fall from Eden, a loss of innocence, both a disappointment and a betrayal. Yet, it is a positive event because it sets us in motion on our journey, circling on our way in search of experience and identity. The poet Rainer Maria Rilke gave voice to the positive side of the solitary quest:

I live my life in growing orbits,
which move out over the things of the world.
Perhaps I can never achieve the last,
but that will be my attempt.
I am circling around God, around the ancient tower,
and I have been circling for a thousand years.
And I still don't know if I am a falcon,
Or a storm, or a great song.
        – BOOK FOR THE HOURS OF PRAYER,
        1899 TRANSLATED BY ROBERT BLY

Abandonment requires us to adjust, to accept our predicament. 'It is only when one is truly alone,' says analyst Rose-Emily Rothenberg, 'that the creative potential ["the child"] that is carried deep inside has the space and room to emerge into the light of day.' We must take up the challenge of our separateness. The pain of our aloneness forces us to become aware, to open to the experience of our Self as apart from others. Perhaps we will eventually come around and, as T. S. Eliot said, '. . . arrive where we started/And know the place for the first time' (*The Four Quartets*).

For some, abandonment is a wound to the childhood Self that results in a narrowing adaptation in which the child is buried deep inside under layers of resentment, entitlement and cynicism. In the heart of every cynic, however, is a bleeding romantic, an innocent inner child who has been wounded early in life by disillusionment with parents or by a discovery that the world is not all it had been cracked up to be.

For all of us, the challenge of abandonment is to accept our orphanhood, to acknowledge that we are ultimately on our own, which means a lifelong responsibility for the care and nurturance of our inner child. The person who tries to avoid the experience of abandonment and to preserve idealistic innocence into adulthood does so at great peril. Such denial requires a great deal of energy and can only result in the futility of the narcissistic dilemma (a theme we will take up in Part III).

As long as the inner child is not actually brought into being, if it is not a reality for the individual, it is abandoned. Jung went so far as to suggest that inner-child awareness requires periodic renewal through ritual if it is to be realized as something real and internal. 'The Christ Child,' he wrote in his essay on the child archetype, 'is a religious necessity only so long as the majority of men [and women] are incapable of giving psychological reality to the saying: "Except ye become as little children . . ." '

James Hillman's contribution challenges us to move beyond the literalism of actual abandonment and to consider a variety of inner-child scenarios: abandonment of the child in our collective thinking about childhood and in our psychologizing; abandonment of the child in our dreams, in our relationships and in our models of imagination and maturity.

Marion Woodman's concise words bring us to consider the issues of identity that are constellated by our forsaken inner child: 'If we have lived behind a mask all our lives, sooner or later – if we are lucky – that mask will be smashed . . . Perhaps we will look into the terrified eyes of our own tiny child, that child who has never known love and who now beseeches us to repond.'

M. Scott Peck isolates the abandonment theme in parenting and identifies the destructive consequences of using the threat of abandonment – consciously or unconsciously – as a child-rearing tool. 'Children, abandoned either psychologically or in actuality, enter adulthood lacking any deep sense that the world is a safe and protective place,' he writes.

And finally, in a literary *tour de force*, science fiction writer Ursula K. LeGuin asks us to consider the moral dilemma of abandoning our inner child.

ABANDONING THE CHILD
James Hillman

≈

James Hillman writes passionately, no matter what his subject. Here, writing on the child nature in all of us, he is perhaps at his most eloquent. Hillman's sense of abandonment is not that of a literal plight, not the orphan-without-parentage scenario. He sees an unhealthy sentimentalization of childhood that relegates the inner child to some romantic (though immature) state, a cultural attitude that divides the individual into adult vs. child, where the child and its imaginal power have to be regained from a lost, forgotten and childish status. Hillman is not afraid to tackle the ambiguities of language and concept in order to provoke an awareness of the reader's own psychology and, especially, of that aspect that is 'perennially child.'

This essay is excerpted from a lecture delivered by Dr Hillman in the summer of 1971 at the Eranos Conference, Ascona, Switzerland. Hillman is one of the most exciting voices in psychology today. He was formerly director of studies at the C. G. Jung Institute, Zurich, and is today the foremost proponent of archetypal psychology. He is a prolific writer and lecturer, a Jungian analyst, and editor of the respected journal Spring.

WHAT IS THE CHILD?

What is this 'child' – that is surely the first question. Whatever we say about children and childhood is not altogether really about children and childhood. We need but consult the history of painting to see how peculiar are the images of children, particularly when comparing them in their distortions with contemporary exactitude in depicting landscapes and still lives or the portraits of adults. We need but consult the history of family life, education and economics to realize that children and childhood as we use the terms today are a late invention.[1]

What is this peculiar realm we call 'childhood', and what we are doing by establishing a special world with children's rooms and children's toys, children's clothes and children's books, music, language, caretakers, doctors, of playing children so segregated from the actual lives of working men and women? Clearly, some realm of the psyche called 'childhood' is being personified by the child and carried by the child for the adult. How curiously similar this *daseinsbereich* [realm of being] is to the realm of the madhouse some centuries ago and even today, when the madman was considered a child, the ward of the state or under the parental eye of the doctor who cared for his 'children', the insane, like for his family. Again, how extraordinary this confusion of the child with the insane, of childhood with insanity.[2]

The confusion between the real child and his childhood and the fantasy child that obfuscates our perception of child and childhood is classical to the history of depth psychology. You may remember that Freud at first believed that repressed memories causing neuroses were forgotten emotions and distorted scenes from actual childhood. Later he abandoned this child, realizing that a fantasy factor had been placed in childhood events that had never actually happened; a fantasy child was at work and not an actual occurrence in the life of the person. He was obliged then to separate child of fact from that of fantasy, outer child events from inner childhood. Nevertheless, he stuck to his belief that the job of therapy was the analysis of childhood. A statement of 1919 is typical:

Strictly considered . . . analytic work deserves to be recognized as genuine psycho-analysis only when it has succeeded in removing the amnesia which conceals from the adult his knowledge of his childhood from its beginning (that is, from about the second to the fifth year) . . . The emphasis which is laid here upon the importance of the earliest experience does not imply any underestimation of the influences of later ones. But the later impressions of life speak loudly enough through the mouth of the patient, while it is the physician who has to raise his voice on behalf of the claims of childhood.[3]

What childhood did Freud mean? Actual children, as I pointed out here two years ago, were never analysed by Freud. He did not analyse children. Was the 'childhood' which the analyst had to recapture actual childhood? Here, Freud himself remains ambiguous, for the actual small young human we call 'child' merges in Freud with a Rousseauian, even Orphic-Neoplatonic child who is 'psychologically a different thing than an adult . . .'[4] 'Childhood has its own ways of seeing, thinking and feeling; nothing is more foolish than to try to substitute our ways.'[5] The difference lies in the child's special way of reminiscing: '. . . a child catches hold on . . . phylo-genetic experience where his own experience fails him. He fills in the gaps in individual truth with prehistorical truth; he replaces occur-rences in his own life by occurrences in the life of his ancestors. I fully agree with Jung in recognizing the existence of this phylo-genetic inheritance . . .'[6]

The actual child itself was not altogether actual because its ex-periences consisted in the confabulations of 'pre-historic' occur-rences, i.e., non-temporal, mythical, archetypal. And childhood thus refers in Freud partly to *a state of reminiscence*, like the Platonic or Augustinian *memoria*, an imaginal realm which provides the actual child with 'its own ways of seeing, thinking and feeling' (Rousseau). This realm, this mode of imaginal existence, is to be found, according to popular and depth psychology, in primitive, savage, madman, artist, genius and the archeological past; the child-hood of persons becomes merged with the childhood of peoples.[7]

But the child and the childhood are not actual. These are terms for a mode of existence and perception and emotion which we still today insist belongs to actual children, so that we construct a world for them following our need to place this fantasy somewhere in actuality. We do not know what children are in themselves, 'unadulterated' by our need for carriers of the imaginal realm, of 'beginnings' (i.e., 'primitivity', 'creation') and of the archetype of the child. We cannot know what children are until we have understood more of the working of the fantasy child, the archetypal child in the subjective psyche.

Freud gave to the child image and to the fantasy of childhood a group of startling attributes which you may remember: child had no super-ego (conscience) like the adult; no free associations like the adult but confabulated reminiscences. The child's parents and problems were external, rather than internal as with the adult, so that the child had no symbolically transferred psychic life.[8] How close to the mental life of 'madness', of artist, and how close to what we call 'primitive' – this absence of personal conscience, this mixture of behaviour and ritual, or memory and myth.

But more startling than the attributes Freud enunciated are those which we may draw from his ideas. First, Freud gave the child *primacy:* nothing was more important in our lives than those early years and that style of thought and emotion of imaginal existence called 'childhood'. Second, Freud gave the child *body:* it had passions, sexual desires, lusts to kill; it feared, sacrificed, rejected; it hated and longed and it was composed of erogenous zones, preoccupied with faeces, genitals, and deserved the name polymorphous perverse. Third, Freud gave the child *pathology:* it lived in our repressions and fixations; it was at the bottom of our psychic disorders;[9] it was our suffering.

These are startling attributes indeed if they be compared with the child of Dickens, for Dorrit and Nell, Oliver and David had little passion and little body, and no sexuality at all, especially in view of little Hans and little Anna and other children of psychoanalytic literature. Perversity, when it entered in Dickens at all, came from adults, from industry, education and society; pathology was in deathbed scenes that claimed children back to paradise. Against Dickens we can see Freud's vision most sharply, even if in both the child as fact and the child as image were still not disentangled.

Jung's essay 'The Psychology of the Child Archetype' in 1940 moved the matter much further; actual child is abandoned and with it the fantasy of empiricism, the notion that our apperception of the factor in our subjectivity results from empirical observation of actual childhood. Jung writes:

> It may not be superfluous to point out that lay prejudice is always inclined to identify the child motif with the concrete experience 'child', as though the real child were the cause and pre-condition of the existence of the child motif. In psychological reality, however, the empirical idea 'child' is only the means . . . by which to express a psychic fact that cannot be formulated more exactly. Hence by the same token the mythological idea of the child is emphatically not a copy of the empirical child . . . not – and this is the point – a human child.[10]

What accuracy can our studies of the human child have so long as we have not recognized enough the archetypal child in our subjectivity affecting our vision? So let us leave the child and childhood to one side and pursue what Jung calls the 'child motif' and the 'childhood aspect of the collective psyche'.

Our question now becomes what is the child *motif* which projects so vividly and draws such fantasies onto itself? Jung answers:

> The 'child' is all that is abandoned and exposed and at the same time divinely powerful; the insignificant, dubious beginning and the triumphal end. The 'eternal child' in man is an indescribable experience, an incongruity, a handicap, and a divine prerogative; an imponderable that determines the ultimate worth or worthlessness of a personality.[11]

Jung elaborates these general and specific features: futurity, divine heroic invincibility, hermaphroditism, beginning and end, and the motif of abandonment from which my theme is drawn. Jung's elaborations of 1940 should be taken as an addition to those in his previous works where the child motif is related to archaic mythical thinking and the mother archetype[12] and to paradisiacal blissfulness.[13] Some of the aspects that Jung discusses Freud had already described in his language-style. The idea of the creative child occurs in Freud's equation child = penis, and the rejected child in his equation child = faeces. ' "Faeces", "child", and "penis" thus form a unity, an unconscious concept (*sit venia verbo*) – the concept, namely, of a little thing that can become separated from one's body.'[14]

To these features I would add two others from our Western tradition, the first specifically Christian, the second specifically Classical. In the Christian tradition (Legasse) 'child' refers also to the simple, the naïve, the poor and the common – the orphans – of society and of the psyche, as it did in the language of the Gospels, where child meant outcast, the pre-condition for salvation, and was later placed in association with the feelings of the heart opposed to the learning of the mind. In the Classical tradition the child appears in those configurations of masculine psychology represented specifically by Zeus, Hermes and Dionysos, their imagery, mythemes and cults. The child motif there may be kept distinct from the child-and-mother motifs and also the child-hero motifs that have distinctly different psychological import.

Our theme follows Jung literally when he says: 'The child motif represents something not only that existed in the distant past but something that exists *now* . . . not just a vestige but a system functioning in the present whose purpose is to compensate or correct, in a meaningful manner, the inevitable onesidedness and extravagances of the conscious mind.'[15] If, according to Freud, the essence of the psychoanalytic method is to alter something, and if the child, according to Jung, is that which acts as psychological corrector, our reflections require that we bring the child back from his abandonment even while we speak of him. Then the general theme may become specifically focused in the private subjectivity of each and may act to alter the onesidedness of consciousness in regard to the child.

ABANDONMENT IN DREAMS

We find the abandoned child first of all in dreams, where we ourselves or a child of ours or one unknown, is neglected, forgotten, crying, in danger or need, and the like. The child makes its presence known through dreams; although abandoned, we can still hear it, feel its call.

In modern dreams we find the child endangered by: drowning, animals, road traffic, being left behind in a car trunk (the 'chest' motif), or a pram or supermarket cart (the 'basket' motif); kidnappers, robbers, members of the family, incompetents; illness, crippling, secret infections, mental retardation and brain damage (the idiot child); or a wider less specific catastrophe such as war, flood or fire. Sometimes, one wakens in the night with the sensation of having heard a child crying.

Usually the dreamer's response to the motif of abandonment is acute worry, a guilty responsibility: 'I should not have let it happen; I must do something to protect the child; I am a bad parent.' If it is an infant in the dream, we believe we must keep the sense of this 'child' with us all the time, feed it every three hours with thoughtful attention, carry it on our backs like a papoose. We tend to take the child as a moral lesson.

But guilt puts the burden of altering something (Freud) and correcting something (Jung) altogether upon the ego as doer. After all, the dreamer is not only in charge of the child; he also *is* the child. Consequently the emotions of worry, guilt and responsibility, morally virtuous as they may be and even partly corrective of neglect, may also prevent other emotions of fright, loss and helplessness. Sometimes the more we worry over the child the less the child really reaches us. So, as long as we take up any dream mainly from the position of the responsible ego, by reacting to it with guilt and the energetics of seeing matters straight, improving by doing, by changing attitudes, extracting from dreams moral lessons for the ethically responsible ego, we reinforce that ego. We thereby emphasize the parent-child cleavage: the ego becomes the responsible parent, which only further removes us from the emotions of the child.

Crucial in all dream integration – integration, not interpretation, for we are speaking now of integrity with the dream, standing with it and in it, befriending it in all its parts, participating in its whole story – is the emotional experience of *all* its parts. Gestalt therapy attempts to drive this home by demanding that the dreamer feel himself into all the parts: the distraught parent, but also the wild dogs, the flooding river, the secret infection, and the exposed child. It is as important to collapse with the child's crying, and to hate savagely the childish, as it is to go home from the analytical hour resolved to take better care of the new and tender parts that need help to grow.

As interpretation and ego responsibility may strengthen the parent at the expense of the child, so too may amplification not reach the child who is abandoned. An amplification of the child in the river, wandering lost in the forest or attempting a task beyond his strength, in terms of fairytales and myths and initiation rites, may stain the motif accurately so that we see certain aspects clearly – mainly heroic new consciousness emerging – but the staining technique of amplification to bring out the objective meaning also may obliterate the subjective reality of dereliction. Amplification often takes us away from the misery by placing it on a general level. For many psychic events this extension of awareness through amplification is just what is needed, but for precisely this motif it would seem contraindicated because the forsaken child can best be refound by moving closer to subjective misery and noting its precise locus.

Both responsibility and amplification are insufficient methods for this motif. As activities of the reasoned, mature person they distance us yet further from the child.

ABANDONMENT IN MARRIAGE

Because every home established, every nest, niche of habit offers the abandoned child a sanctuary, marriage unavoidably evokes the child. Sometimes an early marriage is obviously intended to find a basket for the child that was inacceptable in the parental house. The pattern may continue long afterwards: husband and wife in tacit agreement taking such care of the abandoned child left from their parental homes that they cannot find the child appropriate to themselves.

Being at home, coming home, heading for home – these are emotions which refer to the child's needs. They indicate abandonment. These emotions transform the actual home, its walls and roof, into a picture-book fantasy with psychic walls and psychic roof in which we place our vulnerability and in which we may be safely exposed to the polymorphous perverse fragmentation of our demands. At home, we are not only mother who embraces and father who captains, but also a little child. What is rejected everywhere else must be allowed here at home.

This reality, which some psychotherapists have called 'the inner child of the past' and others 'neurotic interaction in marriage' is as important in the fantasies which are enacted in a marriage as are the various patterns of the conjunction described by Jung. What prevents the aspirations of the conjunction are the fierce incest demands of the child, whose desires for union are of another order than the marriage quaternio[16] and whose image of 'contained' and 'container'[17] is wholly in terms of his anxious dereliction. Where else can he go? This is his home too, and more important to him than wife and husband are mother and father, nursing and protection, omnipotence and idealizations.

A purpose of marriage has been defined in terms of procreating and caring for children. But there is also the archetypal child who is constellated by marriage and whose need for care would wreck the actual marriage by insisting that it rehearse archetypal patterns that are 'pre'-marital (uninitiated, infantile, incestuous). Then there occur those struggles between the actual children and the psychic child of the parents as to whom will be abandoned. Then divorce threatens not only the actual children, but the abandoned child of the parents that found containment in marriage.

The concentration of abandonment in marriage because there is no other home for it makes marriage the principal scene for enacting the child archetype (not the conjunctio). In marriage we find the idealizations of the child: marriage as alpha and omega of life, hermaphroditism lived as 'role-sharing', futurity lived as the planning of hopes and fears, and defensive vulnerability. The couple's attempts to contain the child (not each other) produce a familiar pattern alternating between emotionalism and none at all, marriage stiffened into a social norm. Lost in the oscillation is the imagination which the child can bring. Imagination is blown off in affects or concretizes into plans and habits that keep the child cribbed. If we may speak of a 'marriage therapy' then it would be based not on the 'neurotic interaction' of the *couple*, but on the child as central factor in marriage, and the child's imagination, i.e., the cultivation of the imaginal psyche, the peculiar fantasy life that plays between your child and mine.

BAPTISING THE CHILD

Usually we feel something fundamentally wrong in regard to the child, which wrong we then place into or onto the child. Societies have to do something with children in order to make right this wrong. We do not take children as they are given; they must be removed out of childhood. We initiate, educate, circumcise, innoculate, baptise. And if in the Romantic manner we idealize the child – and idealizations are always a sign of distance – calling the child a *speculum naturae*, we do not altogether trust this nature. Even the child Immanuel (Isaiah 7:14–16) has first to eat butter and honey before he can distinguish between good and evil. The child *per se* makes us uneasy, ambivalent; we are anxious about the human propensities concentrated by the child symbol. It evokes too much of what has been left out or is unknown, becoming easily associated with primitive, mad and mystical.

When one looks at the early controversies over infant baptism one wonders just what psychological content was so exercising these excellent Patristic minds. Their energy spent on the child is comparable to that of ours spent on childhood in modern psychology. At first, though, they (Tertullian, Cyprian) did not urge early baptism, and Gregory of Nazianzus preferred some degree of mind, about the age of three, before baptism. But Augustine was adamant. Because man was born in original sin he brought it with him into the world, as Augustine himself had done from his pagan past. Only baptism could wash this from the child. Augustine was sharp about the child's need of salvation, writing: 'Those who plead for the mimesis of children ought not love their ignorance, but their innocence.'[18] And what is innocent? 'It is the weakness of the faculties of the child that is innocent, not the soul.'[19] How Freudian: the child cannot perform with its still-too-young faculties, those latent perversities that are in the soul. The soul carried not mere general sin, but the specific sin of pre-Christian, un-Christian impulses of polytheistic paganism, which Freud was later to discover and baptise 'polymorphously perverse', and which Jung was later more comprehensively to describe as the archetypes. Baptism could redeem the soul from childhood, from that imaginal world of a multitude of archetypal forms, gods and goddesses, their cults and the unchristian practices they substantiated.

Inasmuch as the child is not a vestige but a system functioning now, and inasmuch as a sacrament is not a vestige of a one-time historical happening but continues now, then the baptism of the child is *always going on*. We are continually baptising the child, lustrating the psyche's 'childhood', its 'beginnings', its reminiscing, with the apotropaic rites of our Augustinian culture, cleansing the soul of its polytheistic imaginal possibility which is carried emblematically by the child, thereby taking the child of the psyche a 'prisoner for Christ' (Gregory of Nazianzus, 'In Praise of Basil'), much as the early church replaced the infants of the hero cults and pagan pantheon with the Jesus child.

This Christening goes on whenever we connect to the child motifs in our dreams and feelings using only Christian models. Then we regard the polymorphic potential of our inherent polytheism as fundamentally in need of updating by transformation into unity. Thus we prevent the child from performing its function of that which alters. We correct it, rather than let it correct us.

REGRESSION, REPRESSION

Baptism served two functions for which we have modern names: it prevented regression; it offered repression. Our most immediate experience of the child today is through these experiences.

What depth psychology has come to call regression is nothing other than a return to the child. Since this is so, we might inquire more fundamentally into psychology's notion of maturity, which has regression as its counterpart, and into psychology's idea of development, which requires that the child be abandoned. Regression is the unavoidable shadow of linear styles of thinking. A developmental model will be plagued by its counter-movement, atavism; and reversion will be seen, not as a return through likeness to imaginal reality along Neoplatonic lines (Proclus, Plotinus), but as a regression to a worse condition. Psychology presents 'going back' as 'going down', a devolution to prior and inferior patterns. Maturity and regression become incompatible. For regression we lose respect, forgetting the need of living things to 'go back' to 'beginnings'.

Regression is made tolerable in theory today only in terms of a 'regression in the service of the ego' (E. Kris, *Psychoanalytic Explorations in Art*, 1952). Even in Jung, regression is mainly compensatory, a *reculer pour mieux sauter*. In Maslow, Erikson, Piaget, Gesell, as well as in Freudian ego psychology, if we do not advance along certain well-researched paths from stage to stage we become fixated in 'childhood' and show regressed behaviour, styles called puerile and infantile. Behind every forward step into 'reality' there is the threatening shadow of the child – hedonistic or mystical depending upon how we regard the reversion to primordiality. This child we propitiate with sentimentality, superstition and kitsch, with indulgent holidays and treats, and with psychotherapy which partly owes its existence and earns its living from the regressive pull of the child.

Our model of maturity tends to make regression attractive. At a distance we idealize the angelic state of childhood and its creativity. By abandoning the child we place it in arcadia, borne by the sea, cradled, rocking softly at water level among reeds and rushes, nour-ished by nymphs who delight in its whims, shepherds, kindly old caretakers who welcome the childish, the regressed. Then of course the counter-movement sets in again; the here constellates; from the abandoned child the great leap forward, the draining of the Zuyder Zee with which Freud compared the work of psychoanalysis.[20]

Because the major content of repression is the child, the contem-porary revolution on behalf of the repressed – black or poor, feminine or natural or undeveloped – becomes unavoidably the revolution of the child. The formulations become immature, a touch pathetic, the behaviour regressed, and the ambition invincible and vulnerable at the same time. Hermaphroditism of the archetype also plays its role in the revolution, as does that peculiar mixture of beginning and end: hope exemplified in apocalyptic destruction. Our theme thus touches upon psychology's relation to the times and its struggle with the child, all of which suggests that it might be profitable to reflect the statements of [Herbert] Marcuse, [R. D.] Laing and [Norman O.] Brown concerning the contemporary revolution of the repressed in the light of archetypal psychology, i.e., as expressions of the cult of the child.

Preferable to the division into child and adult and the consequent patterns of abandonment which we have been sketching, would be a psychology less given over to the child, its woes and romanticism. We might then have a psychology descriptive of man, an aspect of whom is perennially child, carrying his incurable weakness and nurse to it, enacting the child neither by development nor by abandonment, but bearing the child, the child contained. Our subjective experience might then be mirrored by a psychology both more exact in its description and more sophisticatedly classical, where the child is contained within the man who carries in his face and mien the shame of the childish, its unchanging psychopathology – untran-scended, untransformed – and the invincible high hopes together with the vulnerability of these hopes, who bears his abandonment in dignity, and whose freedom comes from the imaginal redeemed from the amnesia of childhood.

THE SOUL CHILD

Marion Woodman

This is an impassioned piece for the inner 'abandoned one': 'That child who is our very soul cries out from underneath the rubble of our lives, often from the core of our worst complex, begging us to say, "You are not alone. I love you." '

As you will undoubtedly notice when you read this essay, Canadian Jungian analyst Marion Woodman has a way with words. They overflow from her as amazing succour, giving nurture to many who hunger for psychological insight and who have had the good fortune to come into contact with her work. Her writings are highly relevant to contemporary lives. This chapter is an excerpt from her book The Pregnant Virgin.

I have found that individuals tend to repeat the pattern of their own actual birth every time life requires them to move onto a new level of awareness. As they entered the world, so they continue to re-enter at each new spiral of growth. If, for example, their birth was straightforward, they tend to handle passovers with courage and natural trust. If their birth was difficult, they become extremely fearful, manifest symptoms of suffocating, become claustrophobic (psychically and physically). If they were premature, they tend to be always a little ahead of themselves. If they were held back, the rebirth process may be very slow. If they were breech-birth, they tend to go through life 'ass-backwards'. If they were born by Caesarian section, they may avoid confrontations. If their mother was heavily drugged, they may come up to the point of passover with lots of energy, then, suddenly, for no apparent reason, stop, or move into a regression, and then wait for someone else to do something. Often this is the point where addictions reappear – bingeing, starving, drinking, sleeping, overworking – anything to avoid facing the reality of moving into a challenging world.

Many delightful babies appear in dreams, and just as many little tyrants who need firm and loving discipline. One child, however, is noticeably different from the others. This is the abandoned one, who may appear in bullrushes, in straw in a barn, in a tree, almost always in some forgotten or out-of-the-way place. This child will be radiant with light, robust, intelligent, sensitive. Often it is able to talk minutes after it is born. It has Presence. It is the Divine Child, bringing with it the 'hard and bitter agony' of the new dispensation – the agony of Eliot's Magi. With its birth, the old gods have to go.

Since the natural gradient of the psyche is toward wholeness, the Self will attempt to push the neglected part forward for recognition. It contains energy of the highest value, the gold in the dung. In the Bible it is the stone that was rejected that becomes the cornerstone.[1] It manifests either in a sudden or subtle change in personality, or, conversely, in a fanaticism which the existing ego adapts in order to try to keep the new and threatening energy out. If the ego fails to go through the psychic birth canal, neurotic symptoms manifest physically and psychically. The suffering may be intense, but it is based on worshipping false gods. It is not the genuine suffering that accompanies efforts to incorporate the new life. The neurotic is always one phase behind where his reality is. When he should be moving into maturity, he hangs onto youthful folly. Never congruent with himself or others, he is never where he seems to be. What he cannot do is live in the *now*.

Many people are being dragged toward wholeness in their daily lives, but because they do not understand initiation rites, they cannot make sense of what is happening to them. They put on a happy face all day, and return to their apartment and cry all night. Perhaps their beloved has gone off with someone else; perhaps they are coping with a fatal illness; perhaps a loved one has died. Perhaps, and this is worst of all, everything has begun to go wrong for no apparent reason. If they have no concept of rites of passage, they experience themselves as victims, powerless to resist an overwhelming Fate. Their meaningless suffering drives them to escape through food, alcohol, drugs, sex. Or they take up arms against the gods and cry out, 'Why me?'

They are being presented with the possibility of rebirth into a different life. Through failures, symptoms, inferiority feelings and overwhelming problems, they are being prodded to renounce life attachments that have become redundant. The possibility of rebirth constellates with the breakdown of what has gone before. That is why Jung emphasized the positive purpose of neurosis.[2] But because they do not understand, people cling to the familiar, refuse to make the necessary sacrifices, resist their own growth. Unable to give up their habitual lives, they are unable to receive new life.

Unless cultural rituals support the leap from one level of consciousness to another, there are no containing walls within which the process can happen. Without an understanding of myth or religion, without an understanding of the relationship between destruction and creation and rebirth, the individual suffers the mysteries of life as meaningless mayhem – alone. To ease the meaningless suffering, addictions may develop that are an attempt to repress the confusing demands of the growth process which cultural structures no longer clarify or contain.

The burning question when one enters analysis is 'Who am I?' The immediate problem, however, as soon as powerful emotions begin to surface, is often a psyche/soma split. While women tend to talk about their bodies more than men, both sexes in our culture are grievously unrelated to their own body experience. Women say, 'I don't like this body'; men say, 'It hurts'. Their use of the third-person neuter pronoun in referring to their body makes quite clear their sense of alienation. They may talk about 'my heart', 'my kidneys', 'my feet', but their body as a whole is depersonalized. Repeatedly they say, 'I don't feel anything below the neck. I experience feelings in my head, but nothing in my heart.' Their lack of emotional response to a powerful dream image reflects the split. And yet, when they engage in active imagination with that dream image located in their body, their muscles release undulations of repressed grief. The body has become the whipping post. If the person is anxious, the body is starved, gorged, drugged, intoxicated, forced to vomit, driven into exhaustion or driven to frenzied reactions against self-destruction. When this magnificent animal attempts to send up warning signals, it is silenced with pills.

Many people can listen to their cat more intelligently than they can listen to their own despised body. Because they attend to their pet in a cherishing way, it returns their love. Their body, however, may have to let out an earth-shattering scream in order to be heard at all. Before symptoms manifest, quieter screams appear in dreams: a forsaken baby elephant, a starving kitten, a dog with a leg ripped out. Almost always the wounded animal is either gently or fiercely attempting to attract the attention of the dreamer, who may or may not respond. In fairytales it is the friendly animal who often carries the hero or heroine to the goal because the animal is the instinct that knows how to obey the goddess when reason fails.

It is possible that the scream that comes from the forsaken body, the scream that manifests in a symptom, is the cry of the soul that can find no other way to be heard. If we have lived behind a mask all our lives, sooner or later – if we are lucky – that mask will be smashed. Then we will have to look in our mirror at our own reality. Perhaps we will be appalled. Perhaps we will look into the terrified eyes of our own tiny child, that child who has never known love and who now beseeches us to respond. This child is alone, forsaken before we left the womb, or at birth, or when we began to please our parents and learned to put on our best performance in order to be accepted. As life progresses, we may continue to abandon our child by pleasing others – teachers, professors, bosses, friends and partners, even analysts. That child who is our very *soul* cries out from under the rubble of our lives, often from the core of our worst complex, begging us to say, 'You are not alone. I love you.'

The following is a recurring childhood dream which continued to haunt a fifty-year-old woman until it was worked through in analysis:

I am four or five years old. I'm with my mother in a crowded building, probably a department store. My mother is wearing dark clothes, a coat and a hat in brown or black, and throughout I see only her back. As we leave the building, I am slowed down by the crowd, and my mother, unknowing, moves ahead and disappears among the people. I try to call to her, but she doesn't hear me, nor does anyone else. I'm very frightened, not only at being lost but at my mother's not noticing we've been separated.

I come out of the building onto a long flight of broad steps, rather like those outside the National Gallery in London, but higher. The

The Scream (1895), Edvard Munch. (Bettmann Archive.)

steps lead down into a large square, empty of any objects, but with similar steps leading to buildings on the other sides. The square, the steps and the buildings are very clean and white. From my vantage point I look around the square, hoping to see my mother. She is nowhere to be seen. I am alone on the steps. There are other people in the square, but they are unaware of me. I know nothing I do will make them notice me.

I am panic-stricken and overwhelmed with a sense of loss, of having been abandoned. It's as though I've ceased to exist for my mother, that she won't bother to come back for me, may even have forgotten about me, that in fact I can't make anyone aware that I exist.

For a moment, and at the same time, I'm an adult observer across the square who sees the small child standing alone at the top of the steps, trying to call out. This is also I, a grown woman who feels enormous pity for this child, longs to comfort and reassure her, but is unable to reach her. Something – the unconsciousness of the other people or the child's own panic – prevents communication between the child and the adult who cares and understands.

The woman associated this dream with Edvard Munch's painting *The Scream*, which evoked in her a similar panic. 'The background is dark and murky,' she said, 'while in my dream the environment is very clear, white and hard-edged, dotted with dark, ill-defined but equally hard-edged figures. The screamer is trying to escape from his environment; the child on the steps is trying to connect with hers.' Many men and women are trapped in lives of quiet desperation until they turn to help that child within.

LOVE AND THE FEAR
OF ABANDONMENT

M. Scott Peck

≈

This selection, an excerpt from M. Scott Peck's enormously popular book
The Road Less Traveled, *looks at the nature of destructive love, the kind*
that produces fear and uncertainty in the child's emotional environment
and that results in a major deficit for the child within the adult. 'To the
child,' says psychiatrist Peck, 'abandonment by its parents is the equival-
ent of death.' He suggests that the parental threat of abandonment sacri-
fices loving involvement for control over the child. It is one of the most
indecent, cruel interactions between parent and child producing existen-
tial angst and poor self-concept, with devastating results for the inner
child.

It is not that the homes of unself-disciplined children are lacking in
parental discipline. More often than not these children are punished
frequently and severely throughout their childhood – slapped,
punched, kicked, beaten and whipped by their parents for even
minor infractions. But this discipline is meaningless – because it is
undisciplined discipline.

One reason that it is meaningless is that the parents themselves
are unself-disciplined, and therefore serve as undisciplined role
models for their children. They are the 'Do as I say, not as I do'
parents. They may frequently get drunk in front of their children.
They may fight with each other in front of the children without
restraint, dignity or rationality. They may be slovenly. They make
promises they don't keep. Their own lives are frequently and obviously in disorder and disarray, and their attempts to order the lives of

their children seem therefore to make little sense to these children.

If father beats up mother regularly, what sense does it make to a boy when his mother beats him up because he beat up his sister? Does it make sense when he's told that he must learn to control his temper? Since we do not have the benefit of comparison when we are young, our parents are godlike figures to our childish eyes. When parents do things a certain way, it seems to the young child the way to do them, the way they should be done. If a child sees his parents day in and day out behaving with self-discipline, restraint, dignity and a capacity to order their own lives, then the child will come to feel in the deepest fibres of his being that this is the way to live. If a child sees his parents day in and day out living without self-restraint or self-discipline, then he will come in the deepest fibres of being to believe that this is the way to live.

Yet even more important than role modelling is love. For even in chaotic and disordered homes genuine love is occasionally present, and from such homes may come self-disciplined children. And not infrequently parents who are professional people – doctors, lawyers, club women and philanthropists – who lead lives of strict orderliness and decorum but yet lack love, send children into the world who are as undisciplined and disorganized as any child from an impoverished and chaotic home.

Ultimately love is everything . . .

When we love something it is of value to us, and when something is of value to us we spent time with it, time enjoying it and time taking care of it. Observe a teenager in love with his car and note the time he will spend admiring it, polishing it, repairing it, tuning it. Or an older person with a beloved rose garden, and the time spent pruning and mulching and fertilizing and studying it. So it is when we love children; we spend time admiring them and caring for them. We give them our time.

Good discipline requires time. When we have no time to give our children, or no time that we are willing to give, we don't even observe them closely enough to become aware of when their need for our disciplinary assistance is expressed subtly. If their need for discipline is so gross as to impinge upon our consciousness, we may still ignore the need on the grounds that it's easier to let them have their own way – 'I just don't have the energy to deal with them today.' Or, finally, if we are impelled into action by their misdeeds and our irritation, we will impose discipline, often brutally, out of anger rather than deliberation, without examining the problem or even taking the time to consider which form of discipline is the most appropriate to that particular problem.

The parents who devote time to their children even when it is not demanded by glaring misdeeds will perceive in them subtle needs for discipline, to which they will respond with gentle urging or reprimand or structure or praise, administered with thoughtfulness and care. They will observe how their children eat cake, how they study, when they tell subtle falsehoods, when they run away from problems rather than face them. They will take the time to make these minor corrections and adjustments, listening to their children, responding to them, tightening a little here, loosening a little there, giving them little lectures, little stories, little hugs and kisses, little admonishments, little pats on the back.

So it is that the quality of discipline afforded by loving parents is superior to the discipline of unloving parents. But this is just the beginning. In taking the time to observe and to think about their children's needs, loving parents will frequently agonize over the decisions to be made, and will, in a very real sense, suffer along with their children. The children are not blind to this. They perceive it when their parents are willing to suffer with them, and although they may not respond with immediate gratitude, they will learn also to suffer. 'If my parents are willing to suffer with me,' they will tell themselves, 'then suffering must not be so bad, and I should be willing to suffer with myself.' This is the beginning of self-discipline.

The time and the quality of the time that their parents devote to them indicate to children the degree to which they are valued by their parents. Some basically unloving parents, in an attempt to cover up their lack of caring, make frequent professions of love to their children, repetitively and mechanically telling them how much they are valued, but not devoting significant time of high quality to them. Their children are never totally deceived by such hollow words. Consciously they may cling to them, wanting to believe that they are loved, but unconsciously they know that their parents' words do not match up with their deeds.

On the other hand, children who are truly loved, although in moments of pique they may consciously feel or proclaim that they are being neglected, unconsciously know themselves to be valued. This knowledge is worth more than any gold. For when children know that they are valued, when they truly feel valued in the deepest parts of themselves, then they feel valuable.

The feeling of being valuable – 'I am a valuable person' – is essential to mental health and is a cornerstone of self-discipline. It is a direct product of parental love. Such a conviction must be gained in childhood; it is extremely difficult to acquire it during adulthood. Conversely, when children have learned through the love of their parents to feel valuable, it is almost impossible for the vicissitudes of adulthood to destroy their spirit.

This feeling of being valuable is a cornerstone of self-discipline because when one considers oneself valuable one will take care of oneself in all ways that are necessary. Self-discipline is self-caring. For instance – since we are discussing the process of delaying gratification, of scheduling and ordering time – let us examine the matter of time. If we feel ourselves valuable, then we will feel our time to be valuable, and if we feel our time to be valuable, then we will want to use it well. The financial analyst who procrastinated did not value her time. If she had, she would not have allowed herself to spend most of her day so unhappily and unproductively. It was not without consequence for her that throughout her childhood she was 'farmed out' during all school holidays to live with paid foster parents although her parents could have taken care of her perfectly well had they wanted to. They did not value her. They did not want to care for her. So she grew up feeling herself to be of little value, not worth caring for; therefore she did not care for herself. She did not feel that she was worth disciplining herself. Despite the fact that she was an intelligent and competent woman she required the most elementary instruction in self-discipline because she lacked a realistic assessment of her own worth and the value of her own time. Once she was able to perceive her time as being valuable, it naturally followed that she wanted to organize it and protect it and make maximum use of it.

As the result of the experience of consistent parental love and caring throughout childhood, such fortunate children will enter adulthood not only with a deep internal sense of their own value but also with a deep internal sense of security. All children are terrified of abandonment, and with good reason. This fear of abandonment begins around the age of six months, as soon as the child is able to perceive itself as an individual, separate from its parents. For with this perception of itself as an individual comes the realization that as an individual it is quite helpless, totally dependent and totally at the mercy of its parents for all forms of sustenance and means of survival. To the child, abandonment by its parents is the equivalent of death. Most parents, even when they are otherwise relatively ignorant or callous, are instinctively sensitive to their children's fear of abandonment and will therefore, day in and day out, hundreds and thousands of times, offer their children needed reassurance: 'You know Mummy and Daddy aren't going to leave you behind'; 'Of course Mummy and Daddy will come back to get you'; 'Mummy and Daddy aren't going to forget about you.' If these words are matched by deeds, month in and month out, year in and year out, by the time of adolescence the child will have lost the fear of abandonment and in its place will have a deep inner feeling that the world is a safe place in which to be and protection will be there when it is needed. With this internal sense of the consistent safety of the world, such a child is free to delay gratification of one kind or another, secure in the knowledge that the opportunity for gratification, like home and parents, is always there, available when needed.

But many are not so fortunate. A substantial number of children actually are abandoned by their parents during childhood, by death, by desertion, by sheer negligence, or, as in the case of the financial analyst, by a simple lack of caring. Others, while not abandoned in fact, fail to receive from their parents the reassurance that they will not be abandoned. There are some parents, for instance, who in their desire to enforce discipline as easily and quickly as possible, will actually use the threat of abandonment, overtly or subtly, to achieve this end. The message they give to their children is: 'If you don't do exactly what I want you to do I won't love you any more, and you can figure out for yourself what that might mean.' It means, of course, abandonment and death. These parents sacrifice love in their need for control and domination over their children, and their reward is children who are excessively fearful of the future. So it is that these children, abandoned either psychologically or in actuality, enter adulthood lacking any deep sense that the world is a safe and protective place. To the contrary, they perceive the world as dangerous and frightening, and they are not about to forsake any gratification or security in the present for the promise of greater gratification or security in the future, since for them the future seems dubious indeed.

In summary, for children to develop the capacity to delay gratification, it is necessary for them to have self-disciplined role models, a sense of self-worth, and a degree of trust in the safety of their existence. These 'possessions' are ideally acquired through the self-discipline and consistent, genuine caring of their parents; they are the most precious gifts of themselves that mothers and fathers can bequeath. When these gifts have not been proffered by one's parents, it is possible to acquire them from other sources, but in that case the process of their acquisition is invariably an uphill struggle, often of lifelong duration and often unsuccessful.

8

THE ONES WHO WALK AWAY FROM OMELAS

Ursula K. Leguin

≈

It is fitting to end this section on abandonment with a story of the scape-goat, an idea that turns on the moral dilemma of sacrifice: one tortured soul exchanged for the happiness of an entire community. This is anal-ogous to the moral problem of the internal community: Can the inner child and its needs be abandoned in order to assure the survival and contentment of the adult personality?

Like Ms LeGuin, I first encountered this motif in Dostoyevsky's Brothers Karamazov, *where Alyosha, the younger brother, is given the moral challenge of establishing a utopian society, heaven on earth, which can happen only if he is willing to sacrifice the life of one human infant. Would he do it?*

Consider your own moral effort: Would you sacrifice (have you aban-doned) the inner child for the promise of perfection? LeGuin asks 'Would you walk away from Omelas?' She has such a wonderful flair for the morally perverse in this tale that her talents wring the feelings right out of you.

This story originally appeared as part of the author's collection of stories, The Wind's Twelve Quarters. *Ms LeGuin is a widely read and honoured writer of fiction.*

≈

The central idea of this psychomyth, the scapegoat, turns up in Dostoyevsky's Brothers Karamazov, and several people have asked me, rather suspiciously, why I gave the credit to William James. The fact is, I haven't been able to re-read Dostoyevsky, much as I loved him, since I was twenty-five, and I'd simply forgotten he used the idea. But when I met it in James's 'The Moral Philosopher and the Moral Life', it was with a shock of recognition. Here is how James puts it.

> Or if the hypothesis were offered us of a world in which Messrs Fourier's and Bellay's and Morris's utopias should all be outdone, and millions kept permanently happy on the one simple condition that a certain lost soul on the far-off edge of things should lead a life of lonely torment, what except a specifical and independent sort of emotion can it be which would make us immediately feel, even though an impulse arose within us to clutch at the happiness so offered, how hideous a thing would be its enjoyment when deliberately accepted as the fruit of such a bargain?

The dilemma of the American conscience can hardly be better stated. Dostoyevsky was a great artist, and a radical one, but his early social radicalism reversed itself, leaving him a violent reactionary. Whereas the American James, who seems so mild, so naïvely gentlemanly – look how he says 'us', assuming all his readers are as decent as himself! – was, and remained, and remains, a genuinely radical thinker. Directly after the 'lost soul' passage he goes on,

> All the higher, more penetrating ideals are revolutionary. They present themselves far less in the guise of effects of past experience than in that of probable causes of future experience, factors to which the environment and the lessons it has so far taught us must learn to bend.

The application of those two sentences to this story, and to science fiction, and to all thinking about the future, is quite direct. Ideals as 'the probable cause of future experience' – that is a subtle and exhilarating remark!

Of course I didn't read James and sit down and say, Now I'll write a story about that 'lost soul'. It seldom works that simply. I sat down and started a story, just because I felt like it, with nothing but the word 'Omelas' in mind. It came from a road sign: Salem (Oregon) backwards.

Don't you read road signs backwards? POTS. WOLS nerdlihc. ocsicnarF naS . . . Salem equals schelomo equals salaam equals Peace. Melas. O melas. Omelas. Homme helas. 'Where do you get your ideas from, Ms LeGuin?' From forgetting Dostoyevsky and reading road signs backwards, naturally. Where else?

With a clamour of bells that set the swallows soaring, the Festival of Summer came to the city of Omelas, bright-towered by the sea. The rigging of the boats in the harbour sparkled with flags. In the streets between houses with red roofs and painted walls, between old moss-grown gardens and under avenues of trees, past great parks and public buildings, processions moved. Some were decorous: old people in long stiff robes of mauve and grey, grave master workmen, quiet, merry women carrying their babies and chatting as they walked. In other streets the music beat faster, a shimmering of gong and tambourine, and the people went dancing, the procession was a dance. Children dodged in and out, their high calls rising like the swallows' crossing flights over the music and the singing. All the processions wound toward the north side of the city, where on the great water-meadow called the Green Fields boys and girls, naked in the bright air, with mud-stained feet and ankles and long, lithe arms, exercised their restive horses before the race. The horses wore no gear at all but a halter without bit. Their manes were braided with streamers of silver, gold and green. They flared their nostrils and pranced and boasted to one another; they were vastly excited, the horse being the only animal who has adopted our ceremonies as his own. Far off to the north and west the mountains stood up half encircling Omelas on her bay. The air of morning was so clear that the snow still crowning the Eighteen Peaks burned with white-gold fire across the miles of sunlit air, under the dark blue of the sky. There was just enough wind to make the banners that marked the race-course snap and flutter now and then. In the silence of the broad green meadows one could hear the music winding through the city streets, farther and nearer and ever approaching, a cheerful faint sweetness of the air that from time to time trembled and gathered together and broke out into the great joyous clanging of the bells.

Joyous! How is one to tell about joy? How describe the citizens of Omelas?

They were not simple folk, you see, though they were happy. But we do not say the words much any more. All smiles have become archaic. Given a description such as this one tends to make certain assumptions. Given a description such as this one tends to look next for the King, mounted on a splendid stallion and surrounded by his noble knights, or perhaps in a golden litter borne by great-muscled slaves. But there was no king. They did not use swords, or keep slaves. They were not barbarians. I do not know the rules and laws of their society, but I suspect that they were singularly few. As they did without monarchy and slavery, so they also got along without the stock exchange, the advertisement, the secret police, and the bomb. Yet I repeat that these were not simple folk, not dulcet shepherds, noble savages, bland utopians. They were not less complex than us. The trouble is that we have a bad habit, encouraged by pedants and sophisticates, of considering happiness as something rather stupid. Only pain is intellectual, only evil interesting. This is the treason of the artist: a refusal to admit the banality of evil and the terrible boredom of pain. If you can't lick 'em, join 'em. If it hurts, repeat it. But to praise despair is to condemn delight, to embrace violence is to lose hold of everything else. We have almost lost hold; we can no longer describe a happy man, nor make any celebration of joy. How can I tell you about the people of Omelas? They were not naïve and happy children – though their children were, in fact, happy. They were mature, intelligent, passionate adults whose lives were not wretched. O miracle! but I wish I could describe it better. I wish I could convince you. Omelas sounds in my words like a city in a fairy tale, long ago and far away, once upon a time. Perhaps it would be best if you imagined it as your own fancy bids, assuming it will rise to the occasion, for certainly I cannot suit you all. For instance, how about technology? I think that there would be no cars or helicopters in and above the streets; this follows from the fact that the people of Omelas are happy people. Happiness is based on a just discrimination of what is necessary, what is neither necessary nor destructive, and what is destructive. In the middle category, however – that of the unnecessary but undestructive, that of comfort, luxury, exuberance, etc. – they could perfectly well have central heating, subway trains, washing machines, and all kinds of marvellous devices not yet invented here, floating light-sources, fuelless power, a cure for the common cold. Or they could have none of that: it doesn't matter. As you like it. I incline to think that people from towns up and down the coast have been coming in to Omelas during the last days before the Festival on very fast little trains and double-decked trams, and that the train station of Omelas is actually the handsomest building in town, though plainer than the magnificent Farmers' Market. But even granted trains. I fear that Omelas so far strikes some of you as goody-goody. Smiles, bells, parades, horses, bleh. If so, please add an orgy. If an orgy would help, don't hesitate. Let us not, however, have temples from which issue beautiful nude priests and priestesses already half in ecstasy and ready to copulate with any man or woman, lover or stranger, who desires union with the deep godhead of the blood, although that was my first idea. But really it would be better not to have any temples in Omelas – at least, not manned temples. Religion, yes, clergy, no. Surely the beautiful nudes can just wander about, offering themselves like divine souffles to the hunger of the needy and the rapture of the flesh. Let them join the procession. Let tambourines be struck above the copulations, and the glory of desire be proclaimed upon the gongs, and (a not unimportant point) let the offspring of these delightful rituals be beloved and looked after by all. One thing I know there is none of in Omelas is guilt. But what else should there be? I thought at first there were no drugs, but that is puritanical. For those who like it, the faint insistent sweetness of *drooz* may perfume the ways of the city, *drooz* which first brings a great lightness and brilliance to the mind and limbs, and then after some hours a dreamy languor, and wonderful visions at last of the very arcane and inmost secrets of the Universe, as well as exciting the pleasure of sex beyond all belief; and it is not habit-forming. For more modest tastes I think there ought to be beer.

What else, what else belongs in the joyous city? The sense of victory, surely the celebration of courage. But as we did without clergy, let us do without soldiers. The joy built upon successful slaughter is not the right kind of joy; it will not do; it is fearful and it is trivial. A boundless and generous contentment, a magnanimous triumph felt not against some outer enemy but in communion with the finest and fairest in the souls of all men everywhere and the splendour of the world's summer: this is what swells the hearts of the people of Omelas, and the victory they celebrate is that of life. I really don't think many of them need to take *drooz*.

Most of the processions have reached the Green Fields by now. A marvellous smell of cooking goes forth from the red and blue tents of the provisioners. The faces of small children are amiably sticky; in the benign grey beard of a man a couple of crumbs of rich pastry are entangled. The youths and girls have mounted their horses and are beginning to group around the starting line of the course. An old woman, small, fat and laughing, is passing out flowers from a basket, and tall young men wear flowers in their shining hair. A child of nine or ten sits at the edge of the crowd, alone, playing on a wooden flute. People pause to listen, and they smile, but they do not speak to him, for he never ceases playing and never sees them, his dark eyes wholly rapt in the sweet, thin magic of the tune.

He finishes, and slowly lowers his hands holding the wooden flute.

As if that little private silence were the signal, all at once a trumpet sounds from the pavilion near the starting line: imperious, melancholy, piercing. The horses rear on their slender legs, and some of them neigh in answer. Sober-faced, the young riders stroke the horses' necks and soothe them, whispering, 'Quiet, quiet, there my beauty, my hope . . .' They begin to form in rank along the starting line. The crowds along the racecourse are like a field of grass and flowers in the wind. The Festival of Summer has begun.

Do you believe? Do you accept the festival, the city, the joy? No? Then let me describe one more thing.

In a basement under one of the beautiful public buildings of Omelas, or perhaps in the cellar of one of its spacious private homes, there is a room. It has one locked door, and no window. A little light seeps in dustily between the cracks in the boards, secondhand from a cobwebbed window somewhere across the cellar. In one corner of the little room a couple of mops, with stiff, clotted, foul-smelling heads, stand near a rusty bucket. The floor is dirt, a little damp to the touch, as cellar dirt usually is. The room is about three paces long and two wide: a mere broom closet or disused tool room. In the room, a child is sitting. It could be a boy or a girl. It looks about six, but actually is nearly ten. It is feeble-minded. Perhaps it was born defective, or perhaps it has become imbecile through fear, malnutrition and neglect. It picks its nose and occasionally fumbles vaguely with its toes or genitals, as it sits hunched in the corner farthest from the bucket and the two mops. It is afraid of the mops. It finds them horrible. It shuts its eyes, but it knows the mops are still standing there; and the door is locked; and nobody will come. The door is always locked; and nobody ever comes, except that sometimes – the child has no understanding of time or interval – sometimes the door rattles terribly and opens, and a person, or several people, are there. One of them may come in and kick the child to make it stand up. The others never come close, but peer in at it with frightened, disgusted eyes. The food bowl and the water jug are hastily filled, the door is locked, the eyes disappear. The people at the door never say anything, but the child, who has not always lived in the tool room, and can remember sunlight and its mother's voice, sometimes speaks. 'I will be good,' it says. 'Please let me out. I will be good!' They never answer. The child used to scream for help at night, and cry a good deal, but now it only makes a kind of whining, 'eh-haa, eh-haa', and it speaks less and less often. It is so thin there are no calves to its legs; its belly protrudes; it lives on a half-bowl of corn meal and grease a day. It is naked. Its buttocks and thighs are a mass of festered sores, as it sits in its own excrement continually.

They all know it is there, the people of Omelas. Some of them have come to see it, others are merely content to know it is there. They all know that it has to be there. Some of them understand why, and some do not, but they all understand that their happiness, the beauty of their city, the tenderness of their friendships, the health of their children, the wisdom of their scholars, the skill of their makers, even the abundance of their harvest and the kindly weathers of their skies, depend wholly on this child's abominable misery.

This is usually explained to children when they are between eight and twelve, whenever they seem capable of understanding; and most of those who come to see the child are young people, though often enough an adult comes, or comes back, to see the child. No matter how well the matter has been explained to them, these young spectators are always shocked and sickened at the sight. They feel disgust, which they had thought themselves superior to. They feel anger, outrage, impotence, despite all the explanations. They would like to do something for the child. But there is nothing they can do. If the child were brought up into the sunlight out of that vile place, if it were cleaned and fed and comforted, that would be a good thing, indeed; but if it were done, in that day and hour all the prosperity and beauty and delight of Omelas would wither and be destroyed. Those are the terms. To exchange all the goodness and grace of every life in Omelas for that single, small improvement: to throw away the happiness of thousands for the chance of happiness of one: that would be to let guilt within the walls indeed.

The terms are strict and absolute; there may not even be a kind word spoken to the child.

Often the young people go home in tears, or in a tearless rage, when they have seen the child and faced this terrible paradox. They may brood over it for weeks or years. But as time goes on they begin to realize that even if the child could be released, it would not get much good of its freedom: a little vague pleasure of warmth and food, no doubt, but little more. It is too degraded and imbecile to know any real joy. It has been afraid too long ever to be free of fear. Its habits are too uncouth for it to respond to humane treatment. Indeed, after so long it would probably be wretched without walls about it to protect it, and darkness for its eyes, and its own excrement to sit in. Their tears at the bitter injustice dry when they begin to perceive the terrible justice of reality, and to accept it. Yet it is their tears and anger, the trying of their generosity and the acceptance of their helplessness, which are perhaps the true source of the splendour of their lives. Theirs is no vapid, irresponsible happiness. They know that they, like the child, are not free. They know compassion. It is the existence of the child, and their knowledge of its existence, that makes possible the nobility of their architecture, the poignancy of their music, the profundity of their science. It is because of the child that they are so gentle with children. They know that if the wretched one were not there snivelling in the dark, the other one, the fluteplayer, could make no joyful music as the young riders line up in their beauty for the race in the sunlight of the first morning of summer.

Now do you believe them? Are they not more credible? But there is one more thing to tell, and this is quite incredible.

At times one of the adolescent girls or boys who go to see the child does not go home to weep or rage, does not, in fact, go home at all. Sometimes also a man or woman much older falls silent for a day or two, and then leaves home. These people go out into the street, and walk down the street alone. They keep walking, and walk straight out of the city of Omelas, through the beautiful gates. They keep walking across the farmlands of Omelas. Each one goes alone, youth or girl, man or woman. Night falls; the traveller must pass down village streets, between the houses with yellow-lit windows, and on out into the darkness of the fields. Each alone, they go west or north, toward the mountains. They go on. They leave Omelas, they leave Omelas, they walk ahead into the darkness, and they do not come back. The place they go toward is a place even less imaginable to most of us than the city of happiness. I cannot describe it at all. But they seem to know where they are going, the ones who walk away from Omelas.

Part Three

ETERNAL YOUTH AND NARCISSISM: THE CHILD'S DILEMMA

INTRODUCTION

≈

Only to a child is pure happiness possible.
Later it is always tainted with the knowledge
that it will not last.

— CHINESE PROVERB

There are special circumstances in the life of a child that can have lifelong debilitating consequences. One such minefield is crossed early in life, when the developing childhood Self begins to separate from the mother or from both parents. This is the narcissistic problem, expressed in the symbol of the *puer aeternus*, the archetype of eternal youth. It is a difficulty that can split the child between attempts to please the parents or to follow the child's developing sense of Self. Narcissism has been called the psychological disturbance of our time. Part 3 is devoted to the problem of the narcissistic relationship to the Self and its consequences for the inner child.

This problem can generally be attributed to defective parental love: the parents, caught in their own impoverished sense of Self, and unable to separate the child from the parental ego, create a bind for the developing Self in the child. The parent's incapacity to see or to meet the child's needs creates in the child an 'as if' Self, one that will please the parents. The nascent real Self of the child is thus split off or hidden and becomes, in effect, the lost inner child.

Those wounds resulting from faulty separation eventually create a complex set of disturbances in the adult personality, which fall under the general term narcissistic disorders, named from the Greek mythological story of Narcissus. At the heart of that great story is the idea of seeing one's own reflection – whether it is in the surface of a pond or in the mirroring face of one's mother – and becoming transfixed there, unable to separate and relate to others. In the myth, Narcissus becomes fixated with his own reflection in a pool and, unable to move from the spot, dies of malnutrition. The story symbolically suggests that the individual child can become fixated at one stage of development, looking to consolidate a sense of his or her true Self but unable to fully accomplish the task of separation for fear of primal rejection by the parent. This unresolved circumstance can later doom the child to a life of restriction, cut off from the Self (the inner child) and unable to deal with the disturbing side of life.

This 'child's dilemma' is a perpetuation of what Joel Covitz calls, in the opening essay of this section, the 'family curse'. As a result of the narcissistic wounds that parents themselves have sustained as children, they are unable to validate their own child's true Self. In turn, they *unconsciously perpetrate* the same fate on their children, demanding perfection and leaving the children feeling inadequate and impaired, believing they can only be loved if they fit the parents' image of perfection. The pain of not being seen, known, loved and cared for *as one is* causes the child to develop a protective set of behaviours to control the anxiety of the situation.

This, then, is the inner child's dilemma: *'How can I identify with my true childhood Self and avoid the pain of primal rejection?'* For the undeveloped ego of a child, this often means choosing to identify with the false, 'as if' Self in order to gain caring attention. The roots of the narcissistic disorders lie here, in the child's resulting fear that no one will love him as he is. The true Self, or inner child, is rejected as inferior or disgusting. As protection from these feelings, the narcissist builds a facade of grandiosity, making the inner child a prisoner of the dilemma.

In the adult, this problem makes it very difficult for an individual to relate to others or to the spiritual reality of the Self. The inner child, thoroughly hidden, is unavailable to the adult. The narcissistic personality is vulnerable to the least failure and craves admiration and adulation to support the false Self, which is maintained with the sacrifice of the inner child. The child in the adult is tormented by feelings of envy and rage, inner despair, isolation and depression.

In the second essay in this section, 'The Search for the True Self,' Alice Miller says that 'It is one of the turning points in analysis when the narcissistically disturbed patient comes to the emotional insight that all the love he has captured with so much effort and self-denial was not meant for him as he really was, that the admiration for his beauty and achievements was aimed at this beauty and these achievements, and not the child himself.'

The narcissistic character as an adult may long for the paradise of childhood and, as Marie-Louise von Franz suggests in the third essay, 'Puer Aeternus,' may adopt a provisional lifestyle, in which life is not quite 'for real' – there is always something missing. In identifying with the *puer aeternus*, the narcissistically injured person can lose the inner child's capacity for life and waste inner riches. 'You feel that such a person has a tremendous wealth and capacity,' says von Franz, 'but there is no possibility of finding a means of realization.'

To be identified with the *puer aeternus* archetype is to lock into the child's dilemma, to indulge in a perpetual fantasy of youth, and deny the experience of real loss and transition that is so essential to development and growth. Only with good fortune and perseverance can one work this through as an adult. However, the *puer* finds it difficult to get into the world of the adult, seeing it as empty and meaningless. 'He has not found a bridge by which he could take over what we would call the true life [the inner child] into adult life,' says von Franz.

Jeffrey Satinover, in his essay 'The Childhood Self and the Origins of *Puer* Psychology,' complements both Miller and von Franz as he elaborates on the theme of the *puer aeternus* as a symbol of the narcissistic relation to the Self. Satinover suggests that a child can become addicted to the grandiose fantasies of the childhood Self as a result of parental disruption of the child's assertiveness, thus avoiding those frustrations that diminish his sense of specialness.

Jung saw the *puer aeternus* as referring to the child archetype, suggesting that its recurring fascination arises from our projection of our inability to renew ourselves. Hence the *puer* does not have an altogether negative connotation. It can embody some of the most positive attributes of the inner child: spontaneity of thought, creativity for problem-solving and original expression, a capacity to risk detachment from one's origins, to exist in a perpetually evolving state, to visualize new beginnings, to seek out opportunities, and to delight others with charm. James Hillman suggests in his book *The Dream and the Underworld* that as long as we are not caught in an identification with the archetype, the *puer aeternus* can endow us with a sense of destiny and meaning.

9

Narcissism: The Disturbance of Our Time

Joel Covitz

≈

This essay sets the tone for Part 3 by giving the general context of the narcissistic dilemma: We live in a time when parenting seems in danger of becoming a lost art. Children's healthy needs and rights are often not understood and frequently are stifled and denied, folded back onto the immature ego of the child with disastrous results. Joel Covitz, a Jungian analyst in Boston, considers this parental negligence to be psychological child abuse. 'Parents have tremendous power,' he says, and the injuries to the soul of the child have lifelong consequences, of which the other essays in this section speak at length. This chapter is an excerpt from Covitz's 1986 book, Emotional Child Abuse: The Family Curse, *which is a useful handbook on healthy parenting styles.*

Each age seems to have its characteristic disturbances. Freud found hysteria a prominent complaint; today's therapist is more likely to see patients who are depressed or compulsive, who feel that their lives lack affection, attention and fulfilling relationships.

When we examine the roots of narcissistic disturbances, it becomes clear that most of them are connected to childhood. Simply stated, a child whose early, healthy narcissistic needs (for attention, affection and respect, as well as for food and shelter) are not met has trouble developing strength, independence and self-esteem. Parents who repeatedly fail to meet these early needs are abusing their children psychologically and emotionally. In almost every case, this is the opposite of what the parents intend; they want to be nurturing and helpful, but it doesn't work out that way. In some cases, they simply don't know how to go about parenting. In others, the parents are so needy themselves – because their early narcissistic needs weren't met – that they cannot meet their child's needs. Until these parents can break this chain of abuse, the effect on their children will be devastating and this destructive pattern will likely be repeated in future generations.

The incidence of physical child abuse in our society raises serious questions about the culture in which we live. Battered children who arrive in hospital emergency rooms bearing the wounds of their parents' anger and frustration will carry those scars for years. But children who are emotionally and psychologically abused also carry scars – harder to see at first, but no less crippling and difficult to heal.

One reason, of course, that the problem is so difficult to solve is that these children are generally unable to fight back in any effective way. As Maria Montessori points out in *The Child in the Family*, 'No social problem is as universal as the oppression of the child . . . No slave was ever so much the property of his master as in the case of the child.'[1] Our society regards children as the parents' property. Parents have tremendous power, and children have few effective means of protest against abuse while they are still young. But eventually the price of that abuse will be exacted on the next generation. In her book *Prisoners of Childhood*, Alice Miller writes, '. . . in twenty years' time these children will be adults who will have to pay it all back to their own children.'[2]

When a child's narcissistic needs are frustrated, he will usually manifest this frustration in anger toward the parents or in depression. But as the child grows older and gets more 'socialized', he tends to repress the anger and tries to behave in a manner that will win or keep his parents' affection (sometimes an impossible task). The repressed rage and hurt must ultimately come out in some form, whether it be a failure to thrive, a poor self-image, self-destructive tendencies, or an adoption of the same mechanisms of defence used by the parents: tyranny, promiscuity, inadequacy. Whatever the adaptive behaviour, the underlying frustration does not go away by itself. Only when a child can dig through his own defences and get to the roots of the problem can he come to terms with his parents' abusive behaviour. Almost always, shadows of that parental behaviour can be recognized in his own. It is impossible to break the family's chain of abuse completely, to cut oneself off entirely from one's emotional heritage (in its good or bad aspect). But an understanding of the basis for that abusive behaviour can help parents and children alike to modify it – with the goal being a step forward for each generation.

There are no secrets from a child's unconscious, although parents sometimes act as though their conscious words and deeds are the only messages they transmit to their children. Much of parents' communication with their children is non-verbal. Subliminally transferred from parent to child, all of the messages will be perceived by the child's unconscious, and he or she will have a fairly accurate perception of the parent's personality. As Jung says in *The Development of Personality*,

> *Children are so deeply involved in the psychological attitude of their parents that it is no wonder that most of the disturbances in childhood can be traced back to disturbed psychic atmosphere in the home . . . There can be no doubt that it is of the utmost value for parents to view their symptoms in the light of their own problems and conflicts. It is their duty as parents to do so. Their responsibility in this respect carries with it the obligation to do everything in their power not to lead a life that could harm the children. Generally far too little stress is laid upon how important the conduct of the parents is for the child, because it is not always words that count, but deeds. Parents should always be conscious of the fact that they themselves are the principle cause of neurosis in their children.*[3]

But it must be remembered that the parents alone are not responsible for the family curse. As Jung also wrote, 'It is not so much the parents as their ancestors – the grandparents and great-grandparents – who are the true progenitors.'[4]

A child can be set up to repeat a parent's inadequacies. For example, Katherine's mother had always considered herself intelligent but not beautiful. Instead of trying to deal with this situation, however, she transmitted to her children the idea that only intelligence was important – not attractiveness or social ease or friendships. Her sons and daughter grew up intellectually accomplished but socially inept. Katherine was taught not to value her clothes or appearance. She was always clean, but she described herself as the kind of child whose kneesocks were always falling down, whose hair was out of place. All of her clothes were handed down from her cousins. Makeup was scorned in the household. The children grew up thinking that they were intelligent but ugly, which was not actually the case. Katherine in particular had trouble adjusting socially. She was a victim of the family curse.

Breaking free completely from one's family curse is almost impossible. But parents *can* become aware of the manifestations of this curse in their children, and can work to change the conditions that foster it. They have an opportunity to change whatever they are able to change in order to make their lives more healthy. And as Jung says, 'Nature has no use for the plea that one "did not know." '[5]

THE ROOTS OF THE PROBLEM

How can so much go wrong so early in a child's life? The basic reasons are twofold: the inadequate personality development of the parents, who nearly always suffered abuse themselves as children, and the frustrations parents feel trying to bring up children in a culture that undervalues parenting.

Our children are victims of the increasingly prevalent view that parenting is a messy, frustrating job that gets in the way of one's growth and life, rather than enriching it. The lack of a creative, functioning culture of child-rearing becomes more grievous when we observe the breakdown in family life today. Children of divorce, of abandonment; children, some under ten years old, who run away from home to live in the streets rather than face abusive parents;

children who vehemently resolve never to have children of their own; children who become parents while they are still teenagers; children who hate themselves and lash out at others – all are victims, not only of abusive parents, but of a culture that has devalued the art of parenting.

To ask a young woman who is raising two toddlers, 'But what are you *doing* with your life?' is to tell this mother that what she is doing – the job of parenting – is not worthy of respect. When a culture removes status from the role of mother or father, the self-esteem from assuming that role is lessened. It is as if society is punishing parents rather than respecting them for tackling a tremendously important task. Only jobs in the 'real world' seem to earn such respect. One such young woman, whose situation reflects that of thousands, decided to go back to work when her child was two months old, even though the cost of day-care and other expenses cut into her salary so much that she actually netted less than a dollar an hour. When asked the reason for the choice, she replied, 'I don't want my self-esteem to come from my husband telling me I prepared a good dinner for the family.'

The desire for self-esteem, and indeed the desire to be a working parent, is not a negative one at all. But it is unfortunate that our culture no longer encourages people to feel self-esteem for the work involved in raising a family. John Bowlby expresses a more encouraging approach with regard to parenting:

> A child needs to feel he is an object of pleasure and pride to his mother; a mother needs to feel an expansion of her own personality in the personality of her child: each needs to feel closely identified with the other. The mothering of a child is not something which can be arranged by rote; it is a live human relationship which alters the characters of both partners.
>
> . . . Continuity is necessary for the growth of a mother. Just as a baby needs to feel that he belongs to his mother, a mother needs to feel that she belongs to her child, and it is only when she has the satisfaction of this feeling that it is easy for her to devote herself to him. The provision of constant attention . . . is possible only for a woman who

derives profound satisfaction from seeing her child grow from baby-hood, through the many phases of childhood, to become an indepen-dent man or woman, and knows that it is her care which made this possible.[6]

But our culture, instead of encouraging *both* parents to develop this 'profound satisfaction' makes parents frustrated with the demands the child makes for 'constant attention'.

For this reason, many couples choose not to have children. They feel that they should have children only if they want them, and they view child-rearing only as an unwanted burden. If this is their view, then their choice is presumably beneficial both to them and to their unborn children. But what does this imply about our culture? And what are the possible reasons for this decision?

The reasons a person decides not to have children are usually related fairly directly to his or her own childhood experiences. The primary reason for the rejection of parenting is that children are being brought up on such negative, dysfunctional households that they instinctively do not want to recreate such environments for any future generation. Many of these children have experienced first-hand what it means to have parents who do not want them. One patient told me she had decided not to have children because she wouldn't be able to stand it if her children rejected her the way she had rejected her mother, and the way her mother had rejected her grandmother.

People who choose not to have children usually have held this resolve for as long as they can remember. These people found child-hood a disaster for themselves, and they feel no desire to take part in the continuation of the life cycle. In light of their experiences, they may be making an understandable choice. But the increasing number of such choices provides a sad commentary on family life today. In an age of individualism, the choice not to be a parent is a person's right – but it may also be a tragic error.

EVALUATING THE PARTICULAR SITUATION

To determine the nature and extent of emotional abuse, each family must be examined in light of its own particular situation. The family as an institution is one thing; the individual family is another. Every element of the parent-child relationship is affected by this specificity. When we look at any family, we are looking at its unique combination of hopes, education, assets and aspirations. The child is aware of and makes allowances for the particular situation in which he is raised. There is a vast difference, for instance, in a rich parent who brings up his child 'poor' and a parent who really has no money to offer.

Keith's father, who was a college professor, said to him, 'When I was your age, I had to work my way through college. I had to earn the money for all of my schooling, and I expect you to do the same.' Keith saw the flaw in his father's reasoning. Because Keith's grandfather had died when Keith's father was six, he was forced to go to work when he was still in his early teens and had grown up in the lower middle class. But by the time Keith was ready for college, his father was part of the upper middle class where parents generally help pay for a child's education. Keith's father functioned as though he were still stuck at a lower socioeconomic level; he refused to be aware of the special needs and expectations of his family. He failed to understand or realize that developing the ability to deal with the family situation as it is – not simply as one experienced it in the past, or as one might like it to be – is an essential part of the art of parenthood.

DEVELOPMENT OF THE GENUINE SELF

Narcissus, as the Greek myth goes, stared endlessly at his own reflection. He had no desire to develop his genuine self; he was in love with what has been called 'the false self', the self that wants to deal only with the beautiful, pleasant, happy side of life. This fixation cut him off from a full range of life experiences and emotional responses such as envy, jealousy and anger. This reluctance to come to terms with the disturbing side of life is characteristic of the narcissistically disturbed individual. There is a portion of life which is not conscious, but that is hidden and unavailable. This unknown side can be called the shadow, as these unknown qualities, be they good or bad, remain obscure or in the dark.

As Jung points out, 'Childhood is not only important because it is the starting point for possible crippling of instinct, but also because this is the time when, terrifying or encouraging, those far-seeing dreams and images come from the soul of the child, which prepares his whole destiny.'[7]

The parents' responsibility at this time is extensive. The genuine self is a treasure which each of us is in the process of discovering. Abusive behaviour on the part of the parents can inhibit the development of the genuine self of the child.

THE SEARCH FOR
THE TRUE SELF
Alice Miller

≈

This chapter is drawn from the celebrated work of Swiss psychoanalyst Alice Miller, an exceptionally readable writer, who since 1981 has provided American readers with a primer on narcissistic disturbances and a searing indictment of modern childrearing practices. She has become, for many, the patroness saint of the inner child.

First with Prisoners of Childhood (renamed The Drama of the Gifted Child in subsequent editions), she outlined the inner child's narcissistic dilemma. The selection reprinted below comprises the core chapter of that book. Then, in For Your Own Good, she defined the 'poisonous pedagogy' behind cruelty to children and described at length the lives of three exemplary children (including Adolf Hitler) whose inner child was tormented and crushed by destructive parenting. In Thou Shalt Not Be Aware, she broke with traditional psychoanalytic drive theory to indict society itself for its betrayal of the child. (An excerpt from that book is included in Part 4 of this collection.)

In the introduction to The Drama of the Gifted Child, Dr Miller confesses that she is telling the story of her own inner child's abuse and suffering, which, she has discovered, is a mirror for many people. 'I realized,' she says, 'that I could not change in the slightest my parents' and teachers' past, which had made them blind. But at the same time I felt that I could and must attempt to point out to today's young parents – and especially to future parents – the danger of misusing their power, that I must sensitize them to this danger and make it easier for them to hear the signals of the child inside them, as well as of children everywhere.'

Introduction

Experience has taught us that we have only one enduring weapon in our struggle against mental illness: the emotional discovery and emotional acceptance of the truth in the individual and unique history of our childhood. Is it possible, then, with the help of psychoanalysis, to free ourselves altogether from illusions? History demonstrates that they sneak in everywhere, that every life is full of them – perhaps because the truth often would be unbearable. And yet, for many people the truth is so essential that they must pay dearly for its loss with grave illness. On the path of analysis we try, in a long process, to discover our own personal truth. This truth always causes much pain before giving us a new sphere of freedom – unless we content ourselves with already conceptualized, intellectual wisdom based on other people's painful experiences, for example that of Sigmund Freud. But then we shall remain in the sphere of illusion and self-deception.

There is one taboo that has withstood all the recent efforts at demystification: the idealization of mother love. The usual run of biographies illustrates this very clearly. In reading the biographies of famous artists, for example, one gains the impression that their lives began at puberty. Before that, we are told, they had a 'happy', 'contented', or 'untroubled' childhood, or one that was 'full of deprivation' or 'very stimulating'. But what a particular childhood really was like does not seem to interest these biographers – as if the roots of a whole life were not hidden and entwined in its childhood. I should like to illustrate this with a simple example.

Henry Moore described in his memoirs how, as a small boy, he massaged his mother's back with an oil to soothe her rheumatism. Reading this suddenly threw light for me on Moore's sculptures: the great, reclining women with the tiny heads – I now could see in them the mother through the small boy's eyes, with the head high above, in diminishing perspective, and the back close before him and enormously enlarged. This may be irrelevant for many art critics, but for me it demonstrates how strongly a child's experiences may endure in his unconscious and what possibilities of expression they may awaken in the adult who is free to give them rein. Now, Moore's memory was not harmful and so could survive intact. But every childhood's conflictual experiences remain hidden and locked in darkness, and the key to our understanding of the life that follows is hidden away with them.

THE POOR RICH CHILD

Sometimes I ask myself whether it will ever be possible for us to grasp the extent of the loneliness and desertion to which we were exposed as children, and hence intrapsychically still are exposed as adults. Here I do not mean to speak, primarily, of cases of obvious desertion by, or separation from, the parents, though this, of course, can have traumatic results. Nor am I thinking of children who were obviously uncared for or totally neglected, and who were always aware of this or at least grew up with the knowledge that it was so.

Apart from these extreme cases, there are large numbers of people who suffer from narcissistic disorder, who often had sensitive and caring parents from whom they received much encouragement; yet, these people are suffering from severe depressions. They enter analysis in the belief, with which they grew up, that their childhood was happy and protected.

Quite often we are faced here with gifted parents who have been praised and admired for their talents and their achievements. Almost all of these analysands were toilet-trained in the first year of their infancy, and many of them, at the age of one and a half to five, had helped capably to take care of their younger siblings. According to prevailing, general attitudes, these people – the pride of their parents – should have had a strong and stable sense of self-assurance. But exactly the opposite is the case. In everything they undertake they do well and often excellently; they are admired and envied; they are successful whenever they care to be – but all to no avail. Behind all this lurks depression, the feeling of emptiness and self-alienation, and a sense that their life has no meaning. These dark feelings will come to the fore as soon as the drug of grandiosity fails, as soon as they are not 'on top', not definitely the 'superstar', or whenever they suddenly get the feeling they failed to live up to some kind of ideal image and measure they feel they must adhere to. Then they are plagued by anxiety or deep feelings of guilt and shame. What are the reasons for such narcissistic disturbances in these gifted people?

In the very first interview they will let the listener know that they have had understanding parents, or at least one such, and if ever they lacked understanding, they felt that the fault lay with them and with their inability to express themselves appropriately. They recount their earliest memories without any sympathy for the child they once were, and this is the more striking since these patients not only have a pronounced introspective ability, but are also able to empathize well with other people. Their relationship to their own childhood's emotional world, however, is characterized by lack of respect, compulsion to control, manipulation, and a demand for achievement. Very often they show disdain and irony, even derision and cynicism. In general, there is a complete absence of real emotional understanding or serious appreciation of their own childhood vicissitudes, and no conception of their true needs – beyond the need for achievement. The internalization of the original drama has been so complete that the illusion of a good childhood can be maintained.

In order to lay the groundwork for a description of these patients' psychic climate, I first will formulate some basic assumptions, which will provide us with a starting point and are close to the work of D.W. Winnicott, Margaret Mahler, and Heinz Kohut.

• The child has a primary need to be regarded and respected as the person he really is at any given time, and as the centre – the central actor – in his own activity. In contradistinction to drive wishes, we are speaking here of a need that is narcissistic, but nevertheless legitimate, and whose fulfilment is essential for the development of a healthy self-esteem.

- When we speak here of 'the person he really is at any given time', we mean emotions, sensations, and their expression from the first day onward. Mahler (1968) writes: 'The infant's inner sensations form the core of the self. They appear to remain the central, the crystallization point of the "feeling of the self" around which a "sense of identity" will become established.'[1]

- In an atmosphere of respect and tolerance for his feelings, the child, in the phase of separation, will be able to give up symbiosis with the mother and accomplish the steps toward individuation and autonomy.

- If they are to furnish these prerequisites for a healthy narcissism, the parents themselves ought to have grown up in such an atmosphere.

- Parents who did not experience this climate as children are themselves narcissistically deprived; throughout their lives they are looking for what their own parents could not give them at the correct time – the presence of a person who is completely aware of them and taken them seriously, who admires and follows them.

- This search, of course, can never succeed fully since it is related to a situation that belongs irrevocably to the past, namely to the time when the self was first being formed.

- Nevertheless, a person with this unsatisfied and unconscious (because repressed) need is compelled to attempt its gratification through substitute means.

- The most appropriate objects for gratification are a parents' *own children*. A newborn baby is completely dependent on his parents, and since their caring is essential for his existence, he does all he can to avoid losing them. From the first day onward, he will muster all his resources to this end, like a small plant that turns toward the sun to survive.[2]

So far, I have stayed in the realm of more or less well-known facts. The following thoughts are derived more from observations made in the course of analyses I have conducted or supervised and also from interviews with candidates for the psychoanalytic profession. In my work with all these people, I found that every one has a childhood history that seems significant to me.

- There was a *mother* who at the core was emotionally insecure, and who depended for her narcissistic equilibrium on the child behaving, or acting, in a particular way. This mother was able to hide her insecurity from the child and everyone else behind a hard, authoritarian, and even totalitarian facade. [*By 'mother' I here understand the person closest to the child during the first years of life. This need not be the biological mother nor even a woman. In the course of the past twenty years, quite often the fathers have assumed this mothering function.]
- That child had an amazing ability to perceive and respond intuitively, that is, unconsciously, to this need of the mother, or of both parents, for him to take on the role that had unconsciously been assigned to him.
- This role secured 'love' for the child – that is, his parents' narcissistic cathexis. He could sense he was needed and this, he felt, guaranteed him a measure of existential security.

This ability is then extended and perfected. Later, these children not only become mothers (confidants, comforters, advisers, supporters) of their own mothers, but also take over the responsibility of their siblings and eventually develop a special sensitivity to unconscious signals manifesting the needs of others. No wonder that they often choose the psychoanalytic profession later on. Who else, without this previous history, would muster sufficient interest to spend the whole day trying to discover what is happening in the other person's unconscious? But the development and perfecting of this differentiated sensorium – which once assisted the child in surviving and now enables the adult to pursue his strange profession – also contains the roots of his narcissistic disturbance.

The Lost World of Feelings

The phenomenology of narcissistic disturbance is well-known today. On the basis of my experience, I would think that its etiology is to be found in the infant's early emotional adaptation. In any case, the child's narcissistic needs for respect, echoing, understanding, sympathy, and mirroring suffer a very special fate, as a result of this early adaptation.

One serious consequence of this early adaptation is the impossibility of consciously experiencing certain feelings of his own (such as jealousy, envy, anger, loneliness, impotence, anxiety) either in childhood or later in adulthood. This is all the more tragic since we are here concerned with lively people who are especially capable of differentiated feelings. This is noticeable at those times in their analyses when they describe childhood experiences that were free of conflict. Usually these concern experiences with nature, which they could enjoy without hurting the mother or making her feel insecure, without reducing her power or endangering her equilibrium. But it is remarkable how these attentive, lively, and sensitive children who can, for example, remember exactly how they discovered the sunlight in bright grass at the age of four, yet at eight might be unable to 'notice anything' or to show curiosity about the pregnant mother or, similarly, were 'not at all' jealous at the birth of a sibling. Again, at the age of two, one of them could be left alone while soldiers forced their way into the house and searched it, and she had 'been good', suffering this quietly and without crying. They have all developed the art of not experiencing feelings, for a child can only experience his feelings when there is someone there who accepts him fully, understands and supports him. If that is missing, if the child must risk losing the mother's love, or that of her substitute, then he cannot experience these feelings secretly 'just for himself' but fails to experience them at all. But nevertheless . . . something remains.

Throughout their later life, these people unconsciously create situations in which these rudimentary feelings may awaken but without the original connection ever becoming clear. The point of this 'play', as Jurgen Habermas (1970) called it, can only be deciphered in analysis, when the analyst joins the cast and the intense emotions experienced in the analysis are successfully related to their original situation. Freud described this in 1914 in his work 'Recollection, Repetition, and Working Through.'

Take, for an example, the feeling of being abandoned – not that of the adult, who feels lonely and therefore takes tablets or drugs, goes to the movies, visits friends, or telephones 'unnecessarily', in order to bridge the gap somehow. No, I mean the original feeling in the small infant, who had none of these chances of distraction and whose communication, verbal or preverbal, did not reach the mother. This was not the case because his mother was bad, but because she herself was narcissistically deprived, dependent on a specific echo from a child that was so essential to her, for she herself was a child in search of an object that could be available to her. However paradoxical this may seem, a child is at the mother's disposal. A child cannot run away from her as her own mother once did. A child can be so brought up that it becomes what she wants it to be. A child can be made to show respect, she can impose her own feelings on him, see herself mirrored in her love and admiration, and feel strong in his presence, but when he becomes too much she can abandon that child to a stranger. The mother can feel herself the centre of attention, for her child's eyes follow her everywhere. When a woman had to suppress and repress all these needs in relation to her own mother, they rise from the depth of her unconscious and seek gratification through her own child, however well-educated and well-intentioned she may be, and however much she is aware of what a child needs. The child feels this clearly and very soon forgoes the expression of his own distress. Later, when these feelings of being deserted begin to emerge in the analysis of the adult, that they are accompanied by such intensity of pain and despair that it is quite clear that these people could not have survived so much pain. That would have only been possible in an empathetic, attentive environment, and this they lacked. The same holds true for emotions connected with the Oedipal drama and the entire drive development of the child. All this had to be warded off. But to say that it was absent would be a denial of the empirical evidence we have gained in analysis.

Several sorts of mechanisms can be recognized in the defence against early feelings of abandonment. In addition to simple denial there is reversal ('I am breaking down under the constant responsibility because the others need me ceaselessly'), changing passive suffering into active behaviour ('I must quit women as soon as I feel that I am essential to them'), projection onto other objects, and introjection of the threat of the loss of love ('I must always be good and measure up to the norm, then there is no risk; I constantly feel that the demands are too great, but I cannot change that, I must always achieve more than others'). Intellectualization is very commonly met, since it is a defence mechanism of great reliability.

All these defence mechanisms are accompanied by repression of the original situation and the emotions belonging to it, which can only come to the surface after years of analysis.

Accommodations to parental needs often (but not always) lead to the 'as-if personality' (Winnicott has described it as the 'false self'). This person develops in such a way that he reveals only what is expected of him, and fuses so completely with what he reveals that – until he comes to analysis – one would scarcely have guessed how much more there is to him, behind this 'masked view of himself.'[3] He cannot develop and differentiate his 'true self', because he is unable to live it. It remains in a 'state of noncommunication', as Winnicott has expressed it. Understandably, these patients complain of a sense of emptiness, futility, or homelessness, for the emptiness is real. A process of emptying, impoverishment, and partial killing of his potential actually took place when all that was alive and spontaneous in him was cut off. In childhood these people have often had dreams in which they experienced themselves as partly dead. I should like to give three examples:

My younger siblings are standing on a bridge and throw a box into the river. I know that I am lying in it, dead, and yet I hear my heart beating; at this moment I always wake [a recurrent dream].

～ 113

This dream combines in her unconscious aggression (envy and jealousy) against the younger siblings, for whom the patient was always a caring 'mother', with 'killing' her own feelings, wishes, and demands, by means of reaction formation. Another patient dreamed:

> *I see a great meadow, on which there is a white coffin. I am afraid that my mother is in it, but I open the lid and luckily, it is not my mother but me.*

If this patient had been able as a child to express his disappointment with his mother – to experience his rage and anger – he could have stayed alive. But that would have led to the loss of his mother's love, and that, for a child, is the same as object loss and death. So he 'killed' his anger and with it a part of himself in order to preserve his self-object, the mother. A young girl used to dream:

> *I am lying on my bed. I am dead. My parents are talking and looking at me, but they don't realize that I am dead.*

The difficulties inherent in experiencing and developing one's own emotions lead to bond permanence, which prevents individuation, in which both parties have an interest. The parents have found in their child's 'false self' the confirmation they were looking for, a substitute for their own missing structures; the child, who has been unable to build up his own structures, is first consciously and then unconsciously (through the introject) dependent on his parents. He cannot rely on his own emotions, has not come to experience them through trial and error, has no sense of his real needs, and is alienated from himself in the highest degree. Under these circumstances he cannot separate from his parents, and even as an adult he is still dependent on affirmation from his partner, from groups, or especially from his own children. The heirs of the parents are the introjects, from whom the 'true self' must remain concealed, and so loneliness in the parental home is later followed by isolation within the self. Narcissistic cathexis of her child by the mother does not exclude emotional devotion. On the contrary, she loves the child, as her self-object, excessively, though not in the manner he needs, and always on the condition that he presents his 'false self'. This is no obstacle to the development of intellectual abilities, but it is one to the unfolding of an authentic emotional life.

IN SEARCH OF THE TRUE SELF

How can psychoanalysis be of help here? The harmony depicted in Katchen von Hollbronn (Heinrich von Kleist's romantic heroine in the drama of the same name, 1810) is probably only possible in fantasy, and particularly understandable arising from the longing of such a narcissistically tormented person as Kleist. The simplicity of Shakespeare's Falstaff – of whom Freud is reported to have said that he embodied the sadness of healthy narcissism – is neither possible nor desirable for these patients. The paradise of pre-ambivalent harmony, for which so many patients hope, is unattainable. But the experience of one's own truth, and the postambivalent knowledge of it, makes it possible to return to one's own world of feelings at an adult level – without paradise, but with the ability to mourn.

It is one of the turning points in analysis when the narcissistically disturbed patient comes to the emotional insight that all the love he has captured with so much effort and self-denial was not meant for him as he really was, that the admiration for his beauty and achievements was aimed at this beauty and these achievements, and not at the child himself. In analysis, the small and lonely child that is hidden behind his achievements wakes up and asks: 'What would have happened if I had appeared before you, bad, ugly, angry, jealous, lazy, dirty, smelly? Where would your love have been then? And I was all these things as well. Does this mean that it was not really me whom you loved, but only what I pretended to be? The well-behaved, reliable, empathetic, understanding, and convenient child, who in fact was never a child at all? What became of my childhood? Have I not been cheated out of it? I can never return to it. I can never make up for it. From the beginning I have been a little adult. My abilities – were they simply misused?'

These questions are accompanied by much grief and pain, but the result always is a new authority that is being established in the analysand (like a heritage of the mother who never existed) – a new empathy with his own fate, born out of mourning. At this point one patient dreamed that he killed a child thirty years ago and no one had helped him to save it. (Thirty years earlier, precisely in the Oedipal phase, those around him had noticed that this child became totally reserved, polite, and good, and no longer showed any emotional reactions.)

Now the patient does not make light of manifestations of his self any more, does not laugh or jeer at them, even if he still unconsciously passes them over or ignores them in the same subtle way that his parents dealt with the child before he had any words to express his needs. Then fantasies of grandeur will be revived, too, which had been deprecated, and so split off. And now we can see their relation to the frustrated and repressed needs for attention, respect, understanding, for echoing and mirroring. At the centre of these fantasies there is always a wish that the patient could never have accepted before. For example: I am in the centre, my parents are taking notice of me and are ignoring their own wishes (fantasy: I am the princess attended by my servants); my parents understand when I try to express my feelings and do not laugh at me (fantasy: I am a famous artist, and everyone takes me seriously, even those who don't understand me); my parents are rich in talents and courage and not dependent on my achievements; they do not need my comfort nor my smile (they are king and queen). This would mean for the child: I can be sad or happy whenever anything makes me sad or happy; I don't have to look cheerful for someone else, and I don't have to suppress my distress or anxiety to fit other people's needs. I can be angry and no one will die or get a headache because of it. I can rage and smash things without losing my parents. In D. W. Winnicott's words: 'I can destroy the object and it will still survive.'[4]

Once these grandiose fantasies (often accompanied by

obsessional or perverse phenomena) have been experienced and understood as the alienated form of these real and legitimate needs, the split can be overcome and integration can follow. What is the chronological course?

1) In the majority of cases, it is not difficult to point out to the patient early in his analysis the way he has dealt with his feelings and needs, and that this was a question of survival for him. It is a great relief to him that things he was accustomed to choke off can be recognized and taken seriously. The psychoanalyst can use the material the patient presents to show him how he treats his feelings with ridicule and irony, tries to persuade himself they do not exist, belittles them, and either does not become aware of them at all or only after several days when they have already passed. Gradually, the patient himself realizes how he is forced to look for distraction when he is moved, upset, or sad. (When a six-year-old's mother died, his aunt told him: 'You must be brave; don't cry; now go to your room and play nicely.') There are still many situations where he sees himself as other people see him, constantly asking himself what impression he is making, and how he ought to be reacting or what feelings he ought to have. But on the whole he feels much freer in this initial period and thanks to the analyst as his auxiliary ego, he can be more aware of himself when his immediate feelings are experienced within the session and taken seriously. He is very grateful for this possibility, too.

2) This will, of course, change. In addition to this first function, which will continue for a long time, the analyst must take on a second as soon as the transference neurosis has developed: that of being the transference figures. Feelings out of various periods of childhood come to the surface then. This is the most difficult stage in analysis, when there is most acting out. The patient begins to be articulate and breaks with his former compliant attitudes, but because of his early experience he cannot believe this is possible without mortal danger. The compulsion to repeat leads him to provoke situations where his fear of object loss, rejection, and isolation has a basis in present reality, situations into which he drags the analyst with him (as a rejecting or demanding mother, for

example), so that afterward he can enjoy the relief of having taken the risk and been true to himself. This can begin quite harmlessly. The patient is surprised by feelings that he would rather not have recognized, but now it is too late, awareness of his own impulses has already been aroused and there is no going back. Now the analysand must (and also is allowed to!) experience himself in a way he had never before thought possible.

Whereas this patient had always despised miserliness, he suddenly catches himself reckoning up the two minutes lost on to his session through a telephone call. Whereas he had previously never made demands of others, now he is suddenly furious that his analyst again is going on vacation. Or he is annoyed to see other people waiting outside the consulting room. What can this be? Surely not jealousy. That is an emotion he does not recognize! and yet . . . 'What are they doing here? Do others besides me come here?' He had not realized that before. At first it is mortifying to see that he is not only good, understanding, tolerant, controlled and, above all, adult, for this was always the basis for his self-respect. But another, weightier mortification is added to the first when this analysand discovers the introjects within himself, and that he has been their prisoner. For his anger, demands, and avarice do not at first appear in a tamed adult form, but in the childish-archaic one in which they were repressed. The patient is horrified when he realizes that he is capable of screaming with rage in the same way that he so hated in his father, or that only yesterday, he has checked and controlled his child, 'practically', he says, 'in my mother's clothes!' This revival of the introjects, and learning to come to terms with them, with the help of the transference, forms the major part of the analysis. What cannot be recalled is unconsciously reenacted and thus indirectly discovered. The more he is able to admit and experience these early feelings, the stronger and more coherent the patient will feel. This in turn enables him to expose himself to emotions that well up out of his earliest childhood and to experience the helplessness and ambivalence of that period.

There is a big difference between having ambivalent feelings toward someone as an adult and, after working back through much of one's previous history, suddenly experiencing one's self as a two-year-old who is being fed by the maid in the kitchen and thinking in despair: 'Why does mother go out every evening? Why does she not take pleasure in me? What is wrong with me that she prefers to go to other people? What can I do to make her stay at home? Just don't cry, just don't cry.' The child could not have thought in these words at the time, but in the session on the couch, this man was both an adult and a two-year-old child, and could cry bitterly. It was not only a cathartic crying, but rather the integration of his earlier longing for his mother, which until now he had always denied. In the following weeks the patient went through all the torments of his ambivalence toward his mother, who was a successful pediatrician. Her previously 'frozen' portrait melted into the picture of a woman with lovable aspects but who had not been able to give her child any continuity in their relationship. 'I hated these beats who were constantly sick and always taking my mother away from me. I hated my mother because she preferred being with them to being with me.' In the transference, clinging tendencies and feelings of helplessness were mingled with long dammed-up rage against the love object who had not been available to him. As a result, the patient could rid himself of a perversion that had tormented him for a long time; its point was now easy to understand. His relationships to women now lost their marked characteristics of narcissistic cathexis, and his compulsion first to conquer and then to desert them disappeared completely.

At this stage in the analysis the patient experienced his early feelings of helplessness, of anger, and of being at the mercy of the loved object in a manner that he could not previously have remembered. One can only remember what had been consciously experienced. But the emotional world of a child with a narcissistic disturbance is itself the result of a selection, which has eliminated the most important elements. These early feelings, joined with the pain of not being able to understand what is going on that is part of the earliest period of childhood, are then consciously experienced for the first time during analysis.

The true self has been in 'a state of noncommunication', as

Winnicott said, because it had to be protected. The patient never needs to hide anything else so thoroughly, so deeply, and for so long a time as he has hidden his true self. Thus it is like a miracle each time to see how much individuality has survived behind such dissimulation, denial, and self-alienation, and can reappear as soon as the work of mourning brings freedom from the introjects. Nevertheless, it would be wrong to understand Winnicott's words to mean that there is a fully developed true self hidden behind the false self. If that were so, there would be no narcissistic disturbance but a conscious self-protection. The important point is that the child does not know what he is hiding. A patient expressed this in the following way:

> I lived in a glass house into which my mother could look at any time. In a glass house, however, you cannot conceal anything without giving yourself away, except by hiding it under the ground. And then you cannot see it yourself either.

An adult can only be fully aware of his feelings if he has internalized an affectionate and empathetic self-object. People with narcissistic disturbances are missing out on this. Therefore they are never overtaken by unexpected emotions, and will only admit those feelings that are accepted and approved by their inner censor, which is their parent's heir. Depression and a sense of inner emptiness is the price they must pay for this control. To return to Winnicott's concept, the true self cannot communicate because it has remained unconscious, and therefore undeveloped, in its inner prison. The company of prison warders does not encourage lively development. It is only after it is liberated in analysis that the self begins to articulate, to grow, to develop its creativity. Where there had only been fearful emptiness or equally frightening grandiose fantasies, there now is unfolding an unexpected wealth of vitality. This is not a homecoming since this home has never existed. It is the discovery of home.

3) The phase of separation begins when the analysand has reliably acquired the ability to mourn and can face feelings from his childhood, without the constant need for the analyst.

PUER AETERNUS

Marie-Louise Von Franz

This is an excerpt from the classic study of the adult struggle with the paradise of childhood, Puer Aeternus. *Dr von Franz's original lectures from the Jung Institute in Zurich have spawned an entire generation of thought on the subject of the puer and the narcissistic character disorders. This is a special case of the inner child motif – a very troublesome one – that is always an 'agent of destiny', according to Jung. Everyone who comes into contact with these ideas about this special archetype is moved by them. Von Franz is a founder of the C. G. Jung Institute, an author, analyst, and world-famous researcher on dreams.*

Puer aeternus is the name of a god of antiquity. The words themselves come from Ovid's *Metamorphoses*[1] and are there applied to the child-god in the Eleusinian mysteries. Ovid speaks of the child-god Iacchus, addressing him as *puer aeternus* and praising him in his role in these mysteries. In later times, the child-god was identified with Dionysus and the god Eros. He is the divine youth who is born in the night in this typical mother-cult mystery of Eleusis, and who is a redeemer. He is a god of life, death, and resurrection – the god of divine youth, corresponding to such oriental gods as Tammuz, Attis, and Adonis. The title *puer aeternus* therefore means 'eternal youth', but we also use it to indicate a certain type of young man who has an outstanding mother complex and who therefore behaves in certain typical ways, which I would like to characterize as follows.

In general, the man who is identified with the archetype of the *puer aeternus* remains too long in adolescent psychology; that is, all those characteristics that are normal in a youth of seventeen or eighteen are continued into later life, coupled in most cases with too great a dependence on the mother. The two typical disturbances of a man who has an outstanding mother complex are, as Jung points out,[2] homosexuality and Don Juanism. In the latter case, the image of a mother – the image of the perfect women who will give everything to a man and who is without any shortcomings – is sought in every woman. He is looking for a mother goddess, so that each time he is fascinated by a woman he has later to discover that she is an ordinary human being. Having lived with her sexually, the whole fascination vanishes and he turns away disappointed, only to project the image anew onto one woman after another. He eternally longs for the maternal woman who will enfold him in her arms and satisfy his every need. This is often accompanied by the romantic attitude of the adolescent.

Generally, great difficulty is experienced in adaptation to the social situation. In some cases, there is a kind of asocial individualism: being something special, one has no need to adapt, for that would be impossible for such a hidden genius, and so on. In addition, an arrogant attitude arises toward other people, due to both an inferiority complex and false feelings of superiority. Such people usually have great difficulty in finding the right kind of job, for whatever they find is never quite right or quite what they wanted. There is always 'a hair in the soup'. The woman is never quite the right woman; she is nice as a girl friend, but . . . There is always a 'but' which prevents marriage or any kind of commitment.

This all leads to a form of neurosis which H. G. Baynes has described as the 'provisional life'; that is, the strange attitude and feeling that the woman is *not yet* what is really wanted, and there is always the fantasy that sometime in the future the real thing will come about. If this attitude is prolonged, it means a constant inner refusal to commit oneself to the moment. Accompanying this neurosis is often, to a smaller or greater extent, a saviour or Messiah complex, with the secret thought that one day one will be able to save the world; that the last word in philosophy, or religion, or politics, or art, or something else, will be found. This can progress to a typical pathological megalomania, or there may be minor traces of it in the idea that one's time 'has not yet come'. The one situation dreaded throughout by such a type of man is to be bound to anything whatsoever. There is a terrific fear of being pinned down, of entering space and time completely, and of being the specific human being that one is. There is always the fear of being caught in a situation from which it may be impossible to slip out again. Every just-so situation is hell. At the same time, there is something highly symbolic – namely, a fascination for dangerous sports, particularly flying and mountaineering – so as to get as high as possible, the symbolism of which is to get away from the mother; i.e., from the earth, from ordinary life. If this type of complex is very pronounced, many such men die at a young age in aeroplane crashes and mountaineering accidents. It is an exteriorized spiritual longing which expresses itself in this form.

A dramatic representation of what flying really means to the *puer* is given in John Magee's poem. Soon after the poem was written, Magee died in an aeroplane accident.

HIGH FLIGHT
Oh! I have slipped the surly bonds of Earth
And danced the skies on laughter-silvered wings;
Sunward I've climbed, and joined the tumbling mirth
Of sun-split clouds, – and done a hundred things

You have not dreamed of – wheeled and soared and swung
High in the sunlit silence. Hov'ring there,
I've chased the shouting wind along, and flung
My eager craft through footless halls of air . . .

Up, up the long delirious, burning blue
I've topped the wind-swept heights with easy grace,
Where never lark, or even eagle, flew –
And, while with silent, lifting mind I've trod
The high untrespassed sanctity of space,
Put out my hand and touched the face of God. [3]

Pueri generally do not like sports which require patience and long training, for the *puer aeternus* – in the negative sense of the word – is usually very impatient by disposition. I know a young man, a classical example of the *puer aeternus*, who did a tremendous amount of mountaineering but so much hated carrying a rucksack that he preferred to train himself even to sleep in the rain or snow outdoors. He would make himself a hole in the snow and wrap himself up in a silk raincoat and, with a kind of yoga breathing, was able to sleep out-of-doors. He also trained himself to go practically without food, simply to avoid carrying any weight. He roamed about for years all over mountains in Europe and other continents, sleeping under trees or in the snow. In a way, he led a very heroic existence, just in order not to be bound to go to a hut or carry a rucksack. You might say that this was symbolic, for such a young man in real life does not want to be burdened with any kind of weight; the one thing he absolutely refuses is responsibility for anything, or to carry the weight of the situation.

In general, the positive quality of such youths is a certain kind of spirituality which comes from a relatively close contact with the collective unconscious. Many have the charm of youth and the stirring quality of a drink of champagne. *Pueri aeterni* are generally very agreeable to talk with; they usually have interesting subjects to talk about and have an invigorating effect upon the listener; they ask deep questions and go straight for the truth; usually they are searching for genuine religion, a search that is typical for people in their late teens. Usually the youthful charm of the *puer aeternus* is prolonged through later stages of life.

However, there is another type of *puer* that does not display the charm of eternal youth, nor does the archetype of the divine youth shine through him. On the contrary, he lives in a continual sleepy daze and that, too, is a typical adolescent characteristic: the sleepy, undisciplined, long-legged youth who merely hangs around, his mind wandering indiscriminately, so that sometimes one feels inclined to pour a bucket of cold water over his head. The sleepy daze is only an outer aspect, however, and if you can penetrate it, you will

find that a lively fantasy life is being cherished within.

The above is a short summary of the main characteristics of certain young men who are caught up in the mother complex and, with it, are identified with the archetype of the *puer*. I have given a mainly negative picture of these people because that is what they look like if viewed superficially, but, as you will see, we have not explained exactly what is the matter. The question to which my words are directed is why the problem of this type, of the mother-bound young man, has become so pronounced in our time. As you know, homosexuality – I do not think Don Juanism is so widely spread – is increasing more and more; even teenagers are involved, and it seems to me that the problem of the *puer aeternus* is becoming increasingly actual. Undoubtedly, mothers have always tried to keep their sons in nest, and some sons have always had difficulty in getting free and have rather preferred to continue to enjoy the pleasures of the nest; still one does not quite see why this in itself, a natural problem, should become such a serious time problem. I think that is the important and deeper question we have to put to ourselves because the rest is more or less self-evident. A man who has a mother complex will always have to contend with his tendencies toward becoming a *puer aeternus*. What cure is there? you might ask. If a man discovers that he has a mother complex, which is something that happened to him – something he did not cause himself – what can he do about it? In *Symbols of Transformation*, Dr Jung spoke of one cure – work – and having said that, he hesitated for a moment and thought, 'Is it really as simple as all that? Is that the only cure? Can I put it that way?' But work is the one disagreeable word which no *puer aeternus* likes to hear, and Dr Jung came to the conclusion that it was the right answer. My experience also has been that it is through work that a man can pull himself out of this kind of youthful neurosis. There are, however, some misunderstandings in this connection, for the *puer aeternus* can work, as can all primitives or people with weak ego complexes, when fascinated or in a state of great enthusiasm. Then he can work twenty-four hours at a stretch or even longer, until he breaks down. But what he cannot do is to work on a dreary, rainy morning when work is boring and one has to kick oneself into it; that is the one thing the *puer aeternus* usually cannot manage and will use any kind of excuse to avoid. Analysis of a *puer aeternus* sooner or later always comes up against this problem. It is only when the ego has become sufficiently strengthened that the problem can be overcome, and the possibility of sticking to the work is given. Naturally, though one knows the goal, every individual case is different. Personally, I have not found that it is much good just preaching to people that they should work, for they simply get angry and walk off.

As far as I have seen, the unconscious generally tried to produce a compromise – namely, to indicate the direction in which there might be some enthusiasm or where the psychological energy would flow naturally, for it is, of course, easier to train oneself to work in a direction supported by one's instinct. That is not quite so hard as working completely uphill in opposition to your own flow of energy. Therefore, it is usually advisable to wait a while, find out where the natural flow of interest and energy lies and then try to get the man to work *there*. But in every field of work there always comes the time when routine must be faced. All work, even creative work, contains a certain amount of boring routine, which is where the *puer aeternus* escapes and comes to the conclusion again that 'this is not it!' In such moments, if one is supported by the unconscious, dreams generally occur which show that one should push on through the obstacle. If that succeeds, then the battle is won.

In a letter Jung says about the *puer*: 'I consider the *puer aeternus* attitude an unavoidable evil. *Identity* with the *puer* signifies a psychological puerility that could do nothing better than outgrow itself. It always leads to eternal blows of fate which show the need for another attitude. But reason accomplishes nothing, because the *puer aeternus* is always an agent of destiny.'[4]

When the child motif turns up, it represents a bit of spontaneity, and the great problem – in each case an ethical individual one – is to decide whether it is now an infantile shadow which must be cut off and repressed, or something creative that is moving toward a future possibility of life. The child is always behind and ahead of us. Behind us, it is the infantile shadow which we leave behind, and infantility which must be sacrificed – that which always pulls us backwards into being infantile and dependent, being lazy, playful, escaping problems, responsibility and life. On the other hand, if the child appears ahead of us it means renewal, the possibility of eternal youth, of spontaneity and of new possibilities – the life flows toward the creative future. The great problem always is to make up one's mind in every situation whether there is now an infantile impulse which only pulls backwards, or an impulse which seems infantile to one's own consciousness but which really should be accepted and lived because it leads forward.

Sometimes, the answer to this dilemma is quite obvious, for the context of the dreams may show very clearly which is meant. Let us say a *puer aeternus* type of man dreams about a little boy; then we can tell from the story of the dream if the apparition of the child has a fatal effect, in which case I treat it as the infantile shadow still pulling backwards. If the same figure appears positively, however, then you can say that it is something which looks very childish and silly but which must be accepted because there is a possibility of life in it. If it were always like that, then the analysis of this kind of problem would be very simple. Unfortunately, like all products of the unconscious, the destructive side and the constructive side, the pull backward and the pull forward, are very closely intertwined and are completely enmeshed in each other. That is why if such figures appear, it is very difficult to decide between them; sometimes it is practically impossible.

If you look at the *puer aeternus* in the negative sense, you can say that he does not want to outgrow his youth or youthful stage, but the growth goes on all the same, until it destroys him; he is killed by the very factor in his soul through which he could have outgrown his problem. If you have to contend with such a problem in actual life, then you see how people refuse to grow, become mature and tackle the problem, and more and more a destructive unconscious piles up. Then you have to say, 'For God's sake, do something, for the thing is growing against you and you will be hit over the head by it.'

But the moment may come . . . when it is too late, for the destructive growth has sucked up all the energy.

The luxuriant growth is also an image of a rich fantasy life, of an inner creative richness. Very often, you find in the *puer aeternus* such a rich fantasy life, but that wealth of fantasy is dammed back and cannot flow into life because the *puer* refuses to accept reality as it is, and thereby piles up life. He dams up his inner life. In actuality, for instance, he gets up at 10:30 A.M., hangs around till lunch time with a cigarette in his mouth, giving way to his emotions and fantasies. In the afternoon he means to do some work but first he goes out with friends and then with a girl, and the evening is spent in long discussion about the meaning of life. He then goes to bed at one, and the next day is a repetition of the one before. In that way, the capacity for life and the inner riches are wasted, for they cannot get into something meaningful but slowly overgrow the real personality. The individual walks about in a cloud of fantasies, fantasies which in themselves are interesting and full of rich possibilities, full of unlived life. You feel that such a person has a tremendous wealth and capacity, but there is no possibility of finding a means of realization. Then the tree – the inner wealth – becomes negative, and in the end kills the personality. That is why the tree is frequently linked up with the negative mother symbol, for the mother complex has that danger; because of it, the process of individuation can become negative in this sense.

The child has a naive view of life, and if you recall your own childhood, you remember you were intensely alive. The child, if it is not already neurotic, is constantly interested in something. Whatever else from which the child may suffer, it does not suffer from remoteness from life, normally – only if it is thoroughly poisoned by the neuroses of its parents. Otherwise, it is fully alive, and that is why people, thinking back to their own childhood, long to have that naive vitality which they have lost in becoming a grown-up. The child is an inner possibility, the possibility of renewal. But how does that get into the actual life of an adult?

THE CHILDHOOD SELF AND THE ORIGINS OF PUER PSYCHOLOGY

Jeffrey Satinover

Jeffrey Satinover's contribution takes up where the preceding essay by von Franz leaves off. He departs by specifically locating the origins of puer psychology in the early development of the child and by directly demonstrating the commonality between puer aeternus psychology and the variety of narcissistic difficulties. Satinover, a psychiatrist and Jungian analyst, understands the sources of the puer dilemma to be at either extreme of parental care – neglect or overindulgence – during the child's earliest experiences of the emerging Self. The parents of narcissistically injured puer aeterni fail to recognize the 'twin needs of the child: for an acceptance of his [or her] grandeur and specialness, unrealistic though it may be, and for the moderate frustrations of reality, painful though these may be.' He suggests that parents who deny their children either the healthy inflations or the common pains of reality have an unresolved puer dilemma of their own, that they are too consumed by reactions to their own inner child's needs to respond to the child's Self. This piece is excerpted from a larger discussion originally published in the journal Quadrant *in 1980.*

What events lead to the *puer?* To answer we need first make a rough sketch of how the Self constellates and of what the consequences of this proper constellation are in the emerging personality. The constellation of the Self in childhood has a definite effect on the ego, similar to late, more conscious experiences of the Self: it catalyses a coalescing of ego fragments to form a functional unity. This coming-together is marked by greatly improved functioning, just as later in life, a loss of the sense of identity is accompanied by a severe decrease in the capacities of the ego as it returns to a state analogous to the one prevailing in childhood before the appearance of the Self.

An example: A woman recalled having awakened one afternoon from a nap at the age of two and a half with the realization of who she was and with a sudden knowledge that *she* could decide for herself whether or not to take a nap. She called her parents into her room and announced to them that from that day hence she was no longer taking afternoon naps.

This early, abrupt kind of experience of identity is marked by specific feelings. These are of a certain specialness and importance, even of grandeur or god-likeness, of omniscience and omnipotence. These feelings themselves suggest that it is, indeed, the Self which, under the surface, has been constellated.

At the core of later adult identity is, therefore, what we might call a necessary inflation. The child, as part of the normal constellation of the Self, need to experience a grandiose enlargement of his sense of who he is. Thus, the two and a half year-old could order his parents into his room with the voice of the Self and assert authority over them.

This is the way that the Self is experienced in childhood. The 'childhood Self,' as I will from now on refer to it, remains at the core of the later experience of identity by providing, beyond all rational argument and relativisms in the face of social and physical reality, a deep belief in one's ultimate worth and value. This early experience of the Self provides the basis, too, of later healthy introversion. That is, the child who has deeply experienced this sense of unity and grandeur knows that, in times of frustration and failure, he can always look inward and touch a sense of worthiness. This act of turning to himself, and so learning to depend on himself, becomes a habit.

In the normal course of development the effect of the childhood Self on the child's identity becomes greatly modified. At the time of its constellation he experiences himself as far more potent than he actually is. This is the time in childhood when imagination is at its peak; where the child can play at being a king or queen, a warrior, a homemaker, a parent, an explorer a villain, all with equal ease. It is as if, in imagination, the full range of what it means to be human – the image of the Anthropos – is available to the child. No human capacity is too great or too demeaning to be embraced in the life of fantasy and play. However, the child is faced with the task of increasing adaptation to mundane reality, and in this his capacities are as undeveloped as the imaginative capacities of the childhood Self are rich.

As the child is impelled into reality by his grandiose fantasies, the inevitable result is frustration. This frustration is a necessary and good thing. If the child experiences it slowly, piece by piece, the fantasies of who he is, generated by the Self, will be slowly modified and made smaller. Simultaneously, the capacities and functions of the ego, through exercise, will grow larger and more efficient. Late in adolescence, ideally, a point will be reached where the idealizations of himself and the pressure to grandeur exerted by the Self will have shrunk to the point where they match his increasing abilities.

At this point a new, adult, and more extraverted process can begin. The young adult still has a deep inner sense of his specialness and worth, the heritage of the childhood Self, but his fantasies of who he is are more limited. The sense of specialness lends to his goals and desires a barely conscious sense of numinosity, making them consistently worth pursuing. But now, instead of the frustration he experienced earlier, when his fantasies were greater than his capacities, he experiences validation of his image of himself. Now his idea of who he is, of his talents and limitations, correspond to his actual abilities. He learns that he is indeed who he has come to hope he is and he gains a renewed sense of satisfaction from his verification. In this way he achieves and reinforces a stable identity.

There are two ways this process can go wrong and produce the *puer* later in life. First, the constellation of the Self can be consistently obstructed; second, having been constellated, the Self can be protected from the limitations of reality which modify and reduce the grandiose sense of identity it generates.

Puer psychology in the man is sometimes traced (von Franz, *Puer Aeternus*) to early experiences of a mother who attacks a boy's emerging masculinity. A classical psychoanalytic view of the same development would trace it to excessive fears of castration by the father (this fear being proportional to the attachment to the mother). Each of these views is similar in locating the origin of *puer* psychology rather later (age 3-5) than I do, by attributing a sexual character to it, and in providing an explanation that lends itself more readily to masculine psychology. However, *puers* are to be found no less commonly among women than men. This, plus the fact that *puers* of each gender tend toward a more or less blurred sexual identity, suggests that the origin of the *puer* is earlier, before identity becomes further differentiated along gender lines.

I would say that the *puer* may result from a parental milieu which, in a roughly eighteen-month- to a two-year-old child, habitually disrupts any sign of *assertiveness*, of action or fantasies that carry not the hallmark of masculinity, but of specialness and grandeur. This kind of assertiveness is equally present, at certain ages, in both boys and girls. Disrupting it will generate later disturbances of identity on top of which problems with masculinity and femininity will be overlaid. The kind of disruption I have in mind is akin to the habit we all share in a greater or lesser degree, of attacking inflations we sense in others (and, indeed, the origin of this habit is in our own early experiences of having it done to us).

The disruption of the childhood Self, as it constellates, will return the child again and again to a preceding state we call fragmentation, unless he can find a haven where his inflation is accepted – with a grandparent, another adult friend, or with a therapist.

If the disruption remains uncountered, the child will come to internalize the parental disapproval of the childhood Self, and the child will then himself later take over the role of undermining his idealizations of himself. If it persists into adulthood, this internal criticism will return whenever a new idea, an enthusiasm, a spirit of hope or a self-gratifying fantasy arises. Every hopeful response to the question, 'Who am I?' will be stopped with, 'Oh, that's just an inflation.' In the child, as part of the innate urge to development, the Self will attempt to constellate. Thus, an internal vicious circle is established; each constellation of the Self, bringing with it a tide of grandiose fantasies, is followed by a tide of self-criticism and re-fragmentation.

This cycling between states of grandeur in which the Self is constellated, and states of despair in which the Self is fragmented, is a typical feature of *puer* psychology and the source of the *puer's* exquisite sensitivity. If he does not himself deliver the blow that ushers in fragmentation, the least criticism from another will do it.

The persistence of a state of fragmentation, though sometimes induced by external events, is not dependent upon them. The Self will reconstellate, in its own time. Thus, apologies and reasonable expla-nations which appeal to the ego have little effect. A person suffering from such a fragmentation will remain depressed, sullen, or angry regardless of attempts to undo the damage, often to the chagrin, frus-tration, and guilt of the one who seemed to have caused it.

When reconstellated in the *puer*, the Self is in its childhood form and thus especially liable to refragmentation. It has not been tempered by the immersion in reality, and it reacts as it does in a child. This sensitivity accounts for the essential similarity between children of insufficiently supportive parents and those of excessively supportive ones. In the latter instance, the Self is allowed to constel-late, but it remains insulated from the frustrations of real life that make identity less grandiose but more cohesive. In this case, the grandiose fantasies are not only accepted, they are pushed. The parents overstimulate the child's sense of specialness and press him to behave and to accomplish beyond his age. Precociousness becomes the currency he exchanges for love and admiration.

Such a child can, in effect, become addicted to the childhood Self. He will later devote much of his life to seeking experiences which maintain or re-establish the grandiose constellation, while avoiding frustrations that diminish his sense of specialness.

Puers from each kind of upbringing strike others as being narcis-sistic: the introversion of each is engaged in a ceaseless effort to maintain the experience of the childhood Self, and each will choose external circumstances – drugs, brief affairs, intense physical or mental activities – that enhance this experience. Both will appear inordinately sensitive, and both are liable to radical and sudden shifts in self-esteem.

There is another source which also can yield *puer* psychology. This third source is the presence of great talent. A gift, in proportion to its strength, can generate varying degrees of *puer* psychology, and thus, in the course of self-exploration, one can set off on a relatively fruitless search for the roots of one's neurosis in the relationship to one's parents. On the other hand, the fantasy of being gifted is one of the most frequent self-definitions generated by the childhood Self, leading to the self-serving redefinition of one's flaws as the necessary price of genius. Since this latter problem may occur as easily in a genuinely gifted individual as in a relatively ungifted one, the matter is confusing. It is important to distinguish between an objective assessment of ability, and the need to consider oneself especially able.

Talent produces *puer* psychology in the following way. As in the ungifted, the constellated childhood self produces fantasies of omnipotence and grandeur in the gifted child; however, he meets with far fewer frustrations in his attempt to realize these fantasies than does the ungifted child. So, for instance, the magical, childish way to play an instrument with little or no practice is, for the musically gifted child, nearly possible. The protean diversity of the Self, the Anthropos, is more than just a rich inflation for the multigifted child. In fact he comes close to being able to do everything.

As a result, the gifted child meets with less pressure to modify his grandiose self-image than does the ungifted child. His capacities meet his fantasies, and he is confirmed in a view of himself, not in late adolescence, but very early on, when that view retains much of its original splendour. His parents, in their astonishment and pride, reflect back to him a true view of himself, and not the artificial inflation of the excessively supportive parent.

Thus, the development of the gifted child resembles the development of the child in an overly supportive environment. He is prey to the essential *puer* feature of unstable identity, because he rests upon a less modified Self than does the normal child, and his sense of identity is consequently more labile. Naturally, the gifted child starves off fragmentation and maintains a high in the fashion he is most adept: by the exercise of his talents. It is, therefore, in this area that he is most sensitive to criticism and why, so commonly, criticism of a creative individual's products ushers in fragmentation of his identity.

PUER PSYCHOLOGY IN THE ADULT

Some of the characteristic features of the *puer* syndrome can be related to the preceding model. The most general feature of this model is that in the *puer*, the sense of identity is closely tied to the cycles of the Self, and relatively little of it is derived from or capable of verification by achievements of the ego in the physical or social worlds. There are two broad categories we can examine from this point of view. One is the area of goals and achievements; the other is the area of personal relationships. In both these areas there are two basic sources for *puer* characteristics. That is, some characteristics stem directly from the states of fragmentation or inflation, while other characteristics stem from defences against experiencing either state.

Within the area of goals and achievements we can look at two things: problems in setting and reaching realistic goals, and fantasies of specialness. A characteristic feature of the *puer* is the pressure of intense, recurrent fantasies of grandeur. These fantasies are the translation in consciousness of, and a way of defining identity, based on the childhood Self. Depending on the degree of modification by experience, the fantasies correspond more or less to the pure image of the Self.

The most common fantasies today can be placed on a scale of decreasing grandeur: 1) Messianic fantasies in which personal identity is equivalent to Self. 2) Fantasies of being spiritually chosen, or of having great spiritual accomplishment. 3) Fantasies of being a genius, or being gifted and especially creative. 4) The wish for great fame or power. 5) The wish for great wealth. 6) The wish for professional success.

Keeping in mind that the core of each fantasy remains the Self, we see that as the pressure exerted by the childhood Self decreases, and realistic capacities increase, a point is reached where the fantasies become realistic. Where the point is reached depends, of course, upon the individual's actual ability. In the course of a successful analysis, the fantasies of grandeur will follow some such descent.

It is often overlooked that these fantasies are not only gratifying; they are painful. The *puer* experiences these fantasies as a call to action, and to the degree that he has a genuine appreciation of reality and its limitations the failure to live up to the call will be experienced as an inner reproach that itself reinduces fragmentation and a sense of worthlessness. He often 'knows' that his fantasies are unrealistic, but the *puer* is unable to experience satisfaction from anything less. Thus he is either forced to greater and greater efforts (often of an exhibitive nature where the feedback is large and immediate) or he splits off the pressure entirely and loses all motivation ('being laid-back'). He never gains any true satisfaction from the achievements he accomplishes since they never can match the demands of the childhood Self.

When the talents of such individuals are sufficient, they will commonly follow a meteoric rise in a profession that keeps them before the approving reflection of the public: thus today's plethora of superstars and the desperate struggle for fame, 'becoming somebody.' *Puers* commonly fantasize or dream of flying. I consider this the essential intrapsychic representation of the pressure to specialness and grandeur exerted by the childhood Self. Such dreams and fantasies (and more generally the experience or symbolic representation of 'being high') are often interpreted as meaning that the individual is out of touch with reality. Conversely, they are interpreted as indications of a spiritual ascent. This interpretation is sometimes correct, if by 'reality' we mean the outside world and its demands, but only secondarily. Rather, the motif of flying represents the way in which the sense of specialness raises a person beyond his limitations. Man's age-old dream of flying has always been the prototypical expression of the urge to escape the restraints of mundane existence. It is fitting that such dreams should have as their source the Self. Likewise, the motif of crashing is as common to *puer* fantasy as that of flying. The two types of dreams represent the polar states of Self: constellation and fragmentation.

Therapeutically, it is crucial that the *puer* become familiar with the way these two states are intertwined and that by experiencing and understanding how behind every high is a sense of desperation, and behind every low a struggle for glory. Dreams often signal the appearance of this realization. For instance, 'I am lifted up by a giant parachute drop machine, but without a parachute. When it gets to the top it drops me and I crash to the earth. There it picks me up again. This happens over and over.'

A common feature of such dreams, as in this instance, is the mechanical nature of the cycling. This corresponds to an introspective feature of *puer* psychology that the individual at least partly aware of his nature will express: 'I cannot help getting high, nor can I prevent the crash that follows.' As a result, accusing such a person of being inflated, when he is, rarely has a beneficial effect. Rather, it exacerbates the underlying feeling of frustration, isolation and helplessness in the face of what he already knows is a problem.

Because of the widespread existence of occult and spiritual groups of every sort, the messianic fantasy – being a guru of greater or lesser following – has become much more acceptable, and commonplace, than it once was. This ambition, and the somewhat lesser of being perfectly enlightened, are common in the *puer* and commonly acted on concretely. Why is this so?

Here again, the rarely mentioned fact is that the grandeur of the idea of perfect spiritual attainment exerts a powerful fascination on the *puer*. By taking on the role of master or disciple he acquires an identity that carries with it the numinosity of the Self in its most undiluted concrete form. Furthermore, the general sense that spiritual attainment can lift one out of the mundane world, particularly since it finds support in certain hermetic approaches to the spirit, relieves the constellated childhood Self of daily frustrations, and preserves it in its original, unmodified form. The tenacity with which the *puer* clings to such cults stems from the price he would pay in sacrificing this attachment: fragmentation of his identity.

In her book on the *puer* [see the previous essay], Dr Marie-Louise von Franz remarks that the *puer* is often engaged in a quest for spirituality of the sort typical of late adolescence. I would add to her observation the following: in later adolescence the spiritual quest often quietly drops away. This happens at the point where the decreasing pressure to specialness and increasing realistic capacities meet. It can be seen that adolescent spirituality often screens a search for identity which is not being consciously acknowledged as such (though years later the person can smilingly admit that, indeed, that's what it was). When identity is found, the spiritual interest can safely be dropped. The same is true for the older *puer* personality. The intense spiritual interests often mask the missing identity. When the personal identity has been successfully forged, the spiritual quest for meaning may drop away.

Of course, this is not always the case. There are individuals whose actual gift is that of spirit. In them, resolution of the *puer* structure will yield a personal identity formed around a complex and realistic orientation towards pressing spiritual questions – Jung would have been such a person. But the spirituality of such individuals is highly modified from the ideal generated by the childhood Self. Because of the conflict with reality, it lacks the degree of intense, covert personal grandeur of *puer* spirituality, and further, it is not attracted to perfected, closed systems with guaranteed results. For such individuals, spirit and meaning are always great open questions; they are led onward by doubt rather than belief; by what they don't know than by what they do. The missing identity makes it impossible for the *puer/puella* to maintain this sort of openness. The lack of internal certainty creates a narcissistic dependency on what is perceived as external truths.

An interesting question in this regard is why Jungian psychology is so attractive to the *puer*, especially when Jung himself conceived of his work as addressed primarily to the questions of later life. The answer, I believe, is this: Jungian psychology holds out the possibility of a close relation to the Self and to the archetypes, and it is this that the *puer* seeks. However, the *puer* seeks it for different reasons, and seeks a different sort of close relation to the Self, than that which concerned Jung. Whereas Jung sought to work out an *objective* relationship between the Self and an ego which sensed an already established personal identity (by objective I mean, precisely, as an object of awareness), the *puer* seeks the Self as subject in order to acquire a personal identity. Jung and his early students found themselves in the way of individuation out of necessity; the *puer* seeks individuation because of its appeal.

Another fantasy related to the wish for individuation and common today to the *puer* is that of being creative. As before, I want to make a clear distinction between creativity *per se*, and the need to consider oneself creative, which may be present in both creative and relatively uncreative individuals. The fantasy of being creative belongs to the constellated childhood Self.

Being creative was not always the hallmark of personal identity that it has become today. During the Middle Ages, much of the most creative work was anonymous (as in the illuminated manuscripts of the monks), or collective (as in the great cathedrals which often required three generations of stonemasons to complete). 'Creativity,' as the word itself implies, was the prerogative of God. Psychologically, therefore, it now appears as a fantasy generated by the Self.

During the Renaissance, the identification of individuals as creators burgeoned, hence the rise of the 'Renaissance Man' and the great concern during the Renaissance with cataloguing the signs of genius. The Romantics, harkening back to the Renaissance in the way that the Renaissance harkened back to the Greeks, disseminated the cult of genius more widely with the poets as, in Shelley's phrase, 'the unacknowledged legislators of mankind.' We, inheriting the Romantic tradition and making of it a popular product, now require creative writing, creative footwear, creative marriages, and creative divorces. Ironically, the fantasy of being creative can be a great obstacle to actually being so. The pressure that this fantasy places on the *puer* is often what inhibits or weakens his expressive capabilities. This leads us to the more general topic of ambition.

In spite of their great ambitions, spiritual, creative, fame-seeking or otherwise, many *puers* are described as lazy. 'Laziness' is not exactly accurate. It is true that *puers* have typical sorts of work disturbances, but I do not believe these disturbances derive from an unwillingness to work. That is, they are not disturbances of the ego, or the will. Indeed, many *puers* know quite well that they have high ambitions but find themselves unable to properly pursue them. The painful tension between ambitions and the incapacity to fulfil them is in my experience the single most common presenting complaint.

And, some *puers* are overworkers who are unable to stop working or enjoy the fruits of their labour. Such individuals seek analysis less frequently because they gain, for a time at least, sufficient satisfaction from the image of themselves as hard-working to obscure the underlying emptiness.

The inability to work coupled with great ambition is a source of distress to many *puers*. They will often come into analysis having failed at work of a creative sort: they have writer's block, or stage fright, or, commonly are unable to complete their Ph.D. theses. Frequently they engage in what appear to be deliberately self-destructive behaviours: they will have dropped out of school in the semester before graduation; they will have failed to study for a final exam or a professional school admissions test (though having performed excellently in all the preceding work or requirements); they put off important tasks until the last minute even though the task may involve no more than a phone call, or they procrastinate on a large project so long that they must do the whole thing in a rush and thereby guarantee an impressive accomplishment but a mediocre product.

More commonly, *puers* will simply not finish projects that they have already begun, either by ceasing work altogether, or by continuing to re-work what they have done, so that it is never finished. In these and similar instances, the problem can be traced to the pressures exerted by the constellated childhood Self. The problem is the fear of failure, and more specifically the fear of a failure where, by definition, failure is guaranteed. The *puer* will commonly acknowledge that fear and that it paralyses him or causes him to undo what he has already done. This is most easily seen in cases of stage fright where the fear and paralysis is acute, intense and evident. It is less easily seen in long-term projects such as a thesis. In all cases, what is less accessible to consciousness is the fact that the project must fail no matter how great the actual success. This stems from the fact that no success can live up to the core fantasy of the childhood Self.

This core is the archetype of the divine child. The individual narcissistically bound to this image for identity can experience satisfaction from a concrete achievement only if it matches the grandeur of this archetypal image. It must have the qualities of greatness, absolute uniqueness, of being the best, and more than anything else it must be prodigiously precocious.

This latter quality explains the enormous fascination of child prodigies, and also explains why even a great success yields no permanent satisfaction for the *puer*: being an adult, no accomplishment is precocious unless he stays artificially young or equates his accomplishments with those of old age (hence the premature striving after the wisdom of those who are much older).

The *puer* lives with a constant, vague sense of having failed since he never quite lives up to the archetypal demand. Projected onto his surroundings, he therefore sees the world around him as similarly having failed. The time of glory was earlier, in his childhood or in the younger days of the culture. Nothing in the present, his present or his society's present, no new accomplishment can ever make up for the defect and so the past is tinged with nostalgia. This attitude strongly affects *puer* aesthetics, which runs to camp tastes and antiquarianism. The yearning backwards is not so much a yearning for the mother nor for the *mundus imaginalis* (the imaginal world), as it has variously been explained, but for the Self and for the time of life when the Self had not yet met up with reality.

The beginning of a project is marked by fantasies of its grandeur and specialness, and particularly by fantasies of the grandeur and specialness of the creator. The project is thus embarked upon with a strong sense of identity whose source is the reconstellated childhood Self. But as the project drags on, the enthusiasm fades; completion nears and it begins to look like simply another book, or thesis, or piece of music like thousands of others. With the dawning of this realization the reestablished sense of identity begins to crumble and depression sets in. The project is either abandoned for a new one that reconstellates the Self or the fragmentation is starved off by endless revisions according to an impossibly high set of standards.

Alternatively, as completion approaches, methods are devised to snatch a grandiose defeat from the jaws of banal victory. To barely pass the admissions test, but without studying at all, comes closer to preserving prodigality than does an excellent performance as a result of strenuous effort. One prefers to be known, and to know oneself, as brilliant if erratic, than as a successful drudge. The *puer* prefers his fantasised potentials to his actual capacities because the former preserves more of the flavour for the childhood Self than the latter.

We need now to return to the time in early childhood when the original constellation of the Self is determined. You will recall that one of the important functions of the parents, usually at this age the mother, is to provide a reflection of the child's emerging Self. By reflecting back to the child his specialness and grandeur, the parent helps to sustain a kind of necessary inflation. This inflation will motivate the child to move into an ever-expanding world where, by suffering tolerable defeats, the inflation will be modified and personal identity sustained more and more by the capacities of the ego.

In situations where this reflection fails – either by its absence or its excess – the interaction of the childhood Self with the world fails to take place and normal development is interrupted. The individual then experiences, into adulthood, a constant pressure to return to the state of the constellated childhood Self so that development can proceed anew. The manifestations of *puer* psychology are therefore not so much pathological, but the expression in adulthood of a normal, long-deferred process that stems from the archetypally determined pathway of development. The reason that this process often does not simply take over and bring about a self-cure is that the individual has internalized from his childhood experiences a faulty introversion – one that either automatically attacks the Self as soon as it is constellated, or protects it from modification when frustration is sensed.

The core of *puer* relationships is this: the *puer* seeks relationships that provide him the kind of reflection he is unable to perform for himself. What appears as extraversion in the *puer* is not that at all. In effect, the *puer* does not relate to objects (in the analytic sense); he relates instead to a missing part of himself which he either sees in another or makes another perform. Objects function for the *puer* primarily as an indirect means of introversion.

A type of *puer* relationship consists in an individual, in order to maintain an identity based on the childhood Self, seeking an admirer or admirers who will reflect back to him his specialness and grandeur. While the most common situation is in friendship or marriage, this also occurs in psychoanalysis.

RECONSTELLATING THE SELF

We can now turn to the final question of this essay: what can we do about all this? I believe there is a concrete and practical approach that can be taken, it is an approach that can be used in day to day relationships, and in therapy as well. The *puer* development is a consequence of the parental response to the constellating Self of the child. We can ask ourselves, now, why does the parent fail to recognize the twin needs of the child; for an acceptance of his grandeur and specialness, unrealistic though it may be, and for the moderate frustrations of reality, painful though these may be? The answer should be clear: the parent fails to understand this, cannot understand it, because he . . . is, due to his own unresolved *puer* psychology, too reactive to his own inner states to recognize and respond to the child's Self.

The pattern of interaction in *puer-puella* dyads, a pattern that repeats, for each, the inappropriate childhood constellation, must be interfered with. The way to do this, in general, is to switch attention from the content of the interaction to the process.

Concretely, this means that the partners must avoid acting out the irritation, anger or rage that they are impelled to by the precipitating fragmentation of their own Self. Instead, they need to look inward and ask what feeling is arousing this anger? Generally, the remark that triggers the irritation has had the effect of making one feel small, worthless, wounded. The response of the tip of the tongue is a response to this inner state, and not truly a response to the other person. The fact of the way one feels – worthless – can be simply and neutrally communicated, in a nonaccusatory way.

The straightforward offering of feelings accomplishes a number of things. First, it is an act of intimacy, even when the feelings are negative. The fact that one is willing to expose his vulnerability to his partner reveals an attitude of trust which stops his further fragmentation. It is therefore an implicit form of the reflection he requires. Second, the fact that one is able to talk neutrally about pain he is experiencing means that there is a part – the part that observes and comments – which is outside the cycle of inflation and fragmentation. Third, one partner perceives the other thus relatively at ease with painful feelings, willing to accept them and not shattered as a result. He therefore experiences less of the implicit accusation that he is at fault for the partner's feelings, and is in this way further stabilized.

In general, the goal to be worked for in personal relationships, as in therapy, is the *creation of a third point of view* which is neither split off from the cycles of inflation and fragmentation, nor completely immersed in either the constellated or fragmented Self. This outside point of view is the nucleus around which a new identity, no longer dependent on the cycles of the Self, will be created.

If the defences of the self are worked through and the individual receives the appropriate reflection, the Self will reconstellate. Proper reflection means that the divine child is being accepted by another and so eventually by oneself. As a result of the ensuing frustration, also properly reflected, the Self will be modified in the fashion that didn't occur in childhood.

Part Four

THE WOUNDED
CHILD WITHIN

INTRODUCTION

≈

The violation of the natural weakness and simplicity of the young child not ready for autonomy can turn into a protective infantilism that lasts through one's life. These wounds may be redeemed through the natural simplicity of loving; indeed, they may offer the gateway through which love may enter.

— JEAN HOUSTON, *THE SEARCH FOR THE BELOVED*

Today, in our socially conscious age of information, we are surrounded by images of the abused child. This outer wounded child has been propelled into our awareness through the innumerable stories of child victims that surface daily in all strata of our society. These incidents, ranging from minor neglect and accidental injury to the morally reprehensible exploitation and sexual abuse of young people, are pathetic manifestations of a social and mental epidemic.

The anxiety that results from mistreatment often leads children to become compliant and, for safety's sake, to identify with a false self in their outer personalities. These fears also can give rise to an inflated grandiosity (as we saw in the problem of the *puer aeternus*), in which smugness and superiority mask deeper feelings of injury and unworthiness. In either case, the authentic and vulnerable childhood Self is disowned and aliveness is diminished. To identify with vulnerability is to feel a pain so frightening to the child's fragile developing ego identity that it seems to threaten its very existence.

Those childhood injuries to the soul create a child within the adult who longs for understanding, love, respect, and possibly justice. Rediscovery of the inner child is often painful, because it returns to consciousness the memories and emotions of childhood wounds. Typically, these wounding experiences have taken place in the family. Reconnecting to the wounded child brings us into contact with our parents, whom we tried to please and satisfy. We must also face our angry, sad, and injured Self. Redeeming this inner problem child means, at the very least, reparenting him or her in ways we have longed to be loved, cared for, and nourished.

To heal the wounded child within, we as adults also must learn to understand our parents' suffering. Because we have internalized these damaged parents as well, we must waive harsh judgment or vindictiveness. If we are to stop abusive family patterns and not transmit them to the next generation, then the internalized parental image also must be recognized as wounded. Such compassionate awareness is a developing phenomenon in the lives of those courageous adults who are overcoming their shame and pain in order to acknowledge and heal the wounded child within.

The wounded inner child is the emergent symbol for this compassionate awareness. It represents the obstructed potential of the inner child. It is the inner victim who has suffered the thousands of hurts and who has been buried inside for protection from further humiliation and injury. This authentic being within us – our vulnerable childhood Self – is caught in an unfortunate web of reactive, self-protective behaviours, and is often debilitated by a confusion of feelings of anxiety, hopelessness, hurt, and rage.

The essays in this section are organized around the theme of injury to the child within; each chapter contains a distinct psychological model and sensibility about the wounding and the healing of the inner child.

Hal Stone and Sidra Winkelman postulate a psychological model in which the wounded child is disowned by the conscious personality very early in life, during the first five years. 'This child cannot exist in our civilized societies,' they say, 'without the protection of a very strong protector/controller' element in the personality that buries the child so that it will not be hurt. The primary qualities of

woundedness in the inner child described in this model are vulnerability and a dissociation from the other parts of the total person.
Healing, according to the authors, is a full integration of the inner
child into conscious awareness, so that an aware ego can properly
take care of the child.

Alexander Lowen relates the personal discovery of woundedness
and betrayal he made in his therapy with the famous psychiatrist
Wilhelm Reich. His story gives us a somatically based model in the
wounded inner child, whose unexpressed pain and hurt are locked
in the musculature of the adult's body. 'The truth about our childhood,' says Alice Miller, 'is stored up in our body,' and that aptly
sums up Lowen's bioenergetic model of the wounded child within.

Alice Miller's article 'Advocating for the Child' describes a model
of injury based on actual child abuse. Her focus is on outer children –
and by implication, on the wounded child within – the ones who
suffer through cruel and unconscious abuse by parental and
authority figures. 'Only when we realize how powerless a child is in
the face of parental expectations,' she says, ' . . . will we grasp the
cruelty of parents' threats to withdraw their love if the child fails to
meet these impossible demands. And this cruelty is perpetuated in
the child.'

Robert M. Stein's depth psychology model explicitly relates outer
abuse to inner wounding: 'Depth psychology assumes that the
external and internal worlds reflect each other . . . We need to ask
what lies within the compulsive need to abuse and sexually molest
the outer child.' In contradistinction to Alice Miller's literalized
model. Stein's wounded child within suffers from polarizations in
the individual and in the culture, splittings of attitudes and beliefs
that deny the natural, elemental being of the child and that cut off
the child from its grounding in instinct.

THE VULNERABLE INNER CHILD
Hal Stone and Sidra Winkelman

≈

Stone and Winkelman are the co-creators of a process called the Voice Dialogue Method, which is based on the idea that each individual contains a multiplicity of selves, or subpersonalities. The selves are in varying degrees of relationship to one another and to what the authors term the protector/controller, which is different from what is commonly thought of as the ego.

Stone and Winkelman suggest that certain troublesome selves become disowned and, therefore, live as unintegrated energy patterns in the unconscious. Dialoguing with these disowned selves, recognizing and objectifying them, enables the aware ego to understand and work with them creatively.

Voice Dialogue is a powerful means of gaining direct access to these subpersonalities or inner voices by engaging each in a dialogue without the interference of a protector/controller. With the assistance of a facilitator, the subpersonality can be addressed directly as an individual entity and as a part of the total personality. This process puts the subject into an altered state of consciousness, which is similar to hypnosis. Eventually, more and more of the subpersonalities can be brought into awareness. 'Our task,' Stone and Winkelman say, 'is to become aware of this fragmentation of selves so that we can make valid choices in our lives.'

A key subpersonality is the abandoned inner child. 'Perhaps the most universally disowned self in our civilized world is the vulnerable child,' say the authors. This chapter demonstrates how the inner child manifests in the Voice Dialogue process. It has been excerpted from the authors' two books, Embracing Our Selves: The Voice Dialogue Manual, *and* Embracing Each Other.

The children of our inner world know how to 'be,' while the rest of our personality knows how to 'do' and how to 'act.' In working with these patterns we are given the opportunity to learn how to 'be' with them; otherwise, they cannot emerge. When dealing with the inner child, the dictum is: 'There's nowhere to go and there's nothing to do.'

The loss of the inner child is one of the most profound tragedies of the 'growing up' process. With its loss we lose so much of the magic and mystery of living, the delight and intimacy of relationship. So much of the destructiveness we express to each other is a function of our lack of connection to our sensitivities, our fears, our own magic. How different the world would be if our political figures could say: 'I feel very bad. You really hurt my feelings when you said that.' Or: 'I want to apologize to my colleagues for my remarks yesterday. My feelings were hurt and I was angry and I am sorry.'

If the inner child is operating in our lives autonomously and without protection, we can be fairly sure that we will end up as some kind of victim. The child, however wonderful, cannot drive our cars any more successfully than any other single energy pattern. It, too, needs balancing. But as long as the protector/controller is in charge of the personality, the child will remain buried and therefore inaccessible.

As we become more aware of the inner child, our aware ego gradually becomes the parent to our child. We can then take responsibility to use the energy of the inner child in our lives and provide it with appropriate protection when needed.

When the aware ego becomes more effective, we can begin to relax, knowing that the fundamental integrity of the system is in good hands. Let us look now at how the inner child manifests in the Voice Dialogue process.

VULNERABILITY – A PRIMARY DISOWNED SELF

Perhaps the most universally disowned self in our civilized world is the vulnerable child. Yet this child may be our most precious subpersonality, the one closest to our essence, the one that enables us to be truly intimate, to fully experience others, and to love. Unfortunately, it usually disappears by the age of five. This child cannot exist in our civilized societies without the protection of a very strong protector/controller. The only way a protector/controller can handle the vulnerable child is to disown it. It is usually so completely disowned that the protector/controller no longer even worries about it.

What is this child like? The most striking quality is its ability to be deeply intimate with another person. The facilitator can feel a physical warmth and a fullness radiating from this child. It is as though the space between the two people is alive and vibrating. When the vulnerable child withdraws (as it does at the slightest provocation), this warmth and fullness disappears, leaving behind a slight chill. This experience is somewhat similar to the special feelings that might occur with a small child or with a dog in a moment of deep affection and mutual trust. This ability to be fully 'with' another human being is most precious.

However, being fully with another brings its share of discomfort as well as pleasure. The vulnerable child is tuned in energetically – it is aware of *everything* that is happening. Words will not fool it for a moment. As you speak, the child will know if there is any change whatsoever in your energetic connection to it. An outside thought may have intruded – you may be wondering what time it is, you may suddenly decide you're hungry – and the child will know you have withdrawn. It is exquisitely sensitive and reacts immediately to any abandonment it perceives. It may not know why the withdrawal has happened, but it will know that one has occurred.

Getting in touch with this subpersonality can open us to the most embarrassing feelings of rejection, such as experiencing a sense of abandonment when a spouse leaves the bed in the morning to go to the bathroom. However, when made conscious, this subpersonality can often tell us who is to be trusted and who is not. It usually recognizes the people who have disowned their vulnerable child and who can, therefore, hurt others, either accidentally or deliberately.

The first dialogue with a vulnerable child may simply involve sitting quietly and encouraging it to come forth. It is often preverbal and may sit quietly or cry. In its initial emergence, it might curl up in a foetal position, cover its head, and weep with great wrenching sobs. Another might be very tentative, checking out the facilitator's ability to sense its presence or absence. Above all, no vulnerable child will appear unless the facilitator can be trusted not to hurt it. It has invariably been hurt in the past and is fearful of being hurt again. This was dramatically illustrated by the vulnerable child of a Jewish woman who had managed to stay alive in Europe through Word War II.

CHILD: It hurts to think of everything that she's been through. I had to go away when she was very, very young (crying). It's too painful to exist. It just feels like a skin full of tears.

FACILITATOR (with concern): Do you want to go away now?

CHILD: No, it feels good to have you here with me. I always go into hiding, but it even hurts worse when I'm alone. I need someone to be with me and let me be sad.

The pain of the vulnerable child is a deep pain that requires respect and empathy. The child will know if you are feeling aloof or rational and it will not emerge. It sometimes demands that a facilitator actually search for it. With Natalie, a therapist, the vulnerable child emerged in a most surprising fashion. Natalie began the session by expressing her discomfort at hugging the facilitator. Actually, this was Natalie's rational voice, as it turned out later, but it certainly sounded like an aware ego at first.

RATIONAL NATALIE: I've been thinking a great deal about this business of hugging you at the end of our sessions and it's not comfortable for me. It seems to me that it's a way of discharging anxiety and it works against the therapy. Also, I don't feel I have free choice in the situation.

FACILITATOR (equally rational to protect her own vulnerable child): Well, why don't we forget about hugging and see how that works? I can certainly see your point about the discharge of anxiety and tension and it's not comfortable for me if it feels compulsive.

At this point, the facilitator noticed a change, a sense of sadness in Natalie.

FACILITATOR: Wait a minute. Let me talk to the part of you that wants me to hug her.

VULNERABLE CHILD (bursts into tears): I was afraid you wouldn't know I was here. She's so sensible – I was afraid she'd hurt your feelings and you wouldn't think of looking for me. I *want* you to hug me. I like it. I *want* you to pay attention to me. (A fresh outburst of tears.)

FACILITATOR: I'd love to pay attention to you. Tell me about yourself.

CHILD: I'm very little, about four years old, and I'm cute. But I'm scared. And I'm hiding. I'm hiding in the closet. And I'm hoping that someone will come looking for me (more sobbing) nobody comes, nobody ever comes. I really want someone to come and look for *me* and pay attention to *me*. She's acted grown up and sensible ever since she was little and nobody has ever thought to look for me. Nobody ever misses me. I need people to notice I'm gone, and to care.

This dialogue is a most touching portrait of the vulnerable child. It wants to be missed, sought after, and valued although the protector/controller and other rational subpersonalities do not want it to exist at all.

   Men have even greater difficulty than women in agreeing to contact their vulnerable children because it is socially unacceptable for men to be vulnerable. Their children, too, are often in hiding. They have been found hidden in closets, under the kitchen sink, in a cave, up in a tree house, in the woods, in a barn, or in an attic.

Sometimes the facilitator can make an initial contact by asking for the part that runs away from people or stays hidden.

FACILITATOR: I know that Mike is very efficient and successful, but I'd like to talk to the part of him that's a little more sensitive and needs to keep away from people; maybe it even needs to hide.

CHILD: I certainly do need to hide. When he was little, I used to go out into the woods when someone hurt my feelings. I'd wait and wait for someone to come looking for me. I was really scared that if they found Mike, they'd hurt my feelings again, but I really wanted them to notice that he was gone and to come looking. And do you know what? They never did. And then I'd really feel bad.

Once Mike knows how his feelings have been hurt, he can speak to his wife about this issue. If he doesn't know, he withdraws into a cold parental subpersonality, and his wife's vulnerable child is hurt by his withdrawal so she becomes even more rejecting to protect herself.

The vulnerable child helps to remove ourselves from painful situations if they cannot be changed. The vulnerable child will also pull us out of an unrewarding relationship or a thankless job, once we listen to it. For instance, Frank was in a relationship with a younger woman who was fond of him but clearly let him know that she didn't love him enough to see their relationship move toward marriage as he hoped it would. Frank had disowned his vulnerable child so completely that at first we could only talk to it through the protector/controller. However, the protector/controller finally agreed to let us consult directly with the child.

FACILITATOR: Would you please tell us how you feel about Frank's relationship with Claire?

CHILD: I don't like it at all. I get hurt all the time. He keeps thinking that she's going to learn to love him but I know she's not. She's just sticking around for what she can get. He's nice and he does things for her so she stays around. I know that she doesn't love him and it makes me feel bad. But he doesn't care how I feel.

FACILITATOR: If you were running Frank's life, what would you do?

CHILD: I'd get away from her. It makes me feel too lonely when he's with her. It's much worse than being alone.

As we have said before, the vulnerable child often sees emotional matters clearly and can give good advice. Frank had to decide what to do with this information. He also consulted other subpersonalities, but in the end he followed his vulnerable child's advice – he confronted the situation and, with tact and diplomacy, ended the relationship.

In contrast with its ability to end an unrewarding relationship, the integration of the vulnerable child into a relationship encourages unparalleled intimacy and depth, as we will see in Suzanne's experience.

Suzanne had been raised by a very cold and rejecting mother. Her vulnerable child was disowned quite early in life and replaced with charm, sophistication, and a whimsical, delightful wit. Suzanne was irresistible to men but very lonely. She was shocked to realize she had vulnerable feelings and her child felt worthless.

CHILD: But what good can I do her? I just get hurt and frightened.

FACILITATOR: I know it feels awfully good to be with you and you have lots to tell both Suzanne and myself. You're delicious.

CHILD: I don't know about that (but she smiles because the energetic contact is good).

FACILITATOR: Tell me, why did you have to hide?

CHILD: Her mother (she starts to cry) – her mother is very mean and she made me cry all the time. She always told Suzanne that she was ugly and stupid and that she didn't want Suzanne in the first place. Do you know that she still tells Suzanne that she never wanted her? (She cries for a while as the impact of this revelation is absorbed.)

FACILITATOR: Well, I can certainly see why you wanted to hide. Tell me more about yourself.

CHILD: I'm really sensitive and lots of things hurt my feelings. Suzanne keeps getting into these relationships where another part of her laughs and I feel bad. Like with Eric. He has lots of girlfriends and he likes them all to think he's terrific but he never really loves them. He just collects them. It hurts my feelings but she just gets sophisticated and laughs.

FACILITATOR: That sounds as though it must be difficult for you. Tell me, how do you like being here now?

CHILD (shyly): I really like it. I trust it and it feels good.

Suzanne embraced her vulnerable child quickly. She enjoyed the special opening of her heart energy that it brought and she wanted to seek it elsewhere. She had a great deal of strength, above-average looks, and the intelligence and social skills to protect her vulnerable child. She used everything she had quite consciously. She calmly and objectively confronted Eric with her child's observations and ended her romantic involvement with him, but not her friendship.

Her next relationship, begun shortly after her introduction to this vulnerable child, was like none she had ever before experienced. She found herself communicating her feelings and reactions immediately and actually discussed her past and her mother with her new partner. She verbalized each 'little' hurt and fear as it arose, and the man did likewise. For each, it was a depth of sharing never before experienced. It took real courage. but Suzanne was a determined woman who learned quickly and her bravery inspired equal intimacy in her partner. As each risk was rewarded with deeper mutual understanding and love, they became less fearful and more daring in this mutual exploration of their complex humanity. Although this was not always easy or pleasant, it was deeply satisfying to each of them. With the information provided by their vulnerable children, they were able to deal practically with pain in the relationship and protect the delicious energetic interchange – that warm pulsating energy that vibrates between people when they are truly open and trusting.

A warning – this is not to say that all is forever perfect. Circumstances beyond the control of the aware ego sometimes cause the vulnerable child to withdraw from a relationship. But once this warmth has been experienced it is something to strive for and return to, and most of us are willing to experience much discomfort in order to do so.

We would like to give you one final example of an excerpt from a Voice Dialogue session with the vulnerable child. In this instance, the facilitator asked questions that would allow the subject's awareness level to witness the requirements of the vulnerable child.

FACILITATOR: We've been talking so far about how lonely things are for you and how much you feel left out in Peter's life. Is there anything that Peter could do that might be helpful to you?

CHILD: I don't know what he could do. He always runs away from me.

FACILITATOR: Well, I know that – but Peter is listening to our conversation and he might learn a thing or two about you. I can't guarantee it, but Peter could learn how to be a proper parent to you. I know that he's never done it before, but it could happen.

CHILD: I'd like that. I'd feel better if he'd take care of me. It's especially when I get scared that I need him, and I get scared a lot.

I wish he would just learn to be with me and not run away all the time. If he would just talk to me I'd feel so much better.

FACILITATOR: So one of the things he could do for you is just learn to be with you.

CHILD: And maybe he could save more money. I get scared when there's no money. He likes to do things with money that are scary to me. I hate the stock market. I hate the feeling that he could lose it all. He likes to gamble.

FACILITATOR: So now we have another thing that would make you feel better. You need the feeling of financial security. Is there anything else?

CHILD: He could let me out more. Nobody knows about me. Everyone thinks Peter is strong and tough. That's what everyone sees. No one ever sees me. That makes me feel lonely. Even Margaret (his wife) doesn't know about me. He never tells her about my feelings.

As a child grows up, it is common for parents to reject its vulnerability because life demands strength. Additionally, parents usually have no conscious relationship to their own vulnerability. So it is that we, as adults, reject our own inner child, further perpetuating this ancestral disowning process. Through dialogue work, we can hear the child's voice and gradually take over the responsibility of child-rearing from the protector/controller.

We have seen individuals do very interesting things as they begin tuning in to the needs of their inner child. Cynthia built a large doll house and furnished it, and then made it clear to her children that it was *her* doll house. John constructed an imaginary home for the child where he would visit him regularly. Ann took her special pillow to sleep on when she went on business trips. Sam started reading spy novels rather than purely redemptive literature. Lianne got a job to help her child feel more secure about money. A multitude of different activities can support the needs of the child.

Once the reality of the child has been established, journal writing becomes an excellent tool for working with it. Prior to making this connection, the question will be: Who is doing the writing? If an aware ego has not separated from the protector/controller, then the protector/controller itself may be doing the writing.

Dialoguing with the inner child is very satisfying and very revealing. One excellent approach to this kind of writing is to use the nondominant hand for the child and the dominant hand for the primary self. This same principle can apply to any primary/disowned self system while doing dialogue work in a journal format.[1] For an aware ego to properly take care of the child, it must have the power energy available to it. Without the protection of the heavyweights, the child will not be safe, and generally it knows this. What we aim at here is an aware ego related to the energies of the heavyweights on the other side, and the vulnerability, playfulness, and magic on the other. This is true empowerment. Learning to be powerful and knowing how to consciously use our heavyweights is generally an important step in attaining this empowerment.

THE VULNERABLE CHILD AND INTIMACY

The entire development of personality or primary selves is aimed at protecting one's vulnerability. When we fall in love, the actual act of falling in love allows the vulnerable child, the carrier of this vulnerability, to surface and to make an intense contact with another human being without the usual protection of these primary selves. This ability to be vulnerable with one another, to allow the emergence of every feeling, thought and reaction and to cherish all of them, makes the process of falling in love a wonderful experience. *It is one's vulnerability which makes intimacy in relationship possible and, conversely, it is this same vulnerability and apparent lack of power which the protective primary selves most fear in relationship.*

Just as it is the inclusion of vulnerability in relationship that allows intimacy, so it is the disowning of this vulnerability that later destroys intimacy. When we disown our vulnerable child, we do not attend to it properly. Since it is imperative for this child to receive adequate care, it will look elsewhere and bond in to the people around us requiring them to provide the care that is otherwise lacking. We will not be aware of this process because we do not know about our vulnerability. So, in an entirely unconscious fashion, we are automatically drawn into powerful parent/child bondings over and over again.

Caring for this inner child through an aware ego gives a feeling of real strength. It represents real empowerment. When the aware ego is caring for the vulnerable child, there is no longer the need to rely solely upon the automatic protective devices provided by the primary selves even though this has given a sense of security in the past. Nor is there the need to rely upon others to assume responsibility for this child. *It is important to know that each one of us is ultimately responsible for parenting the vulnerable child within. When we are caring adequately for our own vulnerability, we are in a position to relate deeply and effectively to others.* When we do not care adequately for our own vulnerable child, it will seek this care elsewhere and bond in deeply and unconsciously to the parental side of others. This idea that we need to love our own child first before we can relate to others in a conscious fashion is similar to the old adage that we must love ourselves before we will be able to love another.

How can we take care of our inner children? The most important step in caring for the inner child is to recognize its presence and to develop an awareness of its particular personality, its needs and its reactions. Once we know about the child and its needs and feelings, we are in a position to do something about them. We must learn to separate far enough from our vulnerable selves to realistically evaluate situations in which they have been activated and then to speak up for them in an objective fashion rather than to put them in a position of taking care of themselves. This ability to be objective, or to use impersonal energies, in considering and then in putting forth

the requirements and reactions of the vulnerable child is a true position of empowerment. It is the most powerful way in which to move
into a truly intimate connection with another person and to avoid
the pitfalls of bonding patterns – or to gently extricate ourselves
once these bondings have been constellated.

The discovery of the inner child is really the discovery of a portal
to the soul. A spirituality that is not grounded in understanding,
experience, and an appreciation of the inner child can move people
away from their simple humanity too easily. The inner child keeps
us human. It never grows up, it only becomes more sensitive and
trusting as we learn how to give it the time, care, and parenting it so
richly deserves.

WHY ARE YOU SO
ANGRY WITH ME?

Alexander Lowen

*This chapter is a personal account of Alexander Lowen's experience in
therapy with Wilhelm Reich, the originator of psychotherapeutic work
with the body. The powerful inner child experience that Lowen recounts
here clearly has had a profound effect on his own creative development as
an innovative therapist and teacher. This piece is an excerpt from the
author's book* Bioenergetics, *which describes the methodology of the
same name that he devised, based on Reich's groundbreaking work, in
collaboration with John Pierrakos.*

I began my personal therapy with Reich in the spring of 1942.
During the preceding year I had been a fairly frequent visitor at
Reich's laboratory. He showed me some of the work he had been
doing with bio preparations and cancerous tissue. Then, one day, he
said to me, 'Lowen, if you are interested in this work, there is only
one way to get into it, and that is by going into therapy.' His statement startled me, for I had not contemplated this move. I told him, 'I
am interested, but what I want is to become famous.' Reich took this
remark seriously, for he replied, 'I will make you famous.' Over the
years I have regarded Reich's statement as a prophecy. It was the
push I needed to overcome my resistance and to launch me into my
lifework.

My first therapeutic session with Reich was an experience I
will never forget. I went with the naïve assumption that there was
nothing wrong with me. It was to be purely a training analysis. I lay
down on the bed wearing a pair of bathing trunks. Reich did not use

a couch since this was a body-oriented therapy. I was told to bend my knees, relax, and breathe with my mouth open and my jaw relaxed. I followed these instructions and waited to see what would happen. After some time Reich said, 'Lowen, you're not breathing.' I answered, 'Of course I'm breathing; otherwise I'd be dead.' He then remarked, 'Your chest isn't moving. Feel my chest.' I placed my hand on his chest and noticed that it was rising and falling with each breath. Mine clearly was not.

I lay back again and resumed breathing, this time with my chest moving outward on inspiration and inward on expiration. Nothing happened. My breathing proceeded easily and deeply. After a while Reich said, 'Lowen, drop your head back and open your eyes wide.' I did as I was told . . . a scream burst forth from my throat.

It was a beautiful day in early spring, and the windows of the room opened onto the street. To avoid any embarrassment with his neighbours, Reich asked me to straighten my head, which stopped the scream. I resumed my deep breathing. Strangely, the scream had not disturbed me. I was not connected to it emotionally. I did not feel any fear. After I had breathed again for a while, Reich asked me to repeat the procedure: Put my head back and open my eyes wide. Again the scream came out. I hesitate to say that I screamed because I did not seem to do it. The scream happened to me. Again I was detached from it, but I left the session with the feeling that I was not as right as I thought. There were other 'things' (images, emotions) in my personality that were hidden from consciousness, and I knew then that they would have to come out.

At that time Reich called this therapy Character Analytic Vegetotherapy. Character analysis had been his great contribution to psychoanalytic theory, one for which he was highly regarded by all analysts. Vegetotherapy referred to the mobilization of feeling through breathing and other body techniques that activated the vegetative centres (the ganglia of the autonomic nervous system) and liberated 'vegetative' energies.

For Reich, then, the first step in the therapeutic procedure was to get the patient to breath easily and deeply. The second was to mobilize whatever emotional expression was most evident in the patient's face or manner. In my case this expression was fear. We have seen what a powerful effect this procedure had on me.

Succeeding sessions followed the same general pattern. I would lie on the bed and breathe as freely as I could, trying to allow a deep expiration to occur. I was directed to give in to my body and not control any expression or impulse that emerged. A number of things happened that gradually brought me into contact with early memories and experiences. At first the deeper breathing to which I was not accustomed produced strong, tingling sensations in my hands which, on two occasions, developed into a severe carpopedal spasm, severely cramping the hands. This reaction disappeared as my body accommodated to the increased energy the deeper breathing produced. Tremors developed in my legs when I moved my knees gently together and apart, and in my lips when I followed an impulse to reach out with them.

Several breakthroughs of feelings and associated memories followed. On one occasion, as I was lying on the bed breathing, my body started to rock involuntarily. The rocking increased until I sat up. Then, without my seeming to do so, I got off the bed, turned to face it, and started to pound it with both fists. As I was doing this, my father's face appeared on the bedsheet, and I suddenly knew I was hitting him for a spanking he had given me when I was a young boy. Some years later I asked my father about this incident. He said it was the only spanking he had ever given me. He explained that I had come home very late and my mother was upset and worried. He had spanked me so that I would not do that again. The interesting part of this experience, as of the scream, was its completely spontaneous and involuntary nature. I was moved to strike the bed as I was to scream, not by any conscious thought but by a force within that had taken over and possessed me.

On another occasion, while on the bed breathing, I began to get an erection. I had an impulse to touch my penis, but I inhibited it. Then I recalled an interesting episode out of my childhood. I saw myself as a boy of five walking through the apartment where I lived, urinating on the floor. My parents were out. I knew I was doing it to get back at my father, who had scolded me the day before for holding my penis.

It took about nine months of therapy for me to find out what had caused the scream in the first session. I had not screamed since then. As time went on, I thought I had the distinct impression that there was an image I was afraid to see. Contemplating the ceiling from my position on the bed, I sensed it would appear one day. Then it did, and it was my mother's face looking down at me with an expression of intense anger in her eyes. I knew immediately that this was the face that had frightened me. I relived the experience as if it were occurring in the present. I was a baby about nine months of age, lying in a carriage outside the door of my home. I had been crying loudly for my mother. She was obviously busy in the house, and my persistent crying had upset her. She came out, furious at me. Lying there on Reich's bed at the age of thirty-three, I looked at her image and, using words I could not have known as a baby, I said, 'Why are you so angry with me? I am only crying because I want you.'

In those days Reich used another technique to implement the therapy. At the beginning of each session he asked his patients to tell him all the negative thoughts they had about him. He believed that all patients had a negative transference to him as well as a positive one, and he did not trust the positive unless negative thoughts and ideas were expressed first. I found this extremely difficult to do. Having made a commitment to Reich and the therapy, I had banished all negative thoughts from my mind. I felt that I had nothing to complain about. Reich had been very generous with me, and I had no doubt about his sincerity, his integrity, or the validity of his concepts. Characteristically, I was determined to make the therapy succeed, and it was not until it almost failed that I opened up my feelings to Reich.

Following the experience of fear when I saw my mother's face, I went through a long stretch of several months during which I made no progress. I was seeing Reich three times a week then, but I was blocked because I couldn't tell Reich my feeling about him. I wanted him to take a fatherly interest in me, not merely a therapeutic one, but knowing this was an unreasonable request, I couldn't express it. Struggling inwardly with the problem, I got nowhere. Reich seemed unaware of my conflict. As hard as I tried, I couldn't let my breathing become deeper and fuller, it just didn't work.

I had been in therapy for about a year when this impasse developed. When it seemed to go on indefinitely, Reich suggested I quit. 'Lowen,' he said, 'you are unable to give in to your feelings. Why don't you give up?' His words were a sentence of doom. To give up meant the failure of all my dreams. I broke down and cried deeply. It was the first time I had sobbed since I was a child. I could no longer hold back my feelings. I told Reich what I wanted from him, and he listened sympathetically.

I do not know if Reich had intended to end the therapy or whether his suggestion that I terminate treatment was a manoeuvre to break through my resistance, but I had the strong impression that he meant it. In either case, his action produced the desired result. I began to move again in the therapy.

For Reich the goal of therapy was the development by the patient of the capacity to give in fully to the spontaneous and involuntary movements of the body that were part of the respiratory process. Thus the emphasis was on letting the breathing take place fully and deeply. If this was done, the respiratory waves produced an undulating movement of the body that Reich called the orgasm reflex.

My therapy with Reich was resumed in the fall of 1945 with sessions once a week. Within a short time the orgasm reflex came through consistently. There were several reasons for this positive development. During the year's leave of absence from therapy, striving to please Reich and gain sexual health was in abeyance, and I was able to assimilate and integrate my previous work with Reich. At this time, too, I saw my first patient as a Reichian therapist, which gave my spirit a tremendous boost. I felt I had come home and was aware of feeling very secure about my life. Surrender to my body, which also meant a surrender to Reich, became very easy. In a few months it was obvious to both of us that my therapy had come to a successful conclusion by his criteria. Years later I realized, however, that I had not resolved many of my major personality problems. My fear of asking for what I wanted even if it was unreasonable had not been fully discussed. My fear of failure and my need to succeed had not been worked through. My inability to cry unless I was pushed to the wall had not been explored. These problems were finally resolved many years later through bioenergetics.

I do not wish to say that the therapy with Reich was ineffective. If it did not fully resolve all my problems, it made me more aware of them. More important, however, it opened a way for me to self-realization and helped me advance toward that goal. It deepened and strengthened my commitment to the body as the basis of the personality. And it gave me a positive identification with my sexuality, which was proved to be the cornerstone of my life.

15

ADVOCATING FOR THE CHILD
Alice Miller

≈

*Psychoanalyst and author Alice Miller is a staunch advocate of enlight-
ened witnesses taking action on behalf of children whom they see being
abused. Adults who have a connection to the inner child need to act, she
says, on behalf of children at risk. 'Had just one person understood what
was happening and come to my defence,' she says in the introduction to
The Drama of the Gifted Child, 'it might have changed my entire life . . .
In our society, with its hostility toward children, such people are still hard
to find, but their number is growing daily.' In addition, as a therapist, she
challenges psychotherapy to work out a new vision of its role in the light of
the new knowledge of the inner child's truth and of what we now know
about the destructive socialization of the child. This excerpt is from Dr
Miller's third book, Thou Shalt Not Be Aware.*

More than eighty years ago Freud claimed he had 'established' that
his patients' memories of being sexually molested as children by
adults were not memories of real events at all but merely fantasies.
How was he able to establish this? Only since I have become more
familiar with the circumstances surrounding sexual abuse has it
struck me that Freud's conclusion, which provides an important
premise for his drive theory and has been repeated in good faith
countless times since by students in examinations, 'establishes'
something that he can only have conjectured; for it can be established with the aid of witnesses that a certain act took place, but we
can never be certain that something did *not* take place if both parties
to the act have an interest in keeping it secret. This is usually the

case with sexual abuse, for even the victim cannot bear the truth because of the accompanying feelings of fear, shame, and guilt.

I cannot emphasize enough the importance of this point, for whether it is understood or not will determine whether the patient in society, like the child in the family, is left alone with his or her trauma or finds the necessary understanding in the therapist, i.e., understanding for the fact that reality is more tragic than all fantasies, which do indeed contain certain aspects of the trauma experienced but essentially serve to conceal the unbearable truth. A particular difficulty – indeed, an actual hindrance – on the path to remembering in therapy comes about as a result of the mechanism of warding off, once required for survival, and which can manifest itself in fantasies and imagery from fairy tales or in chronic perversions. Perversion, addiction, and self-destructive enactments – like fantasies – take on the function of concealment. They organize present suffering in exact accordance with the pattern of the past and in this way guarantee that the earlier, unbearable suffering remains repressed.

There are now, to be sure, numerous techniques that allow feelings from early childhood to come to the surface in a short period of time and that provide temporary relief. These techniques can be learned, but they cannot be called therapy if a sufficient degree of adequate support is not provided at the same time. The application of learned techniques can have such detrimental effects that the patient remains locked in a depression or in the chaos of awakened feelings. Results of this kind are not rare even if the therapist possesses technical skill and has a well-meaning and concerned attitude but shows tendencies that are both pedagogical and sparing of the parents in his or her therapeutic approach.

Thus, therapists' adequate support must be reinforced by their knowledge *and* emotional experience. I have made every effort to call attention to that aspect of knowledge having to do with the actual situation of the child in our society because I think it is a necessary (although not sufficient) condition if therapy is to be successful. When it is lacking, even the best method will be of no avail, and if the treatment fails, it is not necessarily the method that is at fault. But theoretical understanding alone is still not enough. Only therapists who have had the opportunity to experience and work through their own traumatic past will be able to accompany patients on the path to truth about themselves and not hinder them on their way. Such therapists will not confuse their patients, make them anxious, or educate, instruct, misuse, or seduce them, for they no longer have to fear the eruption in themselves of feelings that were stifled long ago, and they know from experience the healing power of these feelings.

But this expanding knowledge will scarcely emanate from authoritative institutions such as universities and institutes. Once the survivors of abuse (sexual and non-sexual) feel truly supported by society and by their therapists so that they are able to find their own voice, therapists will learn more from them than from any teacher. As a result, therapists will find it easier to relinquish many of these misguided beliefs that are based on the pedagogical principles of earlier centuries.

Only liberation from pedagogical tendencies will bring about crucial insights into the child's actual situation. These insights can be summarized in the following points:

1. The child is always innocent.

2. Each child needs among other things: care, protection, security, warmth, skin contact, touching, caressing, and tenderness.

3. These needs are seldom sufficiently fulfilled; in fact, they are often exploited by adults for their own ends (trauma of child abuse).

4. Child abuse has lifelong effects.

5. Society takes the side of the adult and blames the child for what has been done to him or her.

6. The victimization of the child has historically been denied and is still being denied, even today.

7. This denial has made it possible for society to ignore the devastating effects of the victimization of the child for such a long time.

8. The child, when betrayed by society, has no choice but to repress the trauma and to idealize the abuser.

9. Repression leads to neuroses, psychoses, psychosomatic disorders, and delinquency.

10. In neuroses, the child's needs are repressed and/or denied; instead, feelings of guilt are experienced.

11. In psychoses, the mistreatment is transformed into a disguised illusory version (madness).

12. In psychosomatic disorders, the pain of mistreatment is felt but the actual origins are concealed.

13. In delinquency, the confusion, seduction, and mistreatment of childhood are acted out again and again.

14. The therapeutic process can be successful only if it is based on uncovering the truth about the patient's childhood instead of denying that reality.

15. The psychoanalytic theory of 'infantile sexuality' actually protects the parent and reinforces society's blindness.

16. Fantasies always serve to conceal or minimize unbearable childhood reality for the sake of the child's survival; therefore, the so-called invented trauma is a less harmful version of the real, repressed one.

17. The fantasies expressed in literature, art, fairy tales, and dreams often unconsciously convey early childhood experiences in a symbolic way.

18. This symbolic testimony is tolerated in our culture thanks to society's chronic ignorance of the truth concerning childhood;

if the import of these fantasies were understood, they would be rejected.

19. A past crime cannot be undone by our understanding of the perpetrator's blindness and unfulfilled needs.

20. New crimes, however, can be prevented, if the victims begin to see and be aware of what has been done to them.

21. Therefore, the reports of victims will be able to bring about more awareness, consciousness, and sense of responsibility in society at large.

Thanks to these honest reports of childhood experiences, other men and women will be encouraged to confront their own childhood, take it seriously, and talk about it. In so doing, they in turn will provide information to others about what so many human beings have had to undergo at the beginning of life without even knowing about it in later years and without anyone else knowing about it either. Earlier, it simply was not possible to be aware of these matters and there were virtually no published reports by the victims that did not idealize the perpetrators. But now such reports are available and will continue to appear, presumably in growing numbers. I do not believe this process can be reversed.

I have not founded a psychoanalytic school or an institute nor have I established any groups, and I am not in a position to provide names and addresses of therapists. My intention has been to describe the unstated commandment that forbids us to see the true situation of children in our society. Once their plight has become visible, it will be easier to offer therapeutic help through existing channels, and the danger that therapeutic practices will be used to subjugate people (in sects, for instance) will be reduced. Research in the field will also be of more use to therapists than before, once researches have accepted the truth, which is no less true because it is painful and which for that reason has healing and transforming powers.

The truth about our childhood is stored up in our body, and although we can repress it, we can never alter it. Our intellect can be deceived, our feelings manipulated, our perceptions confused, and our body tricked with medication. But someday the body will present its bill, for it is as incorruptible as a child who, still whole in spirit, will accept no compromises or excuses, and it will not stop tormenting us until we stop evading the truth.

16

ON INCEST AND CHILD ABUSE
Robert M. Stein

≈

This short essay revolves around Jungian anaylst Robert M. Stein's belief that 'The way I treat my inner child is the way I am going to treat my outer child.' The near epidemic of child abuse in our culture today reveals a terrible disconnection from the inner child, individually and collectively. Stein's rigorous yet sensitive approach to the subject makes him a leader in understanding the phenomenon of abuse and what we can do to change it. He challenges Alice Miller's view of the 'always innocent' child, suggesting that such a literal idealization of the outer child misses the truth and can be a dangerous way to fall into an unconscious collusion with the anger of the wounded inner child. The debate developing between these two outspoken contributors is a provocative one.

This paper was originally published in the journal Voices *in 1986, then revised for the journal* Spring *the following year.*

Actual child abuse always reflects a lack of connection to and respect for the internal or psychic child. As an archetype, the image of the child is associated with a newly developing aspect of the psyche which is still very much contained in nature. As Kerenyi puts it, being at home in the primeval world is an essential quality of the child archetype.[1] The attitude toward the child which we seem to have inherited from Victorian times, if not much earlier, is that the psyche of a newborn infant is a *tabula rasa* (clean slate), and that the child's development depends entirely on how we educate and shape it. Treating the child as an object to be moulded instead of relating to it as an intelligent soul capable of intentionality and choice is the main psychological root of child abuse. Studies of abusive parents show that the majority claim to have been abused themselves as children. Abuse has been perpetuated internally by a loveless, critical superego that has no understanding or respect for the inner child.

Depth psychology assumes that the external and internal worlds reflect each other. If the prevailing epidemic of incest and child abuse reflects our collective attitude toward the child within, then we need to ask what lies within the compulsive need to abuse and sexually molest the outer child.

The way I treat my inner child is the way I am going to treat my outer child. Why would I want to abuse my inner child? How do I abuse it? If my child is getting out of hand, I want to stop it and that may result in abuse. For example, my child enjoys just playing and being, it doesn't much like schedules and the pressure which I put on it to work, to write this paper, to do anything that isn't fun. I abuse my child primarily by rarely letting it have its way and by putting it down for being so lazy and unproductive. And when it becomes withdrawn and depressed, I do everything possible at first to get it moving, to get it busy doing something worthwhile. The more ego-directed and collective are our attitudes and goals, the more trouble we are likely to have with the inner child, because the archetypal child contains knowledge about its own developmental needs which is often in opposition to our ego orientation. And, those of us who are not clever enough to manipulate and control the child verbally often resort to abusive physical measures to keep it in its place.

Paradoxically, an adult's compulsive need for sexual intimacy may initially have arisen out of deep feelings of compassion for the neglected, abused child. What I am suggesting is that the other side of this hate for the troublesome child is a deep love and compassion for this vulnerable, neglected, abandoned and abused aspect of the soul. The soul's need for union is often expressed in images of sexual intimacy. When an adult suffers from a deep spirit/flesh, mind/body, love/sex split, he or she will often fall under the compulsive power of the sexual drive to literalize those images. Healing does not lie in attempting to overcome these 'perverse' desires, but in being able to experience fully the incestuous desires emotionally and imaginally. In this way the sexual drive is gradually transformed, and the child (inner and outer) can be loved, honoured, and respected as a unique being.

The image of the child as innocent, helpless, unprotected and lacking a sexual drive seems to be more rooted in the archetype of the innocent divine maiden (Kore) than in the empirical realities of childhood. Persephone, the innocent maiden Goddess who is raped and carried off to the underworld by Hades, represents a charming, seductive soul-quality which certainly belongs to the child. This innocent, vulnerable, virginal quality of the soul which is so easily violated – and even invites violation from the dark underworld forces – belongs to the soul's need to be penetrated and deepened. This psychological penetration from below, often experienced as rape, needs to be recognized as a psychological process essential to soul-making or the process will tend to be lived in a literal way, i.e., through identification with the innocent victim or through attachment to others upon whom the archetype is projected. Perhaps the current epidemic of child abuse and sexual molestation is also in part owing to the fact that the Kore archetype has been projected on our children, who then tend to live out this projection for us.

I believe Alice Miller, in her book *Prisoners of Childhood*,[2] describes the child identified with the Kore projection and who is, as a consequence, repeatedly violated because it has no access to the ground of its instinctual being. No healthy young animal would allow itself to be close to anyone it sensed as abusive; nor would it tolerate for an instant anyone taking advantage of its trust and vulnerability. Why should a healthy child be any less capable of protecting itself? My three-year-old granddaughter, who is as vulnerable and seductive as a playful kitten, is also as determined, independent and powerful as a tiger when she wants her way. Miller's image of the child as 'always innocent' and her rejection of Freud's theories of infantile sexuality as a projection of the Victorian patriarchal attitude toward children[3] seem to me rather a regression to the pre-Freudian,

Victorian idealized projection on the child.

Freud destroyed the Victorian image of the child as innocent, pure, helpless and asexual in his seminal work *Three Contributions to the Theory of Sex*.[4] In making us aware of the crucial importance to psychological development of the sexual drive in infancy and childhood, Freud paradoxically established that the sexual instinct and probably other basic human instincts contain an intelligence and intentionality that go beyond the mere physical survival of the species. Thus, when a child is blocked or cut off from its sexual instincts as a consequence of an Oedipal complex, or what I have termed the incest wound, it loses touch with an instinctual power and intelligence that could protect it from abuse and manipulation.

Freud dropped his trauma theory, not because he believed that these childhood memories were of seductions that had not occurred, but because he realized that whether or not these sexual memories were literally true was less important psychologically than the psychic reality of the images. In my book *Incest and Human Love*,[5] I argue that psychologically the incest taboo functions to stimulate the sexual imagination and the formation of the image of marriage as a Sacred Union, the *hieros gamos*; to humanize and transform sexuality; to make us aware of our incompletion and to stimulate our desire to attain completion, first through union with another, but ultimately through an internal union. I also argued that *contained within the polarity of the incest archetype is both the desire and the inhibition, and that the tension between these opposites is essential to psychological development.* I proposed that the repression of either the desire or the inhibition causes a split in the child's psyche between love/sex, mind/body, spirit/flesh, and I used the term *incest wound* to describe these developmental splits. The depth of the incest wound is determined by the severity of the psychic split between love and sex, mind and body, desire and inhibition. In my view, the wounds to the soul from the repression of sexuality can be as damaging as actual sexual contact between parent and child. The current myopic focus on the literal violation of the incest taboo is unfortunate because it has diverted attention away from the deeper and more relevant psychological issues. Alice Miller's anti-psychological literalism suggests that she has fallen into an identification with her own angry, neglected, deprived inner child. Unfortunately, *nothing is more damaging to the child and its rich imaginal life than literalism.*

Is there perhaps a connection between the exploitation and abuse of children in Victorian times and the onset of the industrial age? And is there perhaps a similar connection between the onset of our modern computer age and the epidemic of child abuse? Are we, like our Victorian ancestors perhaps inflated with our new-found power to understand and manipulate the natural forces of the universe? Are we perhaps identified with what Jung would call the all-knowing Old Wise Man or senex archetype?

Identification with an archetype always leads to inflation, one-sidedness and literalism. Cut off from the renewing vitality of the child archetype, the senex becomes progressively narrow, arid and rigid. The greater the internal split between senex and child archetypes, the more desperate is the need of the senex to unite with those qualities of innocent wonder, openness, vulnerability and virginal freshness which the child carries. But the child also needs the stabilizing strength, ancient spiritual wisdom, limits and depths of the senex. Thus, Senex and Child are a polarity that functions creatively for psychological development only when forming a complementary whole rather than an oppositional split. This sort of split is probably a major factor responsible for the compulsive need of so many adults for sexual intimacy with children. As for the child who may be living out this projection of the innocent, virginal Kore archetype, not only has it been deprived of its instinctual power to protect itself from such abuse, but also it is in the grips of an archetypal power needing to unite with its other half.

The current hysteria about incest and sexual molestation intensifies the fear of sensuality and sexuality between parent and child instead of inspiring us to find a new, creative relationship to the incest mystery. I have suggested that the primary function of the incest prohibition is to stimulate the sexual imagination and to bring instincts into the service of love, kinship and creativity. This means that essential to the psychological health and maturation of the child is that it experiences an erotic flow and connection to parents and siblings without fear, guilt or violation.

Let me end these reflections with a few quotes from a superb original paper, 'Oedipal Love in the Countertransference,' by Harold Searles. He proposed that the mutual experience of romantic and erotic feelings between analyst and analysand is an essential aspect of the resolution of the Oedipus complex in analysis:[6]

> *I have found, time after time, that in the course of the work with every one of my patients who has progressed to, or very far toward, a thorough-going analytic cure, I have experienced romantic and erotic desires to marry, and fantasies of being married to the patient.*[7]

He indicates that he has experienced the same phenomenon occurring with both sexes.[8] Searles offers further evidence to support his concepts through his experience as a husband and parent:

> *Toward my daughter, now eight years of age, I have experienced innumerable fantasies and feelings of romantic-love kind, thoroughly complementary to the romantically adoring, seductive behaviour she has shown toward her father often times ever since she was about two or three years of age. I used at times to feel somewhat worried when she would play the supremely confident coquette with me, and I would feel enthralled by her charms; but then I came to the conviction, some time ago, that such moments of relatedness could only be nourishing for her developing personality as well as delightful to me. If a little girl cannot feel herself able to win the heart of her father, who has known her so well and for so long, and who is tied to her by mutual blood ties, I reasoned, then how can the young woman who comes later have deep confidence in the power of her womanliness.*[9]

Part Five

RECOVERING THE CHILD

INTRODUCTION

≈

Return to the beginning;
Become a child again.

— TAO TE CHING

People get absolutely intolerable when they have a creative
idea in their womb and can't bring it out. So one has to help
them bring the child out.

— MARIE-LOUISE VON FRANZ

The essays in this section need little general introduction, for the
theme they have in common is self-evident: They have been selected
for their practical and direct approach to the task of realizing the
inner child, and each discusses how to recover the child's special
gifts and embrace its vitality.

Lucia Capacchione has created a series of exercises to help you
understand and love your child within, based on her discovery of the
linkage between self-expression with the non-dominant hand and
the inner child. Here we have included material for getting to know
your inner child, for healing your vulnerable child, and for meeting
your playful child.

In 'Liberating Your Lost Inner Child,' popular therapist and
teacher John Bradshaw describes a process he calls 'shame reduction' for reclaiming the inner child and the authentic Self.

Jean Houston's article 'Recalling the Child' asks you to befriend
the child you once were and connect this child to your Higher Self, to

evoke what she calls your 'extended sense of being,' to know the living presence of the child within.

The interview excerpt 'Killing the Dragon' comes from the late, great visionary mythologist Joseph Campbell, and speaks to getting in touch with the child that lies within us.

THE POWER OF YOUR OTHER HAND

Lucia Capacchione

Consultant and workshop leader Lucia Capacchione has a great enthusi-asm for the life of the inner child. Her work reads like a coursebook for 'Inner Child 101.' Through her own healing process, she has discovered a way to unlock the child inside. She also generously acknowledges the work of several other of our contributors and describes how to integrate some of their practical techniques, along with her own, into a full-out crash programme for the recovery of the inner child. This selection is excerpted from Capacchione's book of the same title.

Child abuse is a downward spiral, a tragic affliction handed down from one generation to the next. It has always existed, but we've heard more about it in recent years through media coverage. It may have gotten worse or it may simply be that we are willing to bring it out in the open now. And we are shocked at what we find: psycho-logical torment, physical and sexual abuse in families and in schools, child pornography, and kidnapping. More and more chil-dren are escaping into gangs, drugs, and sometimes even suicide.

Since the beginning of modern psychotherapy, the issue of child-hood trauma has been a central factor in many methods of treat-ment. More recently, in the writings of psychoanalyst Alice Miller, we learn how society breeds psychopathology and violence in the home, school, and other institutions. In childhood, most of us were abused to one degree or another. Those of us who have worked as therapists with adults, adolescents, or children will attest to the grim fact that many people prefer to deny the deplorable treatment they received in their early years – the neglect, coercion, or outright violation – in favour of a fantasy memory of 'happy childhood.' As long as the denial continues, there is no way to 'work through' the abuse, so it is passed down to the next generation.

Denial has been a key issue in the families of alcoholics/addicts/obsessive-compulsives. The denial of family problems was so great that, in the case of adult children of alcoholics, it isn't until many years after leaving home that the truth is allowed to surface, sometimes overwhelming the individual with pain, grief, and rage. The problem in the U.S. has reached staggering proportions. In his book, *Healing the Child Within: Discovery and Recovery for Adult Children of Dysfunctional Families*, Charles Whitfield, M.D., writes that new self-help groups for adult children of alcoholics were forming in the late '80s at the rate of one per day. These are non-professional, no-fee organizations patterned after the highly successful twelve-step programme of Alcoholics Anonymous and Alanon. As a participant in these programmes, I can personally attest to their effectiveness. They have given hope to the hopeless and strength to the helpless.

In the fields of psychotherapy, social work, and education, more and more professionals are addressing the problem of child abuse. And in counselling work with adults, the theme of healing the Inner Child is being presented in books, workshops, seminars, and professional training programmes. If Whitfield is correct in his estimation that 80 to 95% of the population did not receive adequate parenting, then healing the Inner Child becomes a task for most of us.

Starting in the '60s and '70s, Hugh Missildine (*Your Child of the Past*) and Eric Berne (*Transactional Analysis*) introduced the concept of the Inner Child. In the '80s, Miller, Whitfield, and Stone and Winkelman have continued with books and therapeutic techniques for finding and healing the Child Within. These experts are all in agreement that there is still a Child living in all of us, a Child who continues to need parenting. But we must become our own parents. We must provide the understanding, compassion and guidance of a parent for our own Inner Child.

The Inner Child consists of all our childlike feelings, instincts, intuitions, spontaneity, and vitality. It is naturally open and trusting unless it learns to shut down for self-protection. It is emotional and expressive until condemned for being what it is – a child. It is playful until it is crushed for being childish. This Inner Child is creative until ridiculed for its expression. It is magical until it is punished for using its imagination. We can bury it, distort it, handicap it, make it sick, but we can't get rid of it.

By the time most of us reach adulthood, our natural, healthy child-like traits are so wounded they are nearly dead. Or they are distorted beyond recognition. Alcoholism, drug addiction, sexual obsession, eating disorders, compulsive spending, and gambling are some of the misguided attempts to return to childhood. The behaviour that results is inappropriate childishness rather than true child-likeness.

Hal Stone and Sidra Winkelman write poignantly about

> the loss of the Inner Child . . . one of the most profound tragedies of the 'growing-up' process. We lose so much of the magic and mystery of living. We lose so much of the delight and intimacy of relationship. So much of the destructiveness that we bring to each other as human beings is a function of our lack of connection to our sensitivities, our fears, our own magic . . . perhaps the most univer-sally disowned self in our civilized world is the Vulnerable Child. Yet this Vulnerable Child may be our most precious sub-personality – the closest to our essence – the one that enables us to become truly intimate, to fully experience others, and to love.

But there is hope. The Child doesn't die. It's still in there and it can be contacted and revived. As Charles Whitfield puts it:

> Our Child Within flows naturally from the time we are born to the time we die and during all our times and transitions in between. We don't have to do anything . . . it just is. If we simply let it be, it will express itself with no particular effort on our part. Indeed, any effort is usually in denying our awareness and expression of it.

And where does this Child live? In our feelings, hunches, likes and dislikes, our wishes and dreams, our fantasies and wildest imaginings. The exercises in this chapter are designed to help you find, understand, and love that Child Within: the Vulnerable Child, the Playful Child, the Magical Child, and all the other subtle nuances of feeling which this part of you contains. You will learn techniques for recovery from the abuses of childhood.

First, you'll have an opportunity to spend some time getting acquainted with your Inner Child. You will discover who that aspect of yourself really is, what it likes and doesn't like, how it feels, and what it needs. You will also have a chance to accept and nurture your Inner Child in a mutually beneficial way. You may even come home to the joy of the Inner Child.

Getting to Know Your Inner Child

1. Picture a place you feel would be comfortable for your Inner Child, such as:

    near a lake, river or ocean
    in a meadow
    in a garden
    in a beautiful room.

2. Now invite your Inner Child to come into the picture. See this child in your mind's eye and ask yourself, Is it a boy or girl? How old? What does the child look like?

3. Now, start writing out a dialogue. Writing with your dominant hand, greet the child, introduce yourself and ask his or her name. Let your Inner Child respond by writing with the *other hand.*

4. Tell the child you want to get to know his or her feelings, needs, likes and dislikes. Then continue the conversation. The Nurturing Parent writes with the dominant hand, the Inner Child with the non-dominant hand.

5. Complete your conversation by asking the Inner Child for one special thing it wants from you. Work out something that is

mutually agreeable, that satisfies the Child's needs as well as those of the Nurturing Parent, who is responsible for following through. Make sure you are willing to keep the agreement made to the Child. If not, don't make any promises, otherwise you will disappoint the Child and cause further hurt.

6. Thank the Child for coming out. If you are willing to meet again, agree on a place and time.

The next exercise will enable you to meet your Vulnerable Child. Since the Vulnerable Child does not fit with the 'adult' image, this might be the disowned part of you. It is probably buried pretty deep. But as we have seen, letting it write with your dominant hand will give it a chance to come out more easily. It may take a little more time, but it will be well worth it, as you will discover for yourself. The energy and vitality that results from these dialogues is quite remarkable.

Healing Your Vulnerable Child
1. Visualize a very safe place, an environment that is sheltered and soothing, such as a cosy little room with soft furniture, or some other space that feels warm and inviting.

2. Picture your Vulnerable Child in detail: age, gender, appearance, place in the room or environment you've created.

3. Greet and invite the Child to be with you. Write out your conversation, using both hands. The Nurturing Self writes with your dominant hand, the Vulnerable Child with the non-dominant.

4. Ask your Vulnerable Child the following questions:
   Who are you?
   How do you feel?
   Why do you feel this way?
   What can I do to help you?

5. Tell your Vulnerable Child exactly what you will do to follow through, and meet its needs. If you can't, don't make any

promises. This will betray your Child's trust and only make matters worse.

6. If you want to visit with your Vulnerable Child again, agree on a place and time. Then thank your Child for coming out and say good-bye for now.

Notice in your everyday life when your Vulnerable Child is present. This usually happens when you experience fatigue, sickness, fear, sadness, shyness, disappointment. Observe what you do with these feelings. Do you allow yourself to truly feel them? Do you block them out with food, drugs, alcohol, extra work, oversocializing, TV?

Just as it is possible to establish a rapport with the Vulnerable Child who lives in us today, it is also possible to heal the Child of the Past. One of my students who healed his Vulnerable Child of the Past is Tom, a distinguished-looking, middle-aged medical doctor and counsellor. He attended my weekly journal-keeping class for himself, but also to learn methods to use with his patients, especially those who were hospitalized.

When Tom came to my class he thought he was right-handed. As it turned out, he was actually a switch-over (a natural lefty forced into right-handedness). There is no question in my mind that such coercion to conform to the 'majority hand' does deep psychological damage to the individual's Vulnerable Child. But the wound can be healed in adulthood, as we will see in Tom's case.

When Tom was given permission to write with his left hand, he re-experienced a situation with an early teacher. While writing, he actually relived some painful events and later told a grim story. In his early childhood, a teacher had forced little Tom (through physical abuse and threats) into right-handedness. He had attempted to fight back, but the teacher won out. He saw the teacher as a witch and was able to feel the rage and frustration he had been forced to repress as a child in the adult's world. Later, he was able to forgive her by changing her from a witch into a woman (a human being who was doing the best she could). By doing this, Tom healed the childhood

Dear Vulnerable Child, I'm so glad I found you again.
Is there anything you'd like to say to me today?

YES. I WANT YOU TO STAY WITH ME.
AND TAKE ME WITH YOU WHEREVER
YOU GO. PLEASE LISTEN TO MY
FEELINGS AND TAKE CARE OF
ME. DON'T LET THOSE OTHER
ONES DROWN ME OUT OR
BE MEAN TO ME. DON'T LET
THEM TALK YOU INTO TRYING
TO LEAVE ME OUT 'CAUSE
YOU CAN'T LEAVE ME OUT.
I'M YOUR VERY OWN
CHILD AND I LIVE INSIDE
YOU. AND I'LL NEVER
GROW UP AND GO
AWAY. I'LL ALWAYS BE HERE,

trauma of being forced to switch from his natural hand.

A few weeks after Tom started to write with his left hand, class members remarked that he smiled more and seemed far more relaxed. Several years later, this is how he described his left handwriting:

> *My left handwriting is more graceful and is actually more legible than writing done with my right hand. If I have time, I write any personal expression with my left hand. My right-hand writing is unpleasing to me now.*

Tom's story had a happy ending: healing his Vulnerable Inner Child. Forced to renounce his left-handedness by a grown-up who was stronger and held authority, Little Tom was denied his natural style of expression. Big Tom finally rescued Little Tom by putting a pen in his natural hand and allowing him to speak.

The next exercise will enable you to revisit and heal a situation that may have overwhelmed you when you were a child. You will be collapsing time, so to speak, and bringing the past into the present moment. You will deal with a concrete situation, with specific feelings and reactions that were buried at the time. You will become your own counsellor. This exercise can empower you to take responsibility for yourself instead of blaming your parents or others from your childhood. If there are still feelings alive in you from past situations, then the Inner Child is still alive. And *you*, the adult, are now its parent. It's up to you to give the Child that kindness and understanding it needs, instead of demanding that others do it for you.

Healing Your Child of the Past

1. Go back to a time in your childhood when you were frightened, sad, lonely, or felt some very strong emotion that you couldn't express at the time.

2. Imagine that the adult of the present visits this Child of the past and sits down to talk with it. Be the Child's counsellor.

3. Have a conversation with the Inner Child of the past. As a counsellor, let the Child tell you about itself, what happened, and what

it needs. Let the counsellor write with your dominant hand; invite the Inner Child of the Past to write with your *other hand*. Ask the Inner Child the following questions:

> What's your name or nickname?
> How old are you?
> Tell me about yourself. What happened to you?
> How do you feel?
> Why do you feel that way?
> What do you need now? How can I help you?

Observe your feelings in everyday life. Watch to see if this Child of the past comes out.

The next exercise is intended to help you meet your Playful Child. This is the part of you that is genuinely fun-loving, spontaneous, and exuberant. It can be silly, have a sense of humour, and experience joy in being alive. The Playful Child is very present in the body and *in the moment*. It enjoys pleasurable sensations: beautiful colours, delicious tastes, the feel of an ocean breeze, moving the body in ways that are enjoyable, a hot bath on a cold day. The Playful Child doesn't do things because they're supposed to be 'good for you.' It does them because they feel good.

So send your 'stuffy' grown-up on a brief vacation (the part of you that's all work and no play), and invite the Playful Child that lives inside of you to come outside.

Playful Child
1. Imagine an environment where your Playful Child would enjoy meeting with you, such as:
    a playroom
    a playground
    a zoo
    an amusement park or carnival
    the beach
    recreation centre

2. Now invite the Child to come out and be with you. Let the Playful Child draw a picture of itself with your non-dominant hand. Ask the Child to tell you its name and print it on the picture.

3. Writing with your dominant hand (as your adult self), have a conversation with your Playful Child (who writes through your non-dominant hand). Ask the Child all about itself.

    What do you like? What don't you like?

    Where do you like to play?

    What kind of things do you like to do when you play?

    Who do you like to play with?

    What do you like to eat and drink?

    What are your favourite places to eat?

    Where do you like to go on vacation?

    What kind of clothes do you like to wear?

    What are your favourite colours?

    What is your favourite room? Favourite place?

4. Ask your Playful Child how it feels about its place in your life at this time. Does it feel wanted and included? Does it feel ignored and left out?

5. Ask your Playful Child for one thing it wants from you. If you are willing to do it, tell the Child exactly how you will meet its request. Be specific. If you are not going to follow through, don't make promises. This will only disappoint the Child and weaken the trust between you.

6. Thank your Playful Child for coming out to talk with you and agree to meet again if you are willing to do that.

Later on, be aware of the Playful Child when it wants to come out in your everyday life. It may want some time to take a hot bath or pick a bunch of flowers or bike ride to the store instead of driving.

LIBERATING YOUR LOST INNER CHILD

John Bradshaw

Counsellor and workshop leader John Bradshaw's ability to synthesize ideas into a truly usable form is impressive. Many people have experienced this quality in his highly acclaimed showcase presentations on the family for PBS television. This piece, a chapter from his book Healing the Shame That Binds You, *represents Bradshaw's current thinking on the inner child. The child within concept is a theme that has surfaced in his work from a variety of sources, but the 12-step alcoholism recovery movement remains his primary model and metaphor for healing and growth. His 'lost inner child meditation,' included here, is of special interest.*

> *Probably I, too, would have remained trapped by this compulsion to protect the parents . . . had I not come in contact with the CHILD IN ME, who appeared late in my life, wanting to tell me her secret . . . filled with an adult's fear of the darkness . . . But I could not close the door and leave the child alone until my death . . . I made a decision that was to change my life profoundly . . . to put my trust in this nearly autistic being who had survived the isolation of decades.*
>
> – ALICE MILLER, 'PICTURES OF CHILDHOOD'

Bradshaw On: The Family describes three distinct phases of my own shame reduction and externalization process. The figure on page 226 gives you a visual picture of these phases.

The first phase is the recovery phase. Through the group's support and mirroring love, I recovered my own sense of worth. I risked coming out of hiding and showing my shame-based self. As I saw myself reflected in the non-shaming eyes of others, I felt good about myself. I reconnected with myself. I was no longer completely alone and beside myself. The group and significant others restored my sense of having an interpersonal bond.

The recovery process is a first-order change. What that means is that I changed one kind of behaviour for another kind of behaviour. I quit drinking and isolating. I shared my experiences, strength and hope. I started talking and sharing my feelings. I started to feel my feelings again. I shifted my dependency to the new family I had discovered. There was still a dependent and shame-based child in me who made the new group into my parents' safeguarding security.

My shame was reduced but still active. This was evidenced by the fact that I was still compulsive and having trouble with intimacy. I chose women who I felt needed me, confusing love with pity. I set up rescuing-type relationships where others became dependent upon me and saw me as all-powerful. I started working 12-hour days, including Saturday. I smoked more and started eating lots of sugar. Indeed I had stopped a life-threatening disease called alcoholism; I had reduced my shame; I felt better about myself, but I was still compulsive and driven. I was not yet free.

In order to get free I had to do my family-of-origin work. I still needed to grow up and truly leave home.

Fritz Perls once said, 'The goal of life is to move from environmental support to self-support.' The goal of life is to achieve independence. Undependence is grounded in a healthy sense of shame. We are responsible for our own lives.

Our source relationships were bathed in poor modelling and abandonment. This created our shame-based identity. Because we had no authentic self, we clung to our caregivers in a fantasy bond or built walls around us where no one could hurt us. These earliest imprints coloured all our subsequent relationships.

I once heard Werner Erhard, the founder of *est*, say, 'Until we resolve our source relationships, we are never really in another relationship.' Leaving home means breaking our source relationships.

And since we carry much of our shame as a result of those relationships, leaving home is a powerful way of reducing shame.

LEAVING HOME

What does leaving home involve? How do we do it?

Leaving home is the second phase of the journey to wholeness. I call it the Uncovery Phase. What it involves is making contact with the hurt and lonely inner child who was abandoned long ago. This child is that part of us that houses our blocked emotional energy. This energy is especially blocked when we have experienced severe abuse. In order to reconnect with the wounded and hurt child, we have to go back and re-experience the emotions that were blocked.

When we form emotional energy blocks, they seriously affect our ability to think and reason. Our mind is narrowed in its range of vision. We are contaminated in our judgment, perception and ability to reason about the concrete personal events in our life. (Such emotional blockage does not seem to impair abstract or speculative modes of thought.)

Once our practical judgment is shut down, the will, which is the executor of our personality, loses its ability to see alternatives, and is no longer grounded in reality. The emotionally shut-down person literally is filled with will, i.e., becomes will-full. Wilfulness is characterized by grandiosity and unbridled attempts to control, and is the ultimate disaster caused by toxic shame. Wilfulness is playing God; it's the self-will riot referred to in the 12-Step programs.

The only way to get our brains out of hock and cure our compulsivity is to go back and re-experience the emotions. The blocked emotions must be re-experienced as they first occurred. The unmet and unresolved dependency needs must be re-educated with new lessons and corrective experiences.

Our lost childhood must be grieved. Our compulsivities are the result of those old blocked feelings (our unresolved grief) being acted

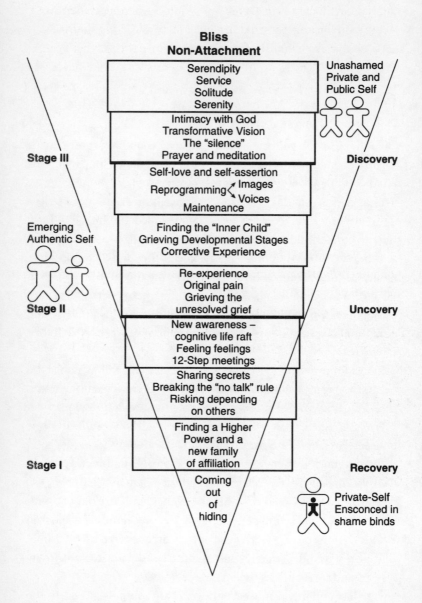

out over and over again. We either work these feelings out by re-experiencing them, or we act them out in our compulsivities. We can also act them in as in depression or suicide, or project them onto others as in the interpersonal strategies for transferring shame.

We must leave home and become our own person in order to cure our compulsivities. Even though I was in recovery, I had never left home. I had never uncovered the sources and set-up for my toxic shame. I had never done the 'original pain' feeling work. I had never dealt with my family or origin.

ORIGINAL PAIN-FEELING WORK

Any shame-based person has been in a family of trauma. Children of trauma experience too much stimulus within a short period of time to be able to adequately master that stimulus. All the forms of the abandonment trauma stimulate grief emotions in children and then simultaneously block their release.

I watched a man and his young daughter in the airport recently. I was getting a haircut and he was sitting two chairs down. He constantly scolded the child, and at one point angrily told her that she was a lot of trouble, just like her mother. I assumed he was separated or divorced. As he walked out, he slapped her a couple of times. It was really painful to watch. As the child cried, he slapped her again. Then he dragged her into the ice cream parlour and bought her ice cream to shut her up. This child is learning at a very early age that she's not wanted, that it's all her fault, that she's not a person, that her feelings don't count and that she's responsible for other people's feelings. I can't imagine where she could find an ally who would sit down with her and validate her sadness and allow her to grieve.

In a healthy respectful family a child's feelings are validated. Trauma is bound to happen somewhere along the way in any normal childhood.

As Alice Miller has repeatedly written, 'It is not the traumas we suffer in childhood which make us emotionally ill but the inability to express the trauma.'

When a child is abandoned through neglect, abuse or enmeshment, there is outrage over the hurt and pain. Children need their pain validated. They need to be shown how to discharge their feelings. They need time to do the discharge work and they need support. Each abandoned child would not become shame-based if there was a nourishing ally who could validate his pain and give him time to resolve it by doing his grief work.

I think of a healthy family I know in which the father was severely injured in a home accident. The six-year-old son was playing outside when he heard an explosion. He was shocked to find his father bleeding and apparently crippled. The father directed him to call an ambulance. A neighbour kept him until his mother returned from work. The boy was in a state of shock. The mother took him to a child play-therapist. He was afraid to go into the basement of the house (where the heater was). He was angry with his mother for not being home and his father for going away (being taken to the hospital).

Over the next months the boy worked his feelings out in the context of symbiotic play. His mum and his dad were both happy that he was able to express his anger toward them. (Shame-based parents would have guilted him for expressing anger.) They gave him support as he worked through his fears of going into the basement where the new heater was. They shared their own feelings with the child.

VALIDATION

In order for grief to be resolved several factors must be present. The first factor is validation. Our childhood abandonment trauma must be validated as real or it cannot be resolved. Perhaps the most damaging consequence of being shame based is that *we don't know how depressed and angry we really are*. We don't *actually feel* our unresolved grief. Our false self and ego defences keep us from experiencing it. Paradoxically, the very defences which allowed us to survive our childhood trauma have now become barriers to our growth. Fritz Perls once said, 'Nothing changes 'til it becomes what it is.' We must uncover our frozen grief.

I remember my paternal grandmother ridiculing me because I was in hysterics over my dad going out to get drunk. He had just had a fight with my mum and left the house in anger, vowing to get drunk. I began to cry and was soon out of control. I was told that I was a 'big sissy' and to get hold of myself. I've never forgotten this experience. Years later I still carried the unresolved grief.

SUPPORT

The greatest tragedy of all this is that we know grief can naturally be healed if we have support. Jane Middleton-Moz has said, 'One of the things we know about grief resolution is that grief is one of the only problems in the world that will heal itself with support.' (For a clear and concise discussion of unresolved grief read *After the Tears* by Jane Middleton-Moz and Lorie Dwinell.)

The reason people go into delayed grief is that there's nobody there to validate and support them. You cannot grieve alone. Millions of us adult children tried it. We went to sleep crying into our pillows or locked in the bathrooms.

Delayed grief is the core of what is called the post-traumatic stress syndrome. As soldiers come back from the war, they have common symptoms of unreality: panic, being numbed-out psychically, easily startled, depersonalization, needing to control, nightmares and sleeping disorders. These same symptoms are common for children from dysfunctional families. They are the symptoms of unresolved grief.

'GRIEF WORK' FEELINGS

After validation and support one needs to experience the feelings that were not allowed. This must be done in a safe non-shaming context. The feelings involved in 'grief work' are anger, remorse, hurt, depression, sadness and loneliness. Grief resolution is a kind of 'psychic work' that has to be done. It varies in duration depending upon the intensity of the trauma. One needs enough time to finish this work. In dysfunctional families, there is never enough time.

At our Centre for Recovering Families in Houston we do four-and-one-half-day 'original pain' workshops. We use the family system roles as a way for people to see how they lost their authentic selves and got stuck in a false self. As a person experiences how he got soul murdered, he begins his grieving. Often the therapy facilitator has to help him embrace the feelings because they are bound in shame. As a person connects with his true and authentic feelings, the shame is reduced. This work continues after the workshop. It may go on for a couple of years.

There are many other methods for doing this original pain work. It must be done if the grief is to be resolved and the re-enactments and compulsive lifestyle stopped.

CORRECTIVE EXPERIENCE

The unresolved grief work is a re-experiencing process, liberating and integrating your lost inner child. Since the neglect of our developmental dependency needs was a major source of toxic shame, it is important to reconnect. Each developmental stage was unique with its own special needs and dynamics. In infancy we needed a mirror of unconditional love. We needed to hear words (nonverbal to an infant) like 'I'm so glad you're here. Welcome to the world. Welcome to our family and home. I'm so glad you're a boy or girl. I want to be near you, to hold you and love you. Your needs are okay with me. I'll give you all the time you need to get your needs met.' These affirmations are adapted from Pam Levin's book *Cycles of Power.*

I like to set up small groups (six to eight people) and let one person sit in the centre of the group. The person in the centre directs the rest of the group as to how close he wants them to be. Some people want to be cradled and held. Some want only touching. Some who were stroke-deprived don't feel safe enough for such closeness. Each person sets his own boundary.

After the group is set, we play lullaby music and each person in the group communicates one of the verbal affirmations while touching, stroking or just sitting near the subject.

Those who have been neglected will start sobbing when they hear the words they needed to hear, but did not hear. If a person was a Lost Child, he will often sob intensely. These words touch the hole in his soul.

After the affirmation the group discusses their experience. I always try to have a mixed group so that a person hears male and female voices. Often a person will report that he especially loved hearing the male voice or the female voice, since he never heard it as a child. Sometimes if a person has been abused by a parent, he will not trust the voice that corresponds to that parent's sex. The group sharing, hearing the affirmations, being touched and supported, offers a corrective kind of experience.

I also suggest other ways people might get their infancy needs met as those needs are recycled in new experiences. They usually need a friend who will give them physical support (lots of touching), and who will feed them (take them out to eat). They need lots of skin satisfaction. They may need a nice warm bath, or wrap up in a blanket. They may want to try a body massage.

We go on to toddler needs, repeating the group process. Since the toddler needs to separate, we let the person sit near but separate from everyone. I usually do an age-regression type meditation, in which I ask the one in the middle to experience himself as a toddler. I give affirmations like, 'It's okay to wander and explore. It's okay to test your limits. It's okay for you to do it and to do it your way. I'll be here. You don't have to hurry. I'll give you all the time you need. It's okay to practice holding on and letting go. I won't leave you.'

Again the group shares after each person has heard these affirmations several times. Frequently people express deep emotions as they share. Often they remember an episode of abandonment that was long forgotten. Some get into more unresolved grief work.

We go through all the developmental stages through adolescence. Adolescence is important because many people went through painful abandonment and shaming incidents during adolescence . . .

I usually ask each person to write a letter to his parent(s) telling them the things he needed that he didn't get.

Wayne Kritsberg has them write the letter with the non-dominant hand. Writing with the non-dominant hand helps create the feeling of being a child. Great emotion is discharged as the person reads his letter to the group. After the letter is read, I ask the group to give the person the affirmations that correspond to the unmet needs that he described in his letter to his parents.

Toward the close of the workshop I have each participant encounter his Lost Child. I cannot describe the power of this exercise. I have put it on several of my cassette tapes. There's no way to convey its power through the written word. I'll outline the meditation. You can put it on a tape recorder and listen to it. I recommend using Daniel Kobialka's 'Going Home' as background music.

MEDITATION: EMBRACING YOUR LOST INNER CHILD

Sit in an upright position. Relax and focus your breathing . . . Spend a few minutes becoming mindful of breathing . . . Be aware of the air as you breathe it in and as you breathe it out . . . Notice the difference in the air as it comes in and as it goes out. Focus on that difference . . . (one minute). Now imagine that you're walking down a long flight of stairs. Walk down slowly as I count down from ten. Ten . . . (ten seconds) Nine . . . (ten seconds) Eight . . . (ten seconds), etc. When you reach the bottom of the stairs, turn left and walk down a long corridor with doors on your right and doors on your left. Each door has a coloured symbol on it . . . (one minute). As you look toward the end of the corridor there is a force field of light . . . Walk through it and go back through time to a street where you lived before you were seven-years-old. Walk down that street to the house you lived in. Look at the house. Notice the roof, the colour of the house and the windows and doors . . . See a small child come out the front door . . . How is the child dressed? What colour are the child's shoes? Walk over to the child . . . Tell him that you are from his future . . . Tell him that you know better than anyone what he has been through . . . His suffering, his abandonment . . . his shame . . . Tell him that of all the people he will ever know you are the only one he will never lose. Now ask him if he is willing to go home with you . . . If not, tell him you will visit him tomorrow. If he is willing to go with you, take him by the hand and start walking away . . . As you walk away see your mum and dad come out on the porch. Wave goodbye to them. Look over your shoulder as you continue walking away and see them getting smaller and smaller until they are completely gone . . . Turn the corner and see your Higher Power and your much cherished friends waiting for you. Embrace all your friends and allow your Higher Power to come into your heart . . . Now walk away and promise your child you will meet him for five minutes each day. Pick an exact time. Commit to that time. Hold your child in your hand and let him shrink to the size of your hand. Place him in your heart . . . Now walk to some beautiful outdoor place . . . Stand in the middle of that place and reflect on the experience you just had . . . Get a sense of communion within yourself, with your Higher Power and with all things . . . Now look up in the sky; see the purple white clouds form the number five . . . See the five become a four . . . and be aware of your feet and legs . . . See the four become a three . . . Feel the life in your stomach and in your arms. See the three become a two; feel the life in your hands, your face, your whole body. Know that you are about to become fully awake – able to do all things with your fully awake mind – see the two become a one and be fully awake, remembering the experience . . .

I encourage you to get an early photo of yourself. Preferably a photo of you before you were seven years old. I suggest you put it in your wallet or purse. Put the picture on your desk so that you can be reminded of this child that lives in you.

Much data supports that the child lives within us in a fully developed stage. This child is the most vital and spontaneous part of us and needs to be integrated into our life.

GETTING CHILD DEVELOPMENTAL NEEDS MET AS AN ADULT

We recycle our developmental needs all through our lives. Each time we start something new we trigger our infancy needs. After we are secure and trust our new environment, our toddler part wants to explore and experiment. Our own children trigger our needs as they go through their various developmental stages. We have an opportunity as an adult to care for us at each of these stages.

As adults we can create a context where we can get our needs met. I was neglected in fathering. I've created a group of men who serve as supporting friends who give me feedback. I've learned that as an adult I can make what I get from others serve my needs. Children never get enough. Adults learn as they mature to make what they get to be enough. So I can take an event of sharing in my group and make fathering out of it. If one of the members is especially nurturing to me, I can allow that to be fathering. I can also let other events in my life serve as fathering and mothering. I can also learn as an adult to get things I specifically need. I can be good to myself and treat myself with nurturing respect and kindness.

THE UNIVERSAL QUEST FOR THE INNER CHILD

It is important to note that the need to find the Inner Child is part of every human being's journey toward wholeness. No one had a perfect childhood. Everyone bears the unresolved unconscious issues of his family history.

The Inner Child journey is the hero's journey. Becoming a fully functioning person is a heroic task. There are trials and tribulations along the way. In Greek mythology, Oedipus kills his father, Orestes kills his mother. Leaving one's parents are obstacles one must encounter on the hero's journey. To kill our parents is a symbolic way to describe leaving home and growing up.

To find our Inner Child is the first leap over the abyss of grief that threatens us all. But finding the Inner Child is just the beginning. Because of his isolation, neglect and neediness, this child is egocentric, weak and frightened. He must be disciplined in order to release his *tremendous spiritual power*.

19

RECALLING THE CHILD

Jean Houston

≈

Teacher and philosopher Jean Houston asks us in this exercise to return to the child and befriend it wholeheartedly. This is a very practical approach for evoking what Ms Houston calls 'an extended sense of being.' It is recommended that you do this exercise with another person serving as guide. 'Recalling the Child' is excerpted from the author's 1982 book, The Possible Human.

What would it be like if you, at your present age and knowing what you now know, could go back and become the great friend and guide of yourself as a child? Many who have explored this possibility with me report that the child in them seems to respond to this friendship in such a way that makes them feel their past life is enriched, although not necessarily changed. In their present adult state they feel the effects that come from experiencing an enriched earlier life, often feeling stronger, more secure and resilient, more creative, and even beginning to lose some disabling and neurotic behaviour that may have started in childhood.

Remember, as you go back in your life to meet the child living within you, to choose to encounter that child at some time when he or she would have been receptive to the arrival of a sympathetic stranger. Very few children are capable of welcoming someone new in the midst of great emotional trauma. Once you and your child have become acquainted and accepting of one another, you can repeat the exercise on other occasions and approach more sensitive areas. You might want to meet your child as he or she goes to school for the first time, or when a tooth is lost, or when your child needs a push on a swing or someone to talk to in the dark.

In the second stage of this exercise you will contact the person you will become in the future, allowing the three of you – yourself now, yourself past and yourself future – to experience the renewal that is inherent in this meeting. It may be possible to go forward in time as well as backward. If we hold this perspective, future selves may be both willing and able to nurture and redeem our present existence. Certainly modern physics has suggested that time is not linear but rather is an omnipresent dimension of reality, and that it is only our experiential limitations which keep us locked into a serial view of this dimension.

PREPARATION

This exercise is best done with one person serving as a guide and reading the instructions. The guide will need a drum or gong to mark the passage across time. If this is not possible, the instructions and the drumming can be put on a tape.

THE EXERCISE

Stage One: Befriending Yourself as a Child

Sitting with your eyes closed, breathe deeply, following your breath in and out. For this exercise act *as if* the following were true: that there still exists in your being yourself as a child, a child who does not know that in some other time frame of its existence it has grown up.

As the drum (or gong) sounds, call upon this child to come forward from wherever it exists. You might even want to open your right hand so that it can be reached by your child. The child, who was yourself, may appear during the sounding of the drum or gong or it may appear at the ending of the sounds. In either case, as soon as you feel your child to be present, be attentive to the child. Some will want to do this with the active imagination, others will actually rock the child or walk around with it, and be very active during this exercise. Find the ways that seem appropriate for you.

You may feel that you actually feel in your right hand a little hand holding yours. Feel the needs and personality of this child. Hold your child in your arms if the child is willing. Talk with your child. Walk with it. Take it, if you like, to some place like the circus or the beach or the zoo, or let it take you somewhere. Play with this child who was you. Give it love, friendship, nurturing, and allow yourself to receive from the child, who may actually have as much if not more to offer you than you have to offer it. You have fifteen minutes to begin the friendship with yourself as a child.

If you go outside, you will be called back by the ringing of a bell.

The guide will then beat a drum or gong slowly thirty to sixty times.

At this point, depending on whether or not you want to go on to the next sequence in this exercise, you can do one of several things. If the exercise has been done in a group, you can meet with one or two others in a small circle, each of you with your child so that adults and 'children' share their experiences. Allow your child to talk and act through you as well as sharing from your mature consciousness. In this kind of group sharing, the reality of the child is honoured and so becomes clearer.

If you are doing this alone, make something with your child – a drawing or clay figure or poem – that will serve to remind you of this meeting and what you have learned. Work with your child as partner in this process.

When this process has been completed, you can tell your child goodbye, assuring it that you will come back and visit often if you plan to do so. If you choose to go on to the next sequence, in which you are befriended by your extended self, tell the child you will call it back in a few minutes.

Stage Two: Becoming Befriended by Your Extended Being

In this next sequence you become as a child to the extended version of yourself. This extended self is the *entelechy* of you – who you said you would be and could be if your potentials were fully realized. This Higher Self is the oak tree of which you at present are still the acorn. We are assuming that in some realm of the psyche this being already exists, just as the child that you were still persists.

Closing your eyes and following the path of your breathing in and out, become aware of the following: Your extended being is about to enter your present reality and be for you as you were for your child. This is the high being of yourself, full of wisdom and grace, free of meanness and pettiness, filled with empowering love, who has multiple ways of knowing, learning, sharing. This is you as Sage, you if you had a hundred more years to consciously work on yourself.

Now as you hear the sound of the gong or drum, this potential being is becoming real, for it truly is real. This richly extended self is coming to meet you from a dimension beyond space and time.

Sound the gong or drum slowly for ten to twenty times.

As this being comes and cares for you, allow yourself to be nourished, empowered and awakened. Let yourself receive and be refined by the gifts that your High Self has for you.

Allow about five to ten minutes for this exercise.

Guided and cared for, loved, acknowledged, and evoked, call forward the child that was you. Hold the child in your arms, as you are being held by your own extended being. The three of you are now together, a trinity that is a perfect oneness. Let a continuum of love, encouragement, and empowerment flow among the three of you so that the child gives its freshness of vision to the extended one, while he or she quickens the child, and you give to both.

Allow about five minutes for this experience.

Release now the child and the extended self so that they may return to their own place of being, knowing that they can be called into your reality frame whenever needed. Know also that each of these parts of yourself has access to the other, and that this communion and communication is a high practice that must be nourished in order to be known.

And coming back now to regular reality, be still for a few minutes as you open your eyes. Reflect upon what has been given to you and what you have given. Sense the extension of yourself flowing through your body as you begin to move around. Share this, if you wish, with another person or by writing in your journal.

DISCUSSION

As I suggested earlier, an extended sense of being is evoked in this exercise. Knowing the living presence of the child within and the promise of the person you are becoming, you are free to draw on these beings, to see the current reality through their eyes and so gain multiple perspectives that still have the integrity of your own experience and your own nature.

While this seems to be true for most people, there is still the possibility of a wide range of individual responses, ranging from poignancy to pathos to falling-out-of-the-chair laughter. One woman who had no memory at all of her father, who had died when she was three, found herself with her two-year-old child being sung to by her father. Others have been surprised to find the great resiliency and strength of their child.

You can extend the power and possibilities of this exercise by allowing your child and your High Self each to have a bit of your day that is theirs, a time in which you might play or listen to music – or pay your bills! – guided by the particular knowing of this being. Some parents and teachers have found that their child within has been most perceptive about the children without, offering helpful advice and insights about the headstrong nine-year-old or tearful adolescent. The High Self provides a different sense of time, putting the drama and trauma, and even the tedium, of the moment into a longer and larger perspective. As these beings become your allies, you extend the horizons of the timebound self.

20

KILLING THE DRAGON
Joseph Campbell

≈

With the death of the great mythologist Joseph Campbell in 1987, a surge of interest in his work seemed to be met synchronistically with the release of books, television programmes, and video. Considering how widely he ranged in his speculations and ideas about the universal nature of mythological motifs, Campbell had curiously little to say about the child or the inner child. However, what he did say was clear, terse, and to the point, as you will see below. The question is quite evident: 'How might we as individuals get in touch with the child that lies within us?'

Here is an excerpt from the interviews Campbell gave on the national public radio programme 'New Dimensions,' in dialogue with host Michael Toms. These transcripts are available in book form, published as An Open Life: Joseph Campbell in Conversation with Michael Toms.

We've been talking about the Eastern guru, but we also have gurus in the West. I think of people in the human potential movement, for example: there are people who have taken on the role of guru.

They themselves are following an Oriental model, I would say. But it must be *really* flattering to say, 'Are you enlightened? I am! So listen! I don't take any guff.' One of the typical things in the Orient is that any criticism disqualifies you for the guru's instruction. Well, in heaven's name, is that appropriate for a Western mind? It's simply a transferring of your submission to the childhood father onto a father for your adulthood, which means you're not growing up.

Similarly, in psychoanalysis there's the whole idea of transference. What do you transfer to the analyst? You transfer all the parental systems of relationships, so you're still bound; you're still a submissive and dependent person.

When you talk about maturity in adulthood, I think of what Jesus said, 'You must become as a little child to enter the kingdom of heaven.' Let's juxtapose that with adulthood and maturity. How do those two come together?

I think what he was talking about is spontaneity. But the answer to your question comes from Nietzsche in the introduction to *Zarathustra*. It's curious to speak of Nietzsche in the same breath as Jesus because typically he's thought to be the anti-Christ; he even thought so himself a little bit. But these are two great teachers, and great teachers frequently say similar things in different languages.

Nietzsche says there are three stages to the spirit. The first is that of the camel. The camel gets down on his knees and says, 'Put a load on me.' This is the condition of youth and learning. When the camel is well loaded, he gets to his feet and runs out into the desert. This is the place where he's going to be alone to find himself and he's transformed into a lion. And the function and deed of the lion is to kill a dragon, and that dragon's name is 'Thou shalt.' On every scale of the dragon a law is written, some dating from 2000 B.C., others from yesterday's paper. When the camel is well loaded, the lion is potent and the dragon *is* killed. You see, there are two quite different things. One is submission, obedience, learning; the other is strong and assertive. And when the dragon is killed, the lion is transformed into a child.

In Nietzsche's words, 'a wheel rolling out of its own centre.' That's what the child represents in this mystical language. The human being has recovered that spontaneity and innocence and thoughtlessness of rules which is so marvellous in childhood. The little one who comes up and says absolutely embarrassing things to the stranger who's visiting your house – that's the child; not the obedient child, but the innocent child who is spontaneous and has the courage to live its impulses.

How might we as individuals get in touch with the child that lives within us?

By killing the dragon, 'Thou shalt.'

By choosing not to live by other people's rules?

Right. Respecting them, but not living by them. Respecting them more or less in the way you respect the red and green lights on the highway. There are other rules which seem advisable – if, in your own intelligence, you see that such a rule represents human decency, for example. But a rule put on you as a rule – 'Thou shalt not' – is another show. I think one can learn to take courage; it also involves taking responsibility for what you're doing – taking the rap, if you have made radical mistakes and hurt people. It can be done.

Part Six

INNER CHILD/OUTER CHILD: THE FUTURE OF PARENTING

≈

INTRODUCTION

≈

The way I treat my inner child is the way I am going to treat my outer child.

— ROBERT M. STEIN

The feeling of being valuable – 'I am a valuable person' – is essential to mental health and is a cornerstone of self-discipline. It is a direct product of parental love. Such a conviction must be gained in childhood; it is extremely difficult to acquire it during adulthood.

— M. SCOTT PECK

Childhood is not only important because it is the starting point for possible cripplings of instinct, but also because this is the time when, terrifying or encouraging, those far-seeing dreams and images come from the soul of the child, which prepare his whole destiny.

— C.G. JUNG

As I suggested at the beginning of this book, the child-rearing task is under siege now as never before. To know, value, and embody the inner child is not, as some would have it, a further episode of self-involvement for the me-generation. Awareness of the inner child must be seen in context as an evolutionary process of transmitting the enlightened laws of individuality to our children and their children. The signs in our culture and the stresses on our children indicate that such explicit measures have become facts of our destiny, the initiatory requirements for children born of an age of millennial transition.

The child within the parent and the inner life of our actual children intersect in the need for spiritual values that nurture wonder and the capacity to experience the mysteries of life. As Robert M. Stein suggested in the preceding essay, the inner child requires a vision of a new and better world. We need contact with the archetype of wholeness, and with the belief that it will eventually be fulfilled, in order for life to have direction, meaning, and balance.

The parents who have realized their own neglected child within also have drawn forward the inner resources of empathy and compassion to enhance the quality of their relations with their children. Such parents have fulfilled the old rabbinical dictum, 'Don't limit children to your own learning, for they were born in another time.' The child beneficiaries of such parents will be equipped to meet the difficult challenges of their time, knowing their own true worth and possessing an uninhibited capacity for renewal.

This section focuses on the benefits of inner-child awareness for improved parenting. All of the contributors are therapists or analysts, looking at the nature of the parental task with the inner child in mind.

The child's connection to the imaginal world is James Hillman's concern in his essay, 'A Note on Story.' Exposure to oral story enhances the ability to see and value the inner life. 'It is good for the soul,' says the author.

Bruno Bettelheim also is concerned with story and imagination, but from a different perspective. In 'storying' their children, he suggests parents have the opportunity to recall important memories from their own childhoods, to realize their inner child while simultaneously stimulating the inner life of their children.

In his short tribute essay to Sigmund Freud, Erik H. Erikson acknowledges the debt we owe to the founder of psychoanalysis for enlightened child attitudes. Freud gave us permission to become conscious of our childhood pasts and exhorted us to apply these insights to better parenting.

Theodore Reik speaks, like a kind and wise uncle, of the reality of the inner child who lives on in each of us, forever playful, forever young.

The final selection of this book is from Samuel O. Osherson, who reminds us of the wounded parent within the adult and of the necessity to bring to a close the unfinished business between the internalized parent and the inner child, so that the adult personality can honour both.

21

A NOTE ON STORY
James Hillman

This is a short and fascinating look at the enriching effects of 'story-awareness' on the inner life of children. 'The first task,' as archetypal psychologist James Hillman sees it, 'is restorying the adult – the teacher and the parent and the grandparent – in order to restore the imagination to a primary place in consciousness in each of us, regardless of age.' Hillman's thoughts are always a cut above most psychologizing. Here, he is reaching toward a poetic basis to reality, a life grounded in symbolic reality. He exhorts us to give the child's imagination the early nurturance it deserves in order to sustain a long and healthy inner life.

This chapter is from the author's collection of essays entitled Loose Ends. *It was originally published in* Children's Literature: The Great Excluded, *vol. III.*

From my perspective as a depth psychologist, I see that those who have a connection with story are in better shape and have a better prognosis than those to whom story must be introduced. This is a large statement and I would like to take it apart in several ways. But I do not want to diminish its apodictic claim: to have 'story-awareness' is *per se* psychologically therapeutic. It is good for soul.

To have had stories of any sort in childhood – and her I mean oral stories, those told or read (for reading has an oral aspect even if one reads to oneself) rather than watching them on a screen – puts a person into a basic recognition of and familiarity with the legitimate reality of story *per se*. It is something given with life, with speech and communication, and not something later that comes with learning and literature. Coming early with life it is already a perspective on life. One integrates life as a story because one has stories in the back of the mind (unconscious) as containers for organizing events into meaningful experiences. The stories are means of finding oneself in events that might not otherwise make psychological sense at all. (Economic, scientific, and historical explanations are sorts of 'stories' that often fail to give the soul the kind of imaginative meaning it seeks for understanding its psychological life.)

Having had story built in with childhood, a person is usually in a better relationship with the pathologized material of obscene, grotesque, or cruel images which appear spontaneously in dream and fantasy. Those who hold to the rationalist and associationist theory of mind, who put reason against and superior to imagination, argue that if we did not introduce such grim tales in early impressionable years, we would have less pathology and more rationality in later years. My practice shows me rather that the more attuned and experienced is the imaginative side of personality, the less threatening and irrational, the less necessity for repression, and therefore the less actual pathology acted out in literal, daily events. In other words, through story the symbolic quality of pathological images and themes finds a place, so that these images and themes are less likely to be viewed naturalistically, with clinical literalism, as signs of sickness. These images find legitimate places in story. They *belong* to myths, legends, and fairy tales where, just as in dreams, all sorts of peculiar figures and twisted behaviours appear. After all, 'The Greatest Story Ever Told,' as some are fond of calling Easter, is replete with gruesome imagery in great pathologized detail.

Story-awareness provides a better way than clinical-awareness for coming to terms with one's own case history. Case history, too, is a fictional form written up by thousands of hands in thousands of clinics and consulting rooms, stored away in archives and rarely published. This fictional form called 'case history' follows the genre of social realism; it believes in facts and events, and takes with excessive literalism all the tales it tells. In deep analysis, the analyst and the patient together rewrite the case history into a new story, creating the 'fiction' in the collaborative work of the analysis. Some of the healing that goes on, maybe even the essence of it, is this collaborative fiction, this putting all the chaotic and traumatic events of a life into a new story. Jung said that patients need 'healing fictions,' but we have trouble coming to this perspective unless there is already a predilection for story-awareness.

Jungian therapy, at least as I practice it, brings about an awareness that fantasy is a creative activity which is continually telling a person into now this story, now that one. When we examine these fantasies we discover that they reflect the great impersonal themes of mankind as represented in tragedy, epic, folk tale, legend, and myth. Fantasy in our view is an attempt of the psyche itself to remythologize consciousness; we try to further this activity by encouraging familiarity with myth and folk tale. Soulmaking goes hand in hand with deliteralizing consciousness and restoring its connection to mythic and metaphorical thought patterns. Rather than interpret the stories into concepts and rational explanations, we prefer to see conceptual explanations as secondary elaborations upon basic stories which are containers and givers of vitality. As Owen Barfield and Norman Brown have written: 'Literalism is the enemy.' I would add: 'Literalism is sickness.' Whenever we are caught in a literal view, a literal belief, a literal statement we have lost the imaginative metaphorical perspective to ourselves and our world. Story is prophylactic in that it presents itself always as 'once upon a time,' as an 'as if,' 'make-believe' reality. It is the only mode of accounting or telling that does not posit itself as real, true, factual, revealed, i.e., literal.

This brings us to the question of content. Which stories need to be told? Here I am orthodox, holding for the old, the traditional, the ones of our own culture: Greek, Roman, Celtic, and Nordic myths; the Bible; legends and folk tales. And these with the least modern marketing (updating, cleaning up, editing, etc.), i.e., with the least interference by contemporary rationalism which is subject to the very narrowing of consciousness which the stories themselves would expand. Even if we be not Celtic or Nordic or Greek in ancestry, these collections are the fundamentals of our Western culture, and they work in our psyches whether we like it or not. We may consider them distorted in their pro-Aryan or pro-male or pro-warrior slant, but unless we understand that these tales depict the basic motifs of the Western psyche, we remain unaware of the basic motives in our psychological dynamics. Our ego psychology still resounds with the motif and motivation of the hero, just as much of the psychology of what we call 'the feminine' today reflects the patterns of the goddesses and nymphs in Greek myth. These thematic tales channel fantasy. Platonists long ago and Jung more recently pointed out the therapeutic value of the great myths for bringing order to the chaotic, fragmented aspect of fantasy. The main body of biblical and classical tales directs fantasy into organized, deeply life-giving psychological patterns; these stories present the archetypal modes of experiencing.

I think children need less convincing of the importance of story than do adults. To be adult has come to mean to be adulterated with rationalist explanations, and to shun such childishness as we find in fairy stories. I have tried to show in my work how adult and child have come to be set against each other: childhood tends to mean wonder, imagination, creative spontaneity, while adulthood, the loss of these perspectives.[1] So the first task as I see it, is restorying the adult – the teacher and the parent and the grandparent – in order to restore the imagination to a primary place in consciousness in each of us, regardless of age.

I have come at this from a psychological viewpoint, partly because I wish to remove story from its too close association with both education and literature – something taught and studied. My interest in story is as something lived in and lived through, a way in which the soul finds itself in life.

22

EXPLORING CHILDHOOD AS AN ADULT
Bruno Bettelheim

≈

Bruno Bettelheim, an eminent child psychologist, encourages parents to go beyond empathy with their offspring and reexplore 'the steps we made in becoming ourselves.' Here is sage advice on how to achieve greater closeness with children by recapturing one's own child of experience. This article is from his most recent book on child-rearing, A Good Enough Parent.

> *We shall not cease from exploration*
> *And the end of all our exploring*
> *Will be to arrive where we started*
> *And know the place for the first time.*
> – T.S. ELIOT

Among the most valuable but least appreciated experiences parenthood can provide are the opportunities it offers for exploring, reliving, and resolving one's own childhood problems in the context of one's relationship to one's child. As T.S. Eliot reminds us, only by exploring and reexploring the steps we made in becoming ourselves can we truly *know* what our childhood experiences were and what they have signified in our lives. If we achieve this knowledge, the impact of these events on our personality will be altered. Our attitude toward our experience will change, as well as our attitude toward parallel experiences with our children. Our growth in self-knowledge must inevitably result in a better comprehension of our children, even more so when the new insights are in consequence of experiences involving these children.

Unfortunately, nearly all of our primary experiences are lost to conscious memory, because they happened too early to leave more than the vaguest traces in our minds. We cannot reexperience them, but we can at least explore imaginatively some of their aspects as we observe how our infant responds to his inner processes, to us, and to his world.

For example, if we realize that the infant's waking world consists of only two opposite experiences – happiness and physical well-being, and unhappiness and pain – this can help us also understand the origin and ambivalent nature of all strong emotions. Since it is normally the parents who change the negative state of the infant's existence, such as hunger pains or the discomfort of soiled nappies, into one of satisfaction by feeding or by changing him, he experiences his parents as all-powerful and the source of all happiness and unhappiness; also as all-giving and all-frustrating. Thus ambivalence is built into our unconscious, particularly in regard to our parents. Later on they and their surrogates, our foremost educators, continue to dispense both pleasure and pain, by praising us, for example, or by criticizing and frustrating us. In this way the original ambivalent feelings, so deeply rooted in our unconsciousness, continue to be fed by the innumerable experiences of daily life.

Understanding this infantile origin of ambivalence, particularly in regard to our parents, can help us comprehend our children better when we are confronted with expressions of ambivalence about us. The more we can accept their ambivalent feelings in relation to us, the greater chance they will have, as they grow up, to neutralize and control these ambivalences – and the less they will need to blow hot one moment and cold the next. By accepted that the negative aspects of this ambivalence must occasionally be ventilated, we reduce the need for our children to repress them; and the less they are repressed, the more accessible they are to rational scrutiny and modification.

As children, we too were torn by our ambivalent emotions. But when we acted out their negative aspects, our parents' disapproval was usually so strong that we were forced to repress these feelings, which thus retained their full force in our unconsciousness. When we are confronted as parents with similar feelings in our children, the experience tends to reactivate some of this repressed material. We can accept that our children will have much less control than we do, as long as their behaviour does not awaken in us feelings we wish to keep repressed; but when our own repressions become remobilized, then we can no longer deal realistically with the negativism of our children.

That we repress the negative aspects of our feelings about our parents is understandable; after all, we need them and don't want to offend or alienate them by openly displaying our hostility. It is harder to comprehend why we also repress our identification with what to us as children seem negative aspects of our parents. Most of us are quite aware that we have made our own many of the things we like about our parents, but we're *not* aware that we have also identified with and internalized the negative aspects of their attitude toward us. Of this we become cognizant – usually to our great surprise – when we hear ourselves scold our children in exactly the same tone, even with the very same words, that our parents used with us. And this although we had objected to their doing so and have thought that we would never behave to our children in such a manner.

On the other hand, when we speak lovingly to our children, we are not at all compelled to use the same terms our parents employed. In our positive expressions and behaviour we are quite our own persons and speak very much with our own voice. The reason for this is once again because there was no cause to repress our positive identification with our parents, it did not become encapsulated in the unconscious but remained accessible to modification as we ourselves developed. The negative identification, in contrast, was repressed and thus remained unchanged.

Very often the relations of the child to the parent of the same sex are more beset by ambivalence than are those to the parent of the other sex. The reason for this is that in relating to the child of our own sex we tend to reexperience some of the more difficult aspects of our own relation to our same-sex parent. Thus it is more likely that a mother will catch herself talking like her own mother when she criticizes her daughter, while a father will find himself repeating in his negative interactions with his son those that took place in his childhood between him and his father.

This is just one example of our tendency to project our own unresolved conflicts onto our children. If we take advantage of the opportunity such situations offer to examine what causes us to behave this way, we may be able at last to solve childhood conflicts we have not resolved before. Such openness to one's feelings will also facilitate our understanding that it is exactly our tremendous importance to our children, and their love for us, that spawns their occasional hostility. It will be clear that when hostility breaks out into the open, what we are being confronted with is but the obverse of their great affection for us. This realization will alter our attitude from annoyance or worse to one of understanding acceptance of the underlying emotional forces, although we still may have to inhibit our child's aggressive behaviour. It may even make us recognize that in restraining him, we are reproducing our parents' conduct in parallel situations. Recalling how unfair we thought our parents were will keep us from overreacting to our child's behaviour. With such deliberations, things out to fall into their rightful place, and what now annoys us about our child will not be fed and aggravated by its connection with all the hostile feelings we have repressed into our unconscious. Most of all, as we realize that despite all the aggressive tendencies we had as children, we did grow up to be nonviolent, law-abiding adults, we will be less likely to bear down too hard on our child's aggressive behaviour out of anxiety that it will become unmanageable once he is grown up.

The repression of the negative side of a child's ambivalent feelings about his parents, if done too severely, can have the consequence of interfering with the expression of the positive feelings, which are but the other side of this ambivalence. I have known many children who were able to form loving attachments to their parents only after they no longer felt the compulsion to repress all their negative feelings about them.

Of course, if we are able to recognize, through introspection, that our feelings toward our children are not entirely free of ambivalence, we no longer need to repress whatever negative feelings may well up in us from time to time. The pretense that our child, because of his immaturity and lack of control, is occasionally having negative feelings about us but that we are entirely free of such feelings about him can cause serious problems in the relations.

UNDERSTANDING NIGHTMARES

What has been said about the origins of our ambivalent feelings about our parents holds true, *mutatis mutandis*, for the entire period of childhood. Our earliest experiences, and those of our child, are mostly unconscious and thus not available in direct form to our memory, but later stages of his development replicate some of our experiences that were not necessarily unconscious or repressed by us, or if so, not so deeply. These memories can be recalled more readily, although this may still require considerable effort.

Few of us can remember in any detail the nightmares from which we suffered, as all children do; even those who can recall to some extent the contents of their nightmares and how upsetting they were have little notion what caused them, beyond the obvious fact that the young child feels helplessly anxious about many things which are incomprehensible to him. Not many people realize that a major source of the nightmares of young children is their developing superegos, which try to punish them for their 'unacceptable,' if not 'sinful,' tendencies. Among others, these may be sexual urges, or the wish to rebel against authority or to get rid of a parent or sibling. As forerunner, an early stage of a more fully integrated conscience, the nightmare plays an important role in the personality development of all of us; it had this role in our development as it now has in that of our child.

Realizing this will help us to treat our child's nightmares with greater care and the respect which a developing conscience deserves. The more we understand about our own nightmares (of which we are not entirely free even in adult life), the better equipped we will be to help our children with theirs. The fact that we have forgotten so much about them suggests that we repressed the childish desires and fears which found expression in those haunting dreams. Underlying such alienation from our childhood experiences is the wish not to know what they were all about, maybe even some dim recognition that the terror we then felt has left in us some residues from which we have failed to free ourselves entirely. Witness the unrealistic anxiety many people still suffer, for example, when confronted with harmless animals, such as garden snakes. Their fear is often rooted in forgotten childhood nightmares in which snakes threatened to devour them.

Thus we can use our children's nightmares as an opportunity to explore and reexplore – as T.S. Eliot suggested – what may have been behind our own, and whatever remnants of them we may still carry with us. Then we shall indeed, for the first time, truly know our nightmares and their meaning in our lives. To the degree we achieve this it will be a boon to us and to our children, since we shall then be able, by understanding ourselves, to help them with their night-mares with a personal sympathy for both the immediate suffering and the significance of such experiences in the formation of their personality, a depth of empathy which otherwise might never be available to either of us.

Unlike our nightmares, which we only vaguely recollect, our anxieties about entering school have stayed with many of us; in fact, some people spend a lifetime demonstrating, to themselves much more than to others, that their childish fears of academic and social failure were unrealistic. Because these worries are usually part of our conscious memories, although often in fragmentary form, we have considerable compassion for our child's anxieties about his first entry into school. Unfortunately, some parents run out of com-passion when an older child develops a school phobia for parallel reasons. This is when an understanding based on one's own experiences would be particularly helpful.

These situations stand for many others which may occur in our interactions with our children; efforts to understand the role played by parallel events in our own development always bring about beneficial changes as they provide new clarity about ourselves. We gain a deeper understanding of what certain experiences have meant in our lives and in our relation to our parents, as well as how these experiences now shape our attitude toward what our child experiences and expresses around some similar occurrence. Such understanding permits us to empathize with whatever moves our child, and this nearly always gives our relation greater depth and meaning, making it a more enjoyable experience for both of us. Thus around some common experience, we not only influence our children's attitudes, but we also change our own, because of a better understanding of what similar events meant to us as children.

Children are very sensitive to their parents' reasons for doing something with or for them. Do parents think they *ought* to do this, or do they really enjoy it? Is Mother reading a story because she wants to quiet me down? Or is it because she thinks it's her duty? Perhaps she thinks I'll enjoy this particular story, or being read to by her, or both? Obviously it is a more rewarding experience for a child if he can sense his mother's desire to give him pleasure.

The child's experience when being read to is radically different from that of the parent, although they engage together in a single activity. However, when parents respond to the story themselves, the two can really share the experience. Perhaps the parent will be moved by the story to recall important memories from his own childhood. I have been told that people who read my book on fairy tales, *The Uses of Enchantment*, suddenly understood why a particular story had been especially significant to them in their childhood. Then it had captivated them in some way, had aroused anxiety or pleasure, or both; but only now did they see why this had been so, with what personal experiences or problems the tale had been connected, so that it became uniquely meaningful to them.

As children these people had wanted a parent to read the story over and over again because, unbeknownst to them at the time but understood now, they had subconsciously hoped that it would convey an important message to the reader. For one it was *The Swiss Family Robinson*; by spinning fantasies about this story, she had found solace from her unhappy family situation. The same book was also very meaningful to another young girl who suffered from the repeated and prolonged absences of her parents, during which she was left in the care of relatives who physically took good care of her but whom she hated, mostly because they took her parents' place. Only as an adult did she realize that she had pestered her parents and relatives to read *The Swiss Family Robinson* aloud to her because she hoped they would get the message that children need to have their parents present. Subconsciously she had hoped that from the story they would understand how much she wanted her parents to either stop travelling or take her with them.

As soon as this woman realized that a child's desire to hear a certain story again and again may derive from his hope that his parent will get the message he thinks the story conveys, reading stories to her own child became a much more rewarding experience for her. Moreover, she began to pay quite different attention to the stories her child requested, for she remembered with particular poignancy how severely disappointed she had been that neither her parents nor her relatives had gotten the message she had tried to send through *The Swiss Family Robinson*.

Reading stories to her son now took on new levels of meaning for her. Before, she had read to him because she remembered how important this activity had been to her, and she wanted to give him this pleasure. Now it occurred to her that by asking for a particular tale, her son might be trying to give something to her – namely, a message about some matter that was of great importance to him. She enjoyed this demonstration of this confidence in her, his desire to tell her – in whatever roundabout form – something of personal significance.

Her experience of the importance *The Swiss Family Robinson* had once had for her gave this mother a new perspective on her own childhood. What she had previously recalled and viewed only as an escape into wish-fulfilling fantasies she now recognized as an intelligent, goal-directed action with a specific purpose: to secure relief from a distressing situation, the long and frequent absence of her parents. Before, she had remembered herself as having been unable to improve the conditions that oppressed her, but now she saw that she had actually done her best to persuade her family to change their ways. Thereafter, when she read stories to her son, she always remembered that this was the experience through which she had gained a more positive image of herself as a child, and with it of herself as a person.

What is said here in respect to story-reading hold true, with the appropriate variations, for many other aspects of child-rearing. Comprehending one's childhood experiences as an adult can provide new and important insights. When this happens, both parent and child have a significant experience through what they are doing together; although they are on different levels, the differences are of less importance than the fact that each is beholden to the other for having gained new insights, and for having provided the setting for such growth. The element of equality in such a shared experience is especially important to the child, because each participant becomes provider and beneficiary at the same time.

Many childhood experiences have become, of necessity, deeply buried in the unconscious during the process of developing one's adult personality. This separation or distancing from one's childhood is no longer needed when the adult personality is fully and securely formed, but by then, the distancing has for most people become a part of that very personality. Separation from one's childhood is temporarily necessary, but if it is permanently maintained it deprives us of inner experiences which, when restored to us, can keep us young in spirit and also permit greater closeness to our children.

23

THE HISTORICAL RELEVANCE OF HUMAN CHILDHOOD

Erik H. Erikson

≈

In keeping with the theme of improved parenting, Freudian psychoanalyst Erik H. Erikson gives us the context from which psychological restoration of the child has arisen, namely the work of Sigmund Freud. A man of indomitable intellect and courage, Freud actually resurrected childhood from its submerged status. 'He invented,' says Erikson, 'a specific method for the detection of that which universally spoils the genius of the child in every human being.'

This chapter pays tribute to the pioneering contribution Freud made, to his perception of the creative potentials in the child, both inner and outer. An excerpt from the author's collection of essays Insight and Responsibility, *it is a portion of a talk he delivered on May 6, 1956, at the University of Frankfurt, in celebration of the 100th birthday of Freud.*

The real value of psychoanalysis is to improve parenting.

— SIGMUND FREUD

That shift in self-awareness [that Freud's discoveries brought about] cannot remain confined to professional partnerships such as the observer's with the observed, or the doctor's with his patient. It implies a fundamentally new *ethical orientation of adult man's relationship to childhood*: to his own childhood, now behind and within him; to his own child before him; and to every man's children around him.

The fields dealing with man's historical dimension are far apart in their appraisal of childhood. Academic minds, whose long-range perspectives can ignore the everyday urgencies of the curative and educative arts, blithely go on writing whole world histories without a trace of women and children, whole anthropological accounts without any reference to the varying styles of childhood. As they record what causal chain can be discerned in political and economic realities, they seem to shrug off as historical accidents due to 'human nature' such fears and rages in leaders and masses as are clearly the residue of childish emotions. True, scholars may have been justly repelled by the first enthusiastic intrusion of doctors of the mind into their ancient disciplines. But their refusal to consider the *historical relevance of human childhood* can be due only to that deeper and more universal emotional aversion and repression which Freud himself foresaw. On the other hand, it must be admitted that in clinical literature (and in literature turned altogether clinical) aversion has given place to a faddish preoccupation with the more sordid aspects of childhood as though they were the final determinants of human destiny.

Neither of these trends can hinder the emergence of a new truth, namely, that the collective life of mankind, in all its historical lawfulness, is fed by the energies and images of successive generations; and that each generation brings to human fate an inescapable conflict between its ethical and rational aims and its infantile fixations. This conflict helps drive man toward the astonishing things he does – and it can be his undoing. It is a condition of man's humanity – and the prime cause of his bottomless inhumanity. For whenever and wherever man abandons his ethical position, he does so only at the cost of massive regressions endangering the very safeguards of his nature.

Freud revealed this regressive trend by dissecting its pathological manifestations in individuals. But he also pointed to what is so largely and so regularly lost in the ambivalent gains of civilization: he spoke of 'the child's radiant intelligence' – the naive zest, the natural courage, the unconditional faith of childhood, which become submerged by excessive ambitions, by fearful teaching and by limited and limiting information.

Now and again, we are moved to say that a genius preserved in himself the clear eye of the child. But do we not all too easily justify man's mass regressions by pointing to the occasional appearance of leaders of genius? Yet, we know (and are morbidly eager to know) how tortured a genius is driven to destroy with one hand as he created with the other.

In Freud, a genius turned a new instrument of observation back on his childhood, back on all childhood. He invented a specific method for the detection of that which universally spoils the genius of the child in every human being. In teaching us to recognize the daimonic evil in children, he urged us not to smother the creatively good. Since then, the nature of growth has been studied by ingenious observers all over the world: never before has mankind known more about its own past – phylogenetic and ontogeny. Thus, we may see Freud as a pioneer in a self-healing, balancing trend in human awareness. For now that technical invention readies itself to conquer the moon, generations to come may well be in need of being more enlightened in their drivenness, and more conscious of the laws of individuality; they may well need to appreciate and preserve more genuine childlikeness in order to avoid utter cosmic childishness.

$$\bigcirc\!\!\!\!24$$

OUT OF THE MOUTHS OF BABES
Theodore Reik

≈

This anecdotal piece is a folksy acknowledgment of the inner child by a consummate psychoanalyst, one of Freud's most brilliant disciples. Theodore Reik says that the psychoanalyst must search for the child in the man, in himself, and in others. 'It would be a serious mistake on the part of the analyst,' he says, 'to underestimate the power of the ideas and ideals of the child who continues his existence in the adult.' Any parent or potential parent can enjoy the wisdom of this kind man's words. This essay is a chapter from Listening with the Third Ear, *the author's fascinating account of the inner experience of a psychoanalyst, first published in 1948.*

Not everything the analyst labours to uncover is repressed material. The area of the unconscious reaches far beyond the sphere attributed to it by many psychoanalytic lecturers. It includes material which is displaced, distorted and disavowed. There are further events and emotions that were never conscious because they happened when the person was too young to grasp their meaning. They belong to the prehistoric period of the individual personality.

We grown-ups are so far removed from the peculiar ways and forms of our childhood that they have become strange to us. Everybody has experiences of this sort. Our parents or old friends of the family have told us that as a small boy we said or did this or that odd thing. In most cases we do not remember the statement or action. And even when we do, we can no longer discover why we acted or spoke like that. We cannot doubt the truth of the story but we do not recognize ourselves in the picture it shows to us. We have to admit that we were this little boy or that little girl, but we cannot acknowledge any psychological identity with our past self. It has vanished like the snows of yesteryear.

Memories of this order come up many times in psychoanalysis. They are conscious in that their content can be ascertained, but their meaning has been lost. This meaning was not repressed. It grew strange because a man cannot recover the thought-processes peculiar to childhood. Loss of an old way of feeling or thinking can be observed already in children themselves. A little girl of eight cannot believe that, once when she was three, she had wanted to catch a snail and had been worried that the snail would run away. If, after some years, children cannot recognize themselves, how can we expect men and women to accept their psychological identity with an infant? The activities, joys, and griefs, the little games children sometimes remember represent their true selves, but the self from the past seems foreign. They are astonished at themselves and cannot imagine what made them so odd or say such funny things. The psychoanalyst frequently has a difficult time with memories of this kind, since no conscious effort on his part, either, can help him regain infantile ways of looking at the world. He would have to study children for a long time and with particular psychological skill in order to understand what his patients tell him about some episodes of their childhood days. Not longing for paradise lost, but his wish for psychological comprehension reminds him of the song by Brahms that goes: 'Oh, if I but knew the way back, the dear way back to childhood days . . .'

Sometimes we realize how remote we are from the child's way of feeling and thinking when we hear the funny things children say. I do not mean the 'bright sayings,' but remarks and comments that we call naive, which make us laugh because we are so charmed. I heard that a little girl on the beach complained about her playmate: 'Mother, Bobby should not take so much water out of the sea. The sea will become quite empty.' The other day I saw a cartoon showing a painter seated before his canvas in a field. He is immersed in his work and pays no attention to the little farm girl who is an attentive observer. The child interrupts the silence suddenly: 'I have had the measles . . .' The two instances, that of the little girl who is worried lest her playmate exhaust the sea, and that of the other child who wants to appear important and opens a conversation with the interesting news that she once had the measles, represent a whole group of sayings that show how differently the world reflects itself in little heads.

Sometimes, in the middle of psychoanalysis, memories occur that puzzle us because we cannot immediately understand what they mean, nor what they meant to the child who twenty or thirty years later is now a patient in our consultation room. Sometimes it is easy enough to grasp their meaning; we have no difficulty in putting ourselves in the emotional world of the child because we find ourselves echoes of the same feeling when we dig down deep enough in our own memories. I believe everybody will hear an echo when I tell what a patient remembered from her childhood.

When she was a very little girl she sneaked from her bedroom into the dining room in the dark because she wanted to know how the furniture, the table, the chairs, and the lamps behaved when they were alone, without people around. She was convinced that the room and the furniture would behave differently when they thought they were not being observed. Children's animistic conceptions of the world are further illustrated by another patient who remembered that he once asked his older brother whether the telegraphic poles speak with the lampposts. We understand immediately that the hum of the wires suggested the question.

Every psychoanalyst has met difficulties dealing with the childhood memories of patients who do not themselves understand the meaning of their recollections. A woman remembers, for example, that as a little girl she once began to cry when her father led her into the lift of a hotel in which the family, interrupting a journey, was to spend the night. Her recollection tells her that the lift was more spacious than any she has seen since and that there were plush benches along three sides. She is also sure that this was the first time she had ever been in an elevator. She clearly remembers that she was desperate when she entered it and that her father tried in vain to console her and stop her tears. Although the recollection recurred several times during her analysis, we could not figure out why she had behaved so strangely at that moment. She denied being scared when the lift began to move because she was already sobbing before that happened. We – the patient and I – were both puzzled until all at once it occurred to her that she must have thought that the spacious lift was a room, and that she, on this, her first visit to a hotel, would have to sleep in this room with her father. She had thought of the upholstered benches as couches. The memory was, of course, significant for the analytic understanding of the patient's relationship with her father.

In other cases the special meaning of a child's behaviour or talk is not so easily grasped. There are times when no learning, no expenditure of conscious intellectual energy, and no hard thinking can penetrate to these lost ways of a child's emotional processes. There is no other path to this hidden area but unconscious identification with the patient as a child.

A man remembered that as a boy he once behaved very strangely on a bus with his mother. A woman who had stepped down from the bus while it was in motion, fell to the pavement without being seriously hurt. The little boy had protested desperately that he had not pushed the woman down. Actually he had been standing at some distance from her so that it would have been impossible for him to attempt anything of the sort. There was no doubt that his memory of the incident was correct. The analytic interpretation of this childhood memory started from the assumption that in some way his emotions must have been appropriate. We learned later that at this time he felt very hostile and aggressive toward his mother, who stood beside him in the bus. In a serious marital conflict between his parents, he had sided with his father. It seemed likely that his hostility against his mother had led to aggressive wishes, which reappeared when the accident on the bus occurred. His feelings toward his mother were displaced upon a stranger. The woman who was hurt was unconsciously thought of as a mother-substitute. When she was hurt he must have felt guilty, as if he were really responsible because he had entertained evil wishes against his mother. It was as if his wishes had become reality in the accident to the other woman. There are many instances that show grown-up people behaving similarly when a crime they wished for is actually committed by others.

I am choosing a relatively simple instance from my psycho-analytic practice in order to demonstrate that only a return to the thought-world of the child can solve the puzzle of a memory that has become unintelligible to the person himself.

A British patient remembered that as a small boy he had said something to his sister (two years older than he) that does not make sense to him now. He recalled the situation precisely. They stood at the window of their country house and it was early evening. They looked at the cows coming home along the village street. The little boy turned to his sister and asked her, 'Can you imagine Uncle Harry being a cow?' Well, that sounds silly enough, and the patient was inclined to dismiss the remembered sentence as one of the funny thoughts children frequently have. He remembered that his sister had roared with laughter and quoted his saying teasingly to him later on.

I tried to convince him that the sentence must have made sense then. His associations seemed to lead him far away, to later memories of Uncle Harry and Aunt Mabel, his wife, to other relatives, and to the contrast between life in the country and in London. The only fact that seemed to be worthy of consideration in these associations was that shortly afterward Aunt Mabel had a baby. I guessed that something in the child's remark alluded to this event, perhaps to the pregnancy, which the little boy had noticed. But I still could not figure out what the sentence, 'Can you imagine Uncle Harry being a cow?' meant. Nothing indicated that the boy had suspicions about Uncle Harry's lack of masculinity. On the contrary, this particular uncle came to be known as quite a philanderer. We did not arrive at a satisfactory solution of the puzzling memory that day. There was only the vague idea that the sentence might have something to do with Aunt Mabel's pregnancy.

The recognition of its meaning occurred to me much later, when the patient, on another occasion and in another context, mentioned that cows sometimes behave strangely in the spring. They jump at each other's backs as if imitating the bull. Everything suddenly became clear. The children, the boy and his sister, must have spoken before about what the grown-ups do in sexual intercourse and compared it with the playful sexual behaviour of the cows. The question 'Can you imagine Uncle Harry being a cow?' had thus the meaning, 'Can you imagine Uncle Harry behaving like a cow jumping at another cow's back?' It therefore meant: 'Can you imagine Uncle Harry in sexual intercourse?' The children might at this time have noticed Aunt Mabel's pregnancy and their thoughts turned to the sexual experiences of their relatives. The boy's question is of a sexual nature. It makes sense now after we have translated it from the child's language into expressions now familiar to us. The laughter of his sister, we understand now, was not only determined by the way the question was put. The girl laughed as an adult would at a sexual allusion that is comical.

It turned out that this interpretation of an unintelligible childhood memory became crucial in the analysis of this patient. He had denied that he had any knowledge of sexual processes before a certain age. No longer understood by the adult, here was perfect proof that he knew what the sexual secret was before that age. His parents postponed sexual information: they seemed to wait with it indefinitely, 'until the cows came home.' But the children knew the secret long before, and the return of the cows only gave them an opportunity to review what they had learned. Often enough just such uncomprehended childhood memories, when psychoanalytically interpreted, give important clues to the life history and the character-formation of our patients.

The child is the father of the man. In reality, there are three persons in the consultation room of the psychoanalyst: the analyst, the patient as he is now, and the child who continues his existence within the patient. We recognized how old childhood convictions live subterraneously side by side with the opinions and views of the adult. Old values consciously discarded long ago operate in the dark and influence the lives of our patients. It would be a serious mistake on the part of the analyst to underestimate the power of the ideas and ideals of the child who continues his existence in the adult. They rise sometimes quite suddenly from their submergence into the bright daylight of conscious living. An adult feels suddenly afraid of the dark and imagines that a picture has come alive. He has revived the animistic belief of childhood days, when every inanimate object had a life and soul of its own. To our astonishment we often realize that childhood beliefs remain intact in us, are not dead and buried, only submerged.

It would be erroneous to neglect this phenomenon. The psychoanalyst must search for the child in the man, in himself, and in others. He will not understand the depth of the emotions if he is not aware of these vestiges of childhood in maturity. Those childhood ideas need not be childish because they are childlike. Some of them are built around a nucleus of early-understood truths and reveal an astonishingly clear vision of the social environment within the narrow circle that makes up the child's world.

About a hundred years ago there lived in Vienna a brilliant satirist and actor, John N. Nestroy, whose witty plays the Viennese loved. In one of them a figure speaks about cobblers' apprentices, who were known as very clever and impudent youngsters, prematurely wise, like the urchins of New York's lower East Side. 'I would like to know,' says this figure, 'what becomes of all those clever, witty cobblers' boys?' Freud, who frequently quoted this line, replied, 'They became stupid shoemakers.' Freud said that at a certain point in childhood sexual repression begins to operate and puts an end to the natural and brilliant intelligence of the child. I think this answer is one-sided. The child learns also to accept authority and to suppress its natural aggressions, rebelliousness, and independence of thinking. Nevertheless, it is true that frequently very bright children suddenly show at a certain age a kind of weakening of their natural powers of observation and judgment, as if the adjustment to society forces them to sacrifice these early personal qualities.

These ideas of children, we said, often contain a grain of truth presented in a childlike manner that sometimes appears funny. A patient was enlightened about the sexual processes by his parents at an early age. Nevertheless, the boy puzzled about the sexuality of men because he tried to imagine it in terms of the animals and the flowers about which his parents had spoken. He imagined that a husband knocks at the bedroom door of his wife on certain evenings and says, 'Mary, the seed is here.' There is no blinking the fact that there is a certain biological truth in the boy's conception. When you remove the trimmings and arrive at the core, you will realize that as little Johnny sees the world, so it is.

We are often reminded in our analytic work that the child lives on in the man and the woman. Life itself bears witness to such survival. When my daughter Miriam was a little girl and we took her to the dentist for the second time, she crawled under a desk and no amount of persuasion could overcome her anxiety. Her mother appealed to her in vain, 'Do you think that a lady would crawl on all fours under a desk in a dentist's office?' My little girl answered, 'They would like to, but they are too big.'

The Wounded Father Within

Samuel Osherson

≈

This touching piece comes from psychotherapist Samuel Osherson's very readable book about unfinished business between men and their fathers, Finding our Fathers. *Although it focuses specifically on a man's inner conflicts, the feeling tones transcend gender: feelings of abandonment, longing, and neediness that both men and women have trouble accepting in themselves. 'Because we have not been more able to nurture the needy, vulnerable parts of ourselves,' Osherson says, 'we carry around within an angry, sad, childlike residue, which often shapes our adult relationships.'*

Yet this essay is specific to men and to male vulnerability: 'My work with men convinces me that there is a male vulnerability in relationships that can be traced back to our early childhood experiences of separation and loss.' Men have a task, suggests Osherson, one that no doubt parallels women's task, to let go of 'distorted and painful misidentifications' with their parents. The clear message is that we must heal the wounded parent within in order to become more nurturing parents to our inner and our outer children. Osherson suggests that this is not only possible, but necessary in order to feel empowered in our lives. This is a liberating note on which to end this book, for both men and women.

Current family situations are rekindling issues of separation and loss that men have not had a chance to work out in growing up. The issues centre on our own vulnerability and dependency as men; uncertainties about our identities and about what it means to be a man; and the needs for support and reassurance many of our own fathers masked beneath the surface of traditional family arrangements and passed along – unmet – to their sons. The normal demands of family life today are powerfully shaped by men's early experiences with father and mother, and by the lessons learned from those experiences about what it means to be male.

Often men's reactions to their wives' involvement with work or with their children reflect childlike feelings of abandonment and the hunger for parental attention and nurturance. When a wife goes off to work, we may feel without realizing it some of the vulnerability and anger we experienced as a child wanting to hold on to Mother and trying to let go of her. The fact that many of our fathers went off to work every day, leaving us alone with our mothers, increased their importance to us and weakened our fathers' roles as the transitional figures necessary to complete the normal process of separation-individuation from mother. And, too, having rarely observed his father taking a secondary place to his mother, a man may not know how confidently to support a wife who works.

One day a successful thirty-eight-year-old lawyer in a luxurious Manhattan office was telling me about his marriage. That confident, engaging man's tone suddenly became plaintive: 'Without wanting to sound patronizing, I always assumed any wife of mine would have a career of her own. I just never anticipated it would be like *this*.' The *this* referred to the mix of loss, feelings of abandonment, and unmet dependency needs he felt on evenings and weekends when his wife devoted her time and energy to her career rather than to him.

The plaintive lawyer was not alone in his feelings of abandonment. A successful university professor also talked about the darker side of a dual-career marriage. Thoughtful and gentle, he was clearly proud of his wife's achievements in becoming established in a counselling centre now that the children were older. Yet he stopped at one point in our talk and reflected that 'confidence is an illusion, you know, and I need my wife to bolster my belief that I *can* be successful, get the writing done I need every week, publish those articles in the tenure race. Since my wife's been working she has much less time to pay attention to me, and I know maintaining confidence in myself is a continuing struggle for me.'

Similarly the arrival of children may rekindle some of our wishes to be taken care of in that blissful way, as well as our desperate desire to prove that we have given up such wishes and are independent. Becoming a father may also spark an identity struggle for the man who, lacking role models in his past, is not at all sure how to be a father who *is* present for his children.

A business executive told me with pride how involved he had been in the birth of his daughter. Yet he spoke sheepishly about how betrayed he felt by his wife's continuing commitment to her demanding career as a lawyer now that their first child was born. For ten years they had shared most of their spare time. Now with his wife juggling her law practice and the care of a one-year-old, it seemed to this man as if 'she has time for everything but me.' Spreading his hands in front of him in a shy gesture of embarrassed neediness, he exclaimed, 'The new baby is doing fine, but how about the old baby? Me!'

There are numerous circumstances in adult life that leave us feeling childlike – needy, helpless, powerless to change things. In growing up men have great difficulty coming to terms with dependency and vulnerability, often because our fathers showed us that such feelings were unacceptable, that to be successful men, to win our fathers' approval, achievement was what counted. Our vulnerability and dependency became papered over by an instrumental, competent pose as adults or by focusing on what we do well: our ability to achieve in the work world.

Yet, despite our self-assurance about work, uncertainties abound there as well. Much of the uncertainty concerns how much of a commitment to make to career success; there is discomfort with the sense of self that the competitive workplace fosters. One puzzled Washington official, the associate director of a powerful government agency, said to me in dismay, after an interview filled with heroic stories of success: 'One major concern does bother me . . . I feel more and more like a well-honed tool for my boss.' Then the clue: 'He's like a father to me.' Many men today wonder, how much like my boss or my mentor do I have to live my life?

Clearly the capacity for autonomy, independence, and a separate identity is essential for healthy adult life. But our emphasis on those qualities in boys obscures the struggle they experience in separating from mother and father. Because we have not been more able to nurture the needy, vulnerable parts of ourselves, we carry them around within an angry, sad, childlike residue, which often shapes our adult relationships with wife, children, boss, and our own parents.

Men used to be protected from their unfinished business with mothers and fathers by the traditional division of labour. But those of us who have grown up during the decades in which the women's movement became a powerful force are experiencing social changes of epic proportions: the clear and direct movement of women into positions of greater power and quality in the workplace, and the movement of men into family life. Regardless of whether men truly are taking greater part in family life (and the evidence suggests there is indeed some small movement in that direction), men are not being sheltered from parts of life they had to repress or devalue in order to grow up.[1] Today, when a wife goes to work, when a baby arrives, or when the family reorganizes upon the departure of children to college, the man is less able to turn to traditional sex roles and expectations. He is often put back in touch with feelings of helplessness and powerlessness that he did not entirely master as a child and is caught by surprise, often feeling a pain he can't really understand.

The volatile nature of this situation is exacerbated by the mutual distrust between the sexes. In this time of changing sex roles men and women often look at each other with suspicion. Many women feel impatient with men's resistance to change, feeling that men are just trying to hold onto their power in relationships or are hopelessly deficient in their capacity for intimacy. Men in turn often become defensive around women, feeling accused and criticized by the women's movement. Some men then try to hide the powerlessness or incompetence they feel behind an emotionally armoured posture. In many marriages today neither spouse has much sympathy or patience for the husband's childlike fears and anxieties as both try to develop new work-family arrangements in their life together.

Both sexes today seem to share a stereotype: that men are distant and unconnected, while relationships are the female speciality. Many people believe that women care more than men about love. Yet the division of the sexes into men as rational and women as feelers is simply untrue, a harmful and dangerous myth. For all that feminism has contributed to our culture, it has also brought with it a subtle idealization of women and a less subtle denigration or misunderstanding of men. My work with men convinces me that there is a male vulnerability in relationships that can be traced back to our early childhood experiences of separation and loss. The key to the unfinished business of manhood is unravelling and letting go of our distorted and painful misidentifications with our fathers.

In order to understand men's adult conflicts with work and intimacy in today's world we have to understand the ways the boy comes to experience himself, women, and men, as well as his ongoing relationships as a grown man with the mother and father of his childhood.

It is possible to heal the wounded father within. Men are not passive victims; much of our wish to be more involved with our children or to become mentors at work, much of the hunger for intimacy that many men reveal, is actually an attempt to heal the wound within ourselves, so that we can become more confident and nurturing as men. As we learn more about the adult life cycle, we are discovering that people reexperience issues of separation and individuation from parents throughout adulthood. Dr George Vaillant, the director of the Grant Study, a longitudinal study of Harvard men, concludes: 'Over and over throughout the study, the lesson was repeated: childhood does not end at 21. Even these men, selected in college for psychological health, continued for the next two decades to wean themselves from their parents.[2]

I have talked to enough men to know that both work and family can be a healing experience for men; particularly in our experiences as nurturing husbands and fathers, we can heal our relationship with our own fathers and mothers, letting go of oppressive fantasies about what happened to us growing up male. Yet too there are many men who continue to act out with bosses and wives unfinished business with their fathers and mothers.

Healing the wounded father within is a psychological and social process that unfolds over time and involves exploring one's own history, testing out and exploring a new sense of self, and understanding the complex crosscurrents within our families which affected us as we grew up. Certainly it means tolerating the angry and needy feelings that our work and family life provoke today, and not trying to discard too quickly those uncomfortable, childlike feelings of powerlessness beneath the pose of male competence and identity.

THE WOUNDED FATHER WITHIN

I saw this little boy within myself one summer day at our cabin in New Hampshire several years ago. It happened during a period when I felt stuck and frustrated in my work. Despite the sunshine outside, I was hard at work inside on a book whose point had completely escaped me. A sinking feeling came over me. I was walking through snowdrifts of words, knee-high, bored by what I was saying, angry and frustrated underneath.

My wife was watching my daily melodrama of frustration. One morning, to cheer me up, she suggested we take a hike on one of our favourite trails.

'No, I can't. I want to finish this chapter, Julie. I can't take time off,' I replied through gritted teeth.

'Well, how's it going?'

'Terrible. I hate this writing. Why am I doing this? Does it have to be so hard?'

I saw an expression of sorrow, irritation, and boredom cross Julie's face, the sort of look people get when they see those they love hurting themselves again. And in the same way. For the nth time. This time she unloaded:

'You've said this a million times, Sam. When are you going to listen to yourself? Why don't you take time off and think things through? You're not sure what you want to say in that book, or even if you're going about it in the right way.

'You're like a kid walking down the street pulling this red wagon full of rocks behind you, crying and asking for help.' As boys look to mother so too men look to their wives to provide us comfort and nurture without our having to take our pain seriously. As a little boy I would go to my mother with my pain (feeling embarrassed and inappropriate), but I never was able satisfactorily to go to my father with it.

I appreciated Julie's concern and ultimately did take her advice to put the book aside. Yet in identifying my expectations and the game I was playing, she was also calling off the game. I felt shamed and angry. An angry inner voice shouted back:

'You owe me!'

Here was the traditional bargain men make with women: I work hard and suffer, and she will be sympathetic and comforting and reassuring. Often men's inability to let go of mother seems like a consolation prize for the absence of a reassuring sense of father.

There I was in this beautiful New Hampshire countryside, suffering – and she was supposed to comfort me, not challenge me to grow up! She wasn't living up to her part in my passion play.

If my anger then had more voice, I might have said, 'You're a woman, you wouldn't understand – you can't possibly know what it feels like to be a man.'

An image of my father watching TV sullenly after a hard day's work comes to mind. My mother seemingly more cheerful, energetic, my father looking beaten down in a way that couldn't really be talked about. He was, after all, a big success at work, but the sense of entrapment he felt was not an appropriate topic for family talk, or so it seemed to me at the time.

To my shock, sitting in that summer cabin several years ago, I saw that as angry as I was at my father's sad, powerless face in our house, that part of him was in me as well. And my wife had pointed to an angry, trapped part of myself that I was afraid to confront.

In some remote recess where we see ourselves clearly, I bumped into a frightening truth: I felt powerless to take control of my life. I was making Julie into my mother while I'd become my father in this passion play, or at least my image of my father. John Updike's lesson came to mind, explored in Rabbi Angstrom's journey through adulthood: The fate of American men is to remain little boys, never gaining their freedom from mother or father.

For men to feel empowered, to come to terms with our identities and deal honestly with our wives, our children, and the demands of careers, means healing the wounded father within, an angry-sad version of ourselves that feels unloved and unlovable. That means coming to terms with that distorted person we never knew well enough: father.

Epilogue: 'May You Stay Forever Young'

≈

The child [within] is therefore . . . both beginning and end, an initial and a terminal creature. The initial creature existed before man was, and the terminal creature will be when man is not. Psychologically speaking, this means that the 'child' symbolizes the pre-conscious and the post-conscious essence of man. His preconscious essence is the unconscious state of earliest childhood; his post-conscious essence is an anticipation by analogy of life after death. In this idea the all-embracing nature of psychic wholeness is expressed.

– C.G. Jung

The child survives within us, joined to us for life: perennially the child, fully alive, an inner possibility awaiting our full and conscious acknowledgment. However, to fixate on the inner child or over-identify with the archtype is inappropriate, psychologically debilitating, just as any unconscious identification with an idea is dangerous.

But to embrace the child, embody it consciously as a healthy expression of our psychic wholeness, is to receive the inner child's gift.

The process begins somewhere, probably in the obvious and the commonplace. A simple recognition, a playful gleam or a grin, and there you go!

At heart, we are all simply children. 'We are but older children, dear,' said Lewis Carroll in *Through the Looking Glass*, 'Who fret to find our bedtime near.'

Alice Miller, in *Pictures of Childhood*, confessed her moment of choice in this way:

Probably I, too, would have remained trapped by this compulsion to
protect the parents . . . had I not come into contact with the Child
Within Me, who appeared late in my life, wanting to tell me her
secret . . . now I was standing at an open door . . . filled with an
adult's fear of the darkness . . . But I could not close the door and
leave the child alone until my death . . . I made a decision that was to
change my life profoundly . . . to put my trust in this nearly autistic
being who had survived the isolation of decades.

I learned the lesson of embracing the child within at a time when I
was most vulnerable. It was the sudden death of my father; I was
twenty-one. I came by the experience through the words of two
loving friends who sent me a telegram. It was an instantaneous
recognition, as soon as I read the words:

Life is a child's spirit within you which does not answer to the ques-
tion why, but she is a loving being and you must embrace her no
matter how she misbehaves. She is joyful and sorrowful, beautiful
and enriching. Yet remember she is always for you (never against).

$$\approx$$

When you experience the child within, it brings you into the world.
We are all here to live out the child's destiny.

'The great ship,' said Whitman, 'the ship of the World. Mariners,
Mariners, gather your skills.'

NOTES

≈

ABBREVIATIONS USED IN NOTES

CW Collected Works of C.G. Jung (Bollingen Series XX), translated by R.F.C. Hull and edited by H. Read, M. Fordham, G. Adler, and William McGuire (Princeton, N.J.: Princeton University Press; and London: Routledge and Kegan Paul, 1953-) cited below by volume number and paragraph or page.
MDR C.G. Jung, *Memories, Dreams, and Reflections* (New York: Random House, 1961).
PC 'The Psychology of the Child Archetype,' in *CW*, vol. 9, part I, *The Archetypes and the Collective Unconscious.*

Introduction/Abrams
All contributors' quotes are from the sources of their respective essays, except where otherwise noted. The subheadings are quoted as follows: 'Where is the life we have lost in living?' – T.S. Eliot; 'It takes a long time to become young.' – Picasso; 'Sing, Muse, the Child!' – Homer

Chapter opening quote: C.G. Jung, *CW*, vol. 17, p. 286.

1. C.G. Jung, *CW*, vol. 16, *The Practice of Psychotherapy* (Princeton, N.J.: Bollingen, 1954), p. 32.
2. Culver Barker, 'Healing the Child Within,' in *The Wake of Jung* (London: Coventure, 1983), p. 48-49.
3. Ronald W. Clark, *Einstein: The Life and Times* (New York: Abrams, 1984), p. 13.
4. Paul A. Schlipp, ed., *Albert Einstein: Philosopher-Scientist* (New York: Tudor, 1951), p. 17 (as quoted in the Goertzels' *Cradles of Eminence;* see bibliography).
5. As quoted in Marshall McLuhan and Quentin Fiore, *The Medium Is the Massage* (New York: Bantam Books, 1967), p. 93.
6. Johann Wolfgang von Goethe, 'The Holy Longing,' 1814, trans. Robert

Bly, as printed in *News of the Universe* (San Francisco: Sierra Club Books, 1980), p. 70.

7. C.G. Jung, 1932, from the Introduction to M. Esther Harding's *The Way of All Women* (New York: C.G. Jung Foundation, 1970), p. xvii.

8. William Butler Yeats, 'The Second Coming,' *Selected Poems and Two Plays of William Butler Yeats*, ed. M.L. Rosenthal (New York: Collier, 1962), p. 91.

9. 'To Find Our Life,' after Ramon Medina Silva, as published in *Technicians of the Sacred*, ed. Jerome Rothenberg (Berkeley: University of California Press, 1968, 1985), p. 232.

Chapter 1/Sullwold

1. George Bernard Shaw, 'Essay on Parents and Children,' in *Prefaces* (London: Constable & Co., 1934), p. 47.

2. William Wordsworth, 'Ode: Intimations of Immortality . . .' in Laurel Poetry Series (New York: Dell, 1968), p. 115.

3. *PC*, p. 170.

Chapter 2/Jung

1. It may not be superfluous to point out that lay prejudice is always inclined to identify the child motif with the concrete experience 'child,' as though the real child were the cause and precondition of the existence of the child motif. In psychological reality, however, the empirical idea 'child' is simply the means (and not the only one) by which to express a psychic fact that cannot be formulated more exactly. Hence by the same token the mythological idea of the child is emphatically not a copy of the empirical child but a *symbol* clearly recognizable as such: it is a wonder-child, a divine child, begotten, born, and brought up in quite extraordinary circumstances, and not – this is the point – a human child. Its deeds are as miraculous or monstrous as its nature and physical constitution. Only on account of these highly unemphical properties is it necessary to speak of a 'child motif' at all. Moreover, the mythological 'child' has various forms: now a god, giant, Tom Thumb, animal, etc., and this points to a causality that is anything but rational or concretely human. The same is true of the 'father' and 'mother' archetypes which, mythologically speaking, are equally irrational symbols.

2. C.G. Jung, *Psychological Types*, in *CW*, vol. 6 (alternative source: trans. by H.G. Baynes [London and New York: 1923]) Def. 48; and *Two Essays on Analytical Psychology*, *CW*, vol. 7, 2d ed. (New York and London: 1966), Index, s.v. 'persona.'

3. – *Psychological Types*, in *CW*, vol. 6, ch. V, 3: 'The Significance of the Uniting Symbol.'

4. – *Psychology and Alchemy*, in *CW*, vol. 12, 2d ed. (New York and London: 1968).

5. – *Two Essays on Analytical Psychology*, in *CW*, vol. 7, pars. 399ff.

6. – *Psychology and Alchemy*, in *CW*, vol. 12, pars. 328ff.

Chapter 3/Singer

1. William Blake, *A Song of Liberty*.

2. *PC*, in *CW* vol. 9, p. i.

3. Cf. also Bacchus, Dionysus.

4. Marie-Louise von Franz, *The Problem of the Puer Aeternus*.

5. Ibid.

6. A full discussion of this archetype and the preceding one appears in James Hillman's essay, 'Senex and Puer: An Aspect of the Historical and Psychological Present,' in *Eranos-Jahrbuch* XXXVI/1967 (Zurich: Rhein-Verlag, 1968).

Chapter 4/Metzner

1. Ramana Maharshi, *The Spiritual Teachings of Ramana Maharshi*, with foreword by C.G. Jung (Boulder, Colo.: Shambhala, 1972).

2. *PC*, p. 164. Jung continues: 'In the psychology of the individual, the 'child' paves the way for a future change of personality. In the individuation process, it anticipates the figure that comes from the synthesis of conscious and unconscious elements in the personality. It is therefore a symbol which unites the opposites; a mediator, a bringer of healing, that is, one who makes whole.'

3. Michael Harner, *The Way of the Shaman* (San Francisco: Harper and Row, 1980).

4. Meister Eckhart, *Meister Eckhart*, trans. Raymond B. Blakney (New York: Harper and Row, 1941).

5. Fritz Meier, 'The Transformation of Man in Mystical Islam,' in *Man and Transformation*, ed. Joseph Campbell; Eranos Yearbooks, vol. 5; Bollingen Series, no. 30 (Princeton, N.J.: Princeton University Press, 1964).

6. King James Version Bible: New Testament, John 3:3.

7. C.G. Jung, 'Concerning Rebirth,' in *The Archetypes and the Collective Unconscious*, p. 121. *CW*, vol. 9, part I.

8. Evelyn Underhill, 'Treatise of the Resurrection,' in *Mysticism* (New York: New American Library, 1955).

9. *PC*, pp. 151-181.

10. Chuang Tsu, *Inner Chapters*, trans. Gia-Fu Feng and Jane English (New York: Random House, 1974).

Chapter 5/Hillman

1. P. Aries, *Centuries of Childhood* [trans. R. Baldrick from *L'Enfant et la vie familiale sous l'ancien regime*, Paris: Plon, 1960] (New York: Knopf and London: Cape, 1962), Part I.

2. M. Foucault, *Madness and Civilization* [trans. R. Howard from *Histoire de*

la Folie, Paris: Plon, 1961] (New York: Pantheon, 1965).
3. S. Freud, *Collected Papers*, vol. II (London: Hogarth, 1924, 1925), p. 177.
4. S. Freud, *New Introductory Lectures on Psycho-Analysis*, trans. Sprott (London: Hogarth, 1933, 1957), p. 190.
5. Rousseau, *Emile*, II.
6. Freud, 'From the history of an infantile neurosis (1918),' in *Collected Papers*, vol. III (London: Hogarth, 1924, 1925), pp. 577-578.
7. Cf. *Collected papers*, vol. III., p. 470: the last paragraph of Freud's discussion of the Schreber case.
8. Freud, *New Introductory Lectures*, p. 190.
9. Freud, *Collected papers*, vol. II, p. 188.
10. *CW*, vol. 9, I, 2d ed. (London: Routledge, 1968), p. 161fn.
11. *CW*, vol. 9, I para. 300.
12. *CW*, vol. 5, passim.
13. *CW*, vol. 6, para. 422f, 442.
14. Freud, *Collected papers*, vol. III, p. 562f.
15. *CW*, vol. 9,I, para. 276.
16. *CW*, vols. 14 and 16, passim.
17. *CW*, 331c and following.
18. St. Augustine, *Enar. in Ps.* XLIV, I.
19. St. Augustine, *Confessions*, I, 7, 11.
20. Freud, *New Introductory Lectures*, p. 106.

Chapter 6/Woodman
1. *King James Version Bible*: Psalms 118:22.
2. C.G. Jung, 'The Tavistock Lectures,' in *CW*, vol. 18, *The Symbolic Life*, para. 389.

Chapter 9/Covitz
1. Maria Montessori, *The Child in the Family* (New York: Hearst Corporation, Aron Books, 1970), pp. 14-15.
2. Alice Miller, *Prisoners of Childhood* (retitled *Drama of the Gifted Child*) (New York: Basic Books, 1981), p. 69.
3. *CW*, vol. 17, *The Development of Personality*, pp. 40-41.
4. *Ibid.*, p. 44.
5. *Ibid.*
6. John Bowlby, *Child Care and the Growth of Love* (Middlesex, England: Penguin Books, Ltd., 1965), pp. 77-78.
7. C.G. Jung, 'On Psychical Energy,' in *CW*, vol. 8, p. 52.

Chapter 10/Miller
1. M. Mahler, *On Human Symbiosis and the Vicissitudes of Individuation* (New York: International Universities Press, 1968), p. 11.
2. Alice Miller, 'Zur Behandlungstechnik bei Sogenannten Narzisstischen

Neurosen,' *Psyche* 25:641-668.

3. J. Habermas, 'Der universalitatsanspruch der Hermeneutik,' in *Kultur und Kritik* (Frankfurt: M. Suhrkamp, 1973).

4. D.W. Winnicott, 'The use of an object,' *International Journal of Psychoanalysis* 50:700, 716, 1969.

Chapter 11/von Franz

1. Ovid, *Metamorphoses*, vol. IV (London and Cambridge, Mass.: Loeb Classical Library, 1946), pp. 18-20.

2. C.G. Jung, *CW*, vol. 5, *Symbols of Transformation*.

3. J.G. Magee, Jr., 'High Flight,' in *The Family Album of Favorite Poems*, ed. P.E. Ernest (New York: Grosset & Dunlap, 1959).

4. Gerhard Adler and Aniela Jaffé, eds. *C.G. Jung: Letters*, 2 vols. (Princeton: Princeton University Press, 1973) vol. I, p. 82, letter dated February 23, 1931.

Chapter 13/ Stone and Winkelman

1. Lucia Capacchione, *The Power of Your Other Hand* (Van Nuys, Calif.: Newcastle Co., Inc. 1988).

Chapter 16/Stein

1. C. Kerenyi and C.G. Jung, *Essays on a Science of Mythology* (New York: Pantheon Books Inc., 1949), p. 40.

2. Alice Miller, *Prisoners of Childhood* (New York: Basic Books, Inc., 1981).

3. Alice Miller, *Thou Shalt Not Be Aware* (New York: Farrar, Straus, Giroux, 1984).

4. Sigmund Freud, *Standard Edition*, vol. VII.

5. Robert M. Stein, *Incest and Human Love: The Betrayal of the Soul in Psychotherapy* (Dallas: Spring Publications, Inc., 1984).

6. Harold Searles, 'Oedipal Love in the Countertransference' (1959), in *Collected Papers on Schizophrenia and Related Subjects* (New York: International University Press, 1965), p. 284.

7. *Ibid.*

8. *Ibid.*, p. 295.

9. *Ibid.*, p. 296.

Part 6: Introduction

Chapter opening quote: 'On Psychic Energy.' C.G. Jung, *CW*, vol. 8, p. 52.

Chapter 21/Hillman

1. James Hillman, 'Abandoning the Child,' in *Loose Ends: Primary Papers in Archetypal Psychology* (Dallas: Spring Publications and the University of Dallas, 1975).

Chapter 25/Osherson

1. J.M. Ross, 'In Search of Fathering: A Review,' in *Father and Child*, ed. Cath, Gurwitz, and Ross.
2. D. Hall, 'My Son, My Executioner,' in *The Alligator Bride* (New York: Harper & Row, 1969).

Epilogue/Abrams

'May You Stay Forever Young': Bob Dylan, 'Forever Young,' 1973, Ram's Horn Music.

Chapter opening quote: C.G. Jung, 'The Psychology of the Child Archetype,' *CW*, vol. 9, i, para. 299.

NOTES ON CONTRIBUTORS

≈

BRUNO BETTELHEIM is Distinguished Professor of Education Emeritus and Professor Emeritus of both psychology and psychiatry at the University of Chicago. His books include *A Good Enough Parent, Love Is Not Enough, Children of the Dream, Freud and Man's Soul*, and *The Uses of Enchantment*. The last won both the National Book Award and the National Book Critics Circle Award in 1977.

JOHN BRADSHAW has worked for the past twenty years as a counsellor, theologian, management consultant, and public speaker. He is host of the nationally televised PBS series *Bradshaw On: The Family* and author of a book by the same title. *Healing the Shame That Binds You* is his most recent work.

JOSEPH CAMPBELL, the great bard and scholar of mythology who died in October 1987, is best known for his work in comparative world mythology. He taught at Sarah Lawrence College in New York City for almost forty years, where the Joseph Campbell Chair in Comparative Mythology was established in his honour. His written works include *The Mythic Image, The Masks of God* (4 volumes), *The Hero with a Thousand Faces, Myths to Live By, The Atlas of World Mythology*, and the posthumous interview transcripts *The Power of Myth* and *An Open Life*.

LUCIA CAPACCHIONE is a registered art therapist, consultant, and workshop leader. Her books include *The Creative Journal, The WellBeing Journal*, and *The Power of Your Other Hand*. Her methods are currently being used with AIDS and cancer patients and in 12-step recovery programmes.

JOEL COVITZ is a clinical psychologist and Jungian analyst in Brookline, Massachusetts, where he lives with his wife and two children. He is the author of *Emotional Child Abuse* and the forthcoming *Visions of the Night: A Study of Jewish Dream Interpretation*.

ERIK H. ERIKSON is one of the leading figures in the field of psychoanalysis and human development. Winner of both the Pulitzer Prize and the National Book Award, he is the author of *Gandhi's Truth, Young Man Luther, Identity: Youth and Crisis, Childhood and Society*, and *Insight and Responsibility*.

MARIE-LOUISE VON FRANZ, a Swiss psychoanalyst, is probably Carl Jung's most important living disciple, having worked directly with him for 31 years. Her work fully embodies the essence of his teachings, although she is in her own right an original and provocative thinker. Many of her lectures have been published and are available in English. Her books include *Number and Time, The Grail Legend* (with Emma Jung), *Puer Aeternus, Projection and Re-Collection in Jungian Psychology, The Feminine in Fairy Tales*, and *On Dreams and Death*.

JAMES HILLMAN, representing the third generation in Jungian thought, is rapidly coming to be seen as one of the most original psychological thinkers in America today. Trained as a Jungian analyst, he calls himself an imaginal or archetypal psychologist, and his writings have captured the imaginations of novelists, poets, feminists, cultural historians, as well as his fellow analysts. He lectures widely and is the editor of the journal *Spring*. His books include *Suicide and the Soul, The Myth of Analysis, Re-Visioning Psychology, Anima* and *Loose Ends*.

JEAN HOUSTON is director of the Foundation for Mind Research in New York. She conducts innovative seminars and works in human development in over thirty-five countries, and has authored more than ten books, including *The Search for the Beloved, The Possible Human, Life Force* and *Mind Games*.

C. G. JUNG, who died in 1961, one of the great personalities of our time, is probably best known as one of the founders of psychoanalysis. His reflections covered the full range of human problems and concerns of the modern soul. His overriding interest was the mystery of consciousness and personality, and their relationship with the great unconscious. His books include *Collected Works* (20 volumes), *Man In Search of a Soul*, and his popular autobiography, *Memories, Dreams, and Reflections*.

URSULA K. LEGUIN is a well-known and beloved novelist and short story writer. Among her books are *Planet of Exile, The Left Hand of Darkness, The Dispossessed*, and the collection *The Wind's Twelve Quarters*. She lives with her family in Portland, Oregon.

ALEXANDER LOWEN, director of the Institute for Bioenergetic Analysis in New York, is the creator of bioenergetics, a practice that incorporates direct work on the body into psychoanalytic process. He is the author of numerous books, including *Love and Orgasm; Betrayal of the Body; Pleasure, Depression and the Body;* and *Bioenergetics.*

RALPH METZNER has been a researcher and teacher in the area of consciousness for over 25 years. He is a psychotherapist and professor of East-West psychology at the California Institute of Integral Studies in San Francisco. His books include *Maps of Consciousness* and *Opening to the Light.*

ALICE MILLER, who lives in Zurich, has devoted herself to writing since 1979, after having practiced and taught for over twenty years as a psychoanalyst. Her best-selling books, *Prisoners of Childhood* (retitled *The Drama of the Gifted Child*), *For Your Own Good,* and *Thou Shalt Not Be Aware,* have created ferment and spawned a movement of activists on behalf of children.

SAMUEL OSHERSON is a research psychologist and practicing psychotherapist in Cambridge, Massachusetts. He is the author of *Holding On or Letting Go* and *Finding Our Fathers* and has written a monthly column for *Boston* magazine.

M. SCOTT PECK is a psychiatrist practicing in New Milford, Connecticut. He is the author of the enormously popular book *The Road Less Traveled,* its sequel *People of the Lie,* and *The Different Drum.*

THEODORE REIK, born in Vienna in 1888, was one of Freud's earliest pupils. He wrote the first doctoral dissertation on psychoanalysis at the University of Vienna. He came to the United States in 1938 and practiced psychoanalysis in New York for many years. His books include *Masochism in Modern Man, A Psychologist Looks at Love,* and *Listening with the Third Ear.*

JEFFREY SATINOVER is a Fellow of the Child Study Center at the Yale University School of Medicine, a director of the Sterling Institute in Weston, Connecticut, and a Jungian analyst in private practice.

JUNE SINGER is a Jungian analyst, author, and member of the faculty at the Institute of Transpersonal Psychology, Palo Alto, California. Her books include *Androgyny, Energies of Love, The Unholy Bible, Boundaries of the Soul,* and *Seeing Through the Visible World.*

ROBERT M. STEIN is a senior training analyst at the Jung Institute of Los Angeles and is in private practice in Beverly Hills. He is author of numerous articles and the book *Incest and Human Love: The Betrayal of the Soul in Psychotherapy.*

HAL STONE is a clinical psychologist and teacher and the director of the Academy of Delos in Northern California, where he and his wife, Sidra Winkelman, offer training groups in Voice Dialogue. He is author of *Embracing Heaven and Earth* and co-author of *Embracing Our Selves* and *Embracing Each Other*.

EDITH SULLWOLD founded the Hilde Kirsch Children's Center at the C. G. Jung Institute of Los Angeles. She was director of Turning Point, a professional group working with seriously ill children. She now teaches and supervises therapists in various parts of the world, most recently in Kenya.

SIDRA WINKELMAN is a psychotherapist, mother, and co-creator of the Voice Dialogue process, which she and her husband, Hal Stone, teach in the United States and abroad. She is co-author of *Embracing Our Selves* and *Embracing Each Other*.

MARION WOODMAN is a Jungian analyst in private practice in Toronto. She travels and lectures widely. Her books include *The Owl Was a Baker's Daughter: Obesity, Anorexia Nervosa, and the Repressed Feminine; Addiction to Perfection: The Still Unravished Bride;* and *The Pregnant Virgin*.

BIBLIOGRAPHY

≈

The works cited below include the sources of the essays in this book, as well as other relevant and related materials on the themes of this collection. I recommend these to the reader, as well as the reference bibliographies in the source books themselves.

Armstrong, Thomas. *The Radiant Child*. Wheaton, Ill.: Quest, 1985.

Bachelard, Gaston. *The Poetics of Reverie*. Translated by Daniel Russell. Boston: Beacon Press, 1971.

—. *Water and Dreams*. Translated by Edith R. Farrell. Dallas: Pegasus Foundation, 1983.

Bettelheim, Bruno. *A Good Enough Parent*. New York: A. Knopf, 1987.

Bly, Robert, ed. *News of the Universe: Poems of Two-fold Consciousness*. San Francisco: Sierra Club, 1980.

Boer, Charles, trans. *The Homeric Hymns*. Dallas: Spring Publications, 1979.

Bradshaw, John. *Bradshaw On: The Family*. Deerfield Beach, Fla.: Health Communications, 1988.

—. *Healing the Shame That Binds You*. Deerfield Beach, Fla.: Health Communications, 1988.

Branden, Nathaniel. *How to Raise Your Self-Esteem*. New York: Bantam, 1987.

Bry, Adelaide, with Marjorie Bair. *Visualization: Directing the Movies of Your Mind*. New York: Barnes and Noble, 1979.

Campbell, Joseph. *The Hero with a Thousand Faces*. Princeton, N.J.: Princeton University Press, Bollingen Series XVII, 1949.

Campbell, Joseph, with Bill Moyers. *The Power of Myth*, New York: Doubleday, 1988.

Campbell, Joseph, with Michael Toms. *An Open Life: Joseph Campbell in Conversation with Michael Toms*. Edited by J.M. Maher and D. Briggs. Burdett, N.Y.: Larsen Publications, 1988.

Capacchione, Lucia. *The Power of Your Other Hand*. North Hollywood, Calif.: Newcastle Publishing, 1988.

Carroll, Lewis. *Through the Looking Glass.* New York: Random House, 1946.

Cott, Jonathan. *Pipers at the Gates of Dawn: The Wisdom of Children's Literature.* New York: Random House, 1981.

Covitz, Joel. *Emotional Child Abuse: The Family Curse.* Boston: Sigo Press, 1986.

Dieckmann, Hans. 'The Favorite Fairy Tale from Childhood,' in *The Analytic Process.* Edited by Joseph Wheelwright. New York: Putnam's, C.G. Jung Foundation, 1971:77-84.

Elkind, David. *The Hurried Child.* Reading, Mass.: Addison-Wesley, 1981.

Erikson, Erik H. *Insight and Responsibility.* New York: W.W. Norton, 1964.

Fordham, Michael. 'Religious Experience in Childhood,' in *The Well-Tended Tree.* Edited by Hilde Kirsch. New York: Putnam's, C.G. Jung Foundation 79-89, 1971.

Frantz, Gilda. 'Birth's Cruel Secret/O I Am My Own Lost Mother/To My Own Sad Child.' *Chiron,* 1985: 157-172.

Franz, Marie-Louis von. *C.G. Jung: His Myth in Our Time.* Translated by W.H. Kennedy. New York: Putnam's, C.G. Jung Foundation for Analytical Psychology, 1975.

—. *Individuation in Fairytales.* Dallas: Spring Publications, 1977.

—. *Puer Aeternus.* Boston: Sigo Press, 1981.

Ghiselin, Brewster, ed. *The Creative Process.* New York: New American Library, 1952.

Giannini, John. 'The Dynamics of the Wounded Child.' *Creation,* vol. 4, no. 6: 32-35.

Goertzel, Victor and Mildred G. *Cradles of Eminence.* Boston: Little Brown, 1962.

Harding, M. Esther. *The 'I' and the 'Not-I'.* Princeton, N.J.: Princeton University Press, Bollingen Series LXXIX, 1965.

Hillman, James. *Loose Ends.* Dallas: Spring Publications, 1975.

—. *Re-Visioning Psychology.* New York: Harper and Row, 1975.

Hillman, James, with Laura Pozzo. *Inter Views.* New York: Harper and Row, 1983.

Hillman, James, et al. *Puer Papers.* Dallas: Spring Publications, 1979.

Houston, Jean. *The Possible Human.* Los Angeles: Jeremy Tarcher, 1982.

Jaffe, Aniela, ed. *C.G. Jung: Word and Image.* Princeton, N.J.: Princeton University Press, Bollingen Series XCVII, 1979.

James, Muriel, and Dorothy Jongeward. *Born to Win: Transactional Analysis with Gestalt Experiments.* Reading, Mass.: Addison-Wesley, 1971.

Jung, Carl Gustav. *Collected Works,* vols. 1-20. Translated by R.F.C. Hull and edited by H. Read, M. Fordham, G. Adler, and William McGuire. (Especially vols. 9i, 16, 17). Princeton, N.J.: Princeton University Press, Bollingen Series XX, 1953-.

—. *Psyche and Symbol.* Edited by Violet de Laszlo. Garden City, N.Y.: Doubleday, 1958.

—. *Memories, Dreams, and Reflections*. Edited by Aniela Jaffe. New York: Random House, Pantheon Books, 1961.

—. *Psychological Reflections*. Edited by Jolanda Jacobi and R.F.C. Hull. Princeton, N.J.: Princeton University Press, Bollingen Series XXXI, 1970.

Jung, Carl Gustav, and Karl Kerenyi. *Essays on A Science of Mythology*. Princeton, N.J.: Princeton University Press, Bollingen Series XXII, 1969.

Keen, Sam. *Apology for Wonder*. New York: Harper and Row, Torchbooks, 1969.

Kehl, Richard. *Silver Departures*. La Jolla, Calif.: Green Tiger, 1983.

Kohut, Heinz. *The Restoration of the Self*. New York: International Universities, 1977.

Lawrence, D.H. *Fantasia of the Unconscious and Psychoanalysis and the Unconscious*. New York: Viking Penguin, 1960.

Liedloff, Jean. *The Continuum Concept*. Reading, Mass.: Addison-Wesley, 1977.

Loudon, John. 'Becoming a Child.' *Parabola*, vol. IV, no. 3 (August 1979): 35-41.

Lowen, Alexander. *Pleasure: A Creative Approach to Life*. New York: Coward, McCann, 1970.

—. *Bioenergetics*. New York: Coward, McCann, 1975.

—. *Narcissism: Denial of the True Self*. New York: Macmillan, Collier Books, 1983.

Luke, Helen. *The Inner Story: Myth and Symbol in the Bible and Literature*. New York: Crossroad, 1982.

—. *Woman: Earth and Spirit*, New York: Crossroad, 1984.

Mahdi, Louise, Steven Foster, and Meredith Little. *Betwixt and Between: Patterns of Masculine and Feminine Initiation*. LaSalle, Ill.: Open Court, 1987.

Metzner, Ralph. *Opening to the Light*. Los Angeles: Jeremy Tarcher, 1986.

Middelton-Moz, Jane, and Lorie Dwinell. *After the Tears: Reclaiming the Personal Losses of Childhood*. Deerfield Beach, Fla.: Health Communications, Inc., 1986.

Miller, Alice. *The Drama of the Gifted Child* (original tile *Prisoners of Childhood*). New York: Basic Books, 1981.

—. *For Your Own Good: Hidden Cruelty in Child-Rearing and the Roots of Violence*. New York: Farrar, Straus, Giroux, 1983.

—. *Thou Shalt Not Be Aware: Society's Betrayal of the Child*. New York: Farrar, Straus, Giroux, 1984.

—. *Pictures of Childhood*. New York: Farrar, Straus, Giroux, 1986.

Mills, Joyce C., and Richard J. Crowley, with Margaret O. Ryan. *Therapeutic Metaphors for Children and the Child Within*. New York: Brunner/Mazel, 1986.

Missildine, W. Hugh. *Your Inner Child of the Past*. New York: Simon and Schuster, 1963.

Neary, John M. 'The Dickens Child: From Infantilism to Wholeness,' *Psychological Perspectives*, Fall, 1982: 138-155.

Neumann, Erich. *The Child.* New York: Putnam's, C.G. Jung Foundation, 1973.

Osherson, Samuel O. *Finding Our Fathers: The Unfinished Business of Manhood.* New York: Random House, Ballantine Books, 1986.

Pearce, Joseph C. *Magical Child: Rediscovering Nature's Plan for Our Children.* New York: Bantam, 1986.

Pearson, Carol. *The Hero Within.* San Francisco: Harper and Row, 1986.

Peck, M. Scott. *The Road Less Traveled.* New York: Simon and Schuster, Touchstone, 1978.

Reik, Theodore. *Listening with the Third Ear.* New York: Arena Books, 1972.

Richards, M.C. 'Recovery of the Child in Manhood,' in *Centering.* Middletown, Conn.: Wesleyan, 1962.

Rothenberg, Rose-Emily. 'The Orphan Archetype.' *Psychological Perspectives*, 1983: 181-194.

Rubin, Theodore. *Compassion and Self-Hate.* New York: Macmillan, Collier, 1975.

Samuels, Andrew. *Jung and the Post-Jungians.* New York: Routledge & Kegan Paul, 1985.

Samuels, Andrew, Bani Shorter, and Fred Plaut, eds. *A Critical Dictionary of Jungian Analysis.* London: Routledge & Kegan Paul, 1986.

Satinover, Jeffrey. 'The Mirror of Doctor Faustus: The Decline of Art in the Pursuit of Eternal Adolescence.' *Quadrant*, Spring, 1984: 23-38.

—. 'Puer Aeternus: The Narcissistic Relation to the Self.' *Quadrant*, Fall, 1980: 75-108.

Schwartz-Salant, Nathan. *Narcissism and Character Transformation.* Toronto: Inner City, 1982.

Short, Susanne. 'Understanding Our Childhood: The Hidden Secret.' *Psychological Perspectives*, Fall, 1989.

Singer, June K. *Boundaries of the Soul.* Garden City, N.Y.: Doubleday, 1972.

Stein, Robert M. *Incest and Human Love: The Betrayal of the Soul in Psychotherapy.* Dallas: Spring Publications, 1973.

—. 'On Incest and Child Abuse.' *Spring 1987*: 61-65.

Stevens, Anthony. *Archetypes: A Natural History of the Self.* New York: Quill, 1983.

Stone, Hal, and Sidra Winkelman. *Embracing Our Selves: The Voice Dialogue Manual.*

—. *Embracing Each Other: Relationship as Teacher, Healer, and Guide.* San Rafael, Calif.: New World Library, 1990.

Sullwood, Edith. 'The Ritual-Maker Within at Adolescence,' in *Betwixt and Between.* Edited by Louise Mahdi, Steen Foster, and Meredith Little. LaSalle, Ill.: Open Court, 1987, 111-131.

Tuby, Molly, ed. *In the Wake of Jung.* London: Coventure, 1983.

Viorst, Judith. *Necessary Losses*. New York: Ballantine, Fawcett, 1986.

Weinrib, Estelle L. *Images of the Self: The Sandplay Therapy Process*. Boston: Sigo Press, 1983.

Whitfield, Charles L. *Healing the Child Within*. Deerfield Beach, Fla.: Health Communications, 1987.

—. *A Gift to Myself: A Workbook and Guide to Healing My Child Within*. Deerfield Beach, Fla.: Health Communications, 1989.

Wickes, Frances G. *The Inner World of Choice*. New York: Harper and Row, 1963.

Woodman, Marion. *The Pregnant Virgin: A Process of Psychological Transformation*. Toronto: Inner City Books, 1985.

Young, James H. 'The Child Archetype.' *Quadrant*, Winter, 1977: 63-72.

PERMISSIONS AND COPYRIGHTS

≈

Chapter 1 is an original essay created especially for this collection by Edith Sullwold. Copyright © 1989 by Edith Sullwold. Used by permission of the author.

Chapter 2 is comprised of excerpts from the essay 'The Psychology of the Child Archetype' by C.G. Jung, from *The Collected Works of C.G. Jung*, trans. R.F.C. Hull, Bollingen Series XX, vol. 9, no. i, *The Archetypes and the Collective Unconscious*. Copyright © 1959, 1969. Reprinted by permission of Princeton University Press.

Chapter 3 is an excerpt from *Boundaries of the Soul* by June K. Singer. Copyright © 1972 by June Singer. Reprinted by permission of Doubleday, a division of Bantam, Doubleday, Dell Publishing Group Inc.

Chapter 4 is an excerpt from *Opening to the Light* by Ralph Metzner. Copyright © 1986 by Ralph Metzner. Reprinted by permission of Jeremy P. Tarcher, Inc., Los Angeles.

Part 2's Introduction contains the poem 'I Life My Life,' by Rainer Maria Rilke, translated by Robert Bly. It is reprinted from *News of the Universe*, copyright 1980, © Robert Bly, used by permission of Robert Bly.

Chapter 5 is comprised of excerpts from *Loose Ends* by James Hillman. Copyright © 1975 by James Hillman. Reprinted by permission of the author and Spring Publications, Inc., Dallas.

Chapter 6 is comprised of excerpts from *The Pregnant Virgin: A Process of Psychological Transformation* by Marion Woodman (Studies in Jungian Psychology by Jungian Analysts, no. 21) Copyright © 1985 by Marion Woodman. Reprinted by permission of Inner City Books, Toronto.

Chapter 17 consists of excerpts from *The Power of Your Other Hand* by Lucia Capacchione. Copyright © 1988 by Lucia Capacchione. Reprinted by permission of Newcastle Publishing Co., Inc., North Hollywood, Calif.

Chapter 18 is comprised of excerpts from *Healing the Shame That Binds You* by John Bradshaw. Copyright © 1988 by John Bradshaw. Reprinted by permission of the author.

Chapter 19 is an excerpt from *The Possible Human* by Jean Houston. Copyright © 1982 by Jean Houston. Reprinted by permission of the publisher, Jeremy P. Tarcher, Inc., Los Angeles.

Chapter 20 is an excerpt from *An Open Life: Joseph Campbell in Conversation with Michael Toms*. Copyright © 1988 by New Dimensions Foundation. Reprinted by permission of the publisher, Larsen Publications, PBPF, 4936 Rte. 414, Burdett, N.Y. 14818.

Chapter 21 is excerpted from *Loose Ends* by James Hillman. Copyright © 1975 by James Hillman. Reprinted by permission of the author and Spring Publications, Inc., Dallas.

Chapter 22 is an excerpt from *A Good Enough Parent* by Bruno Bettelheim. Copyright © 1987 by Bruno Bettelheim. Reprinted by permission of Alfred A. Knopf, Inc.

Chapter 23 consists of a selection from *Insight and Responsibility* by Erik H. Erikson. Copyright © 1964 by Erik H. Erikson. Reprinted by permission of W.W. Norton & Company, Inc.

Chapter 24 is an excerpt from *Listening with the Third Ear* by Theodore Reik. Copyright © 1948 by Theodore Reik. Reprinted by permission of Farrar, Straus, & Giroux, Inc.

Chapter 25 is comprised of excerpts from *Finding Our Fathers: The Unfinished Business of Manhood* by Samuel Osherson. Copyright © 1986 by Samuel Osherson. Reprinted with permission of The Free Press, a division of Macmillan, Inc.

About the Editor

≈

JEREMIAH ABRAMS has worked for the past twenty years as a Jungian therapist, dream analyst, writer, counsellor and consultant. He is currently the director of the Mount Vision Institute, a Centre for Individuation, in Sausalito, California. He lives with his wife and two children in Northern California.